Withdrawn from
Davidson College Library

Library of
Davidson College

THE STRATEGY OF DEVELOPMENT IN BANGLADESH

The Strategy of Development in Bangladesh

Azizur Rahman Khan
Professor of Economics
University of California, Riverside

and

Mahabub Hossain
Director General
Bangladesh Institute of Development Studies, Dhaka

Foreword by

Keith Griffin
Professor and Chairman, Department of Economics
University of California, Riverside

St. Martin's Press   New York

© OECD Development Centre 1990

All rights reserved. For information, write:
Scholarly and Reference Division,
St. Martin's Press, Inc., 175 Fifth Avenue,
New York, NY 10010

First published in the United States of America in 1990

Printed in Great Britain

ISBN 0–312–04210–8

Library of Congress Cataloging-in-Publication Data

Khan, Azizur Rahman.
  The strategy of development in Bangladesh / Azizur Rahman Khan and Mahabub Hossain : foreword by Keith Griffin.
    p. cm.
  Includes bibliographical references.
  ISBN 0–312–04210–8
  1. Bangladesh—Economic policy.   I. Hossain, Mahabub, 1945–
II. Title.
  HC440.8.K54   1990
  338.95492—dc20   89-70064
                                                                        CIP

Dedicated to Professor Nurul Islam
Teacher, Colleague and the Doyen of the
Bangladeshi Economists
to Commemorate the Sixtieth Anniversary of His
Birth

FOREWORD

This volume forms part of a series on economic choices before the developing countries. The experience of economic development over more than four decades is varied and rich and it is possible to learn much from it, both analytically and in terms of economic policy. Already it is clear that there are many paths to development although some no doubt are more circuitous than others. Enough time has elapsed and enough data are available to make it possible to test the strengths and limitations of the most widely-advocated policy approaches or development strategies against actual practice.

This was done within a comparative framework in my book *Alternative Strategies for Economic Development*. That volume as well as this series are part of a research programme on the economic choices or alternatives facing the Third World in the closing years of this century. The research programme and this series, which reports the results of it, were sponsored by the OECD Development Centre in Paris and received the personal and unstinting support of the President of the Development Centre, Louis Emmerij.

The monograph length country studies, of which this is the first, are intended to examine economic policy in depth. It is expected that this first study will be followed by other country monographs on Botswana, the Philippines, Sri Lanka, China and a comparative study of Peru and Colombia; additional country studies may be organised subsequently if resources permit. It is also planned to include in the series a volume which examines economic policy and performance in a broad historical context covering the period 1913-1987. This volume will cover six, mostly rather large, Third World countries in Latin America and Asia, namely, Argentina, Brazil, Mexico, China, India and Korea.

It is appropriate that Bangladesh should be the first of our country studies. Bangladesh is a very large country – the ninth most populous on earth – and one of the poorest. Since its independence in 1971 it has been dismissed as a "basket case" as well as hailed for its adoption of orthodox economic policies. It has experienced a "green revolution"; it has privatised state-owned enterprises; it has raised real rates of interest and it has reduced the overvaluation of the exchange rate. Moreover it has maintained a small public sector in which government revenue accounts for only 8-10 per cent of gross domestic product. Thus

Bangladesh has done many of the things that academic economists, aid donors and international agencies advocate.

The authors of this book, Azizur Rahman Khan and Mahabub Hossain, examine the evidence carefully and soberly. They consider the effects of economic policy on the aggregate rate of growth, on agriculture and industrial output, and on the average standard of living. They explore the effects of capital inflows and government policy on the rate of savings and hence on the ability of the country to generate self-sustained expansion. They examine the implications of the development strategy for employment, the incidence of poverty, levels of nutrition and the distribution of income. And finally, they examine the impact on human development, particularly changes in the rate of literacy and in the pattern and quality of education.

The volume thus is comprehensive in its coverage. Indeed it is the most comprehensive study of the economy of Bangladesh available and will be of interest to everyone concerned with the development of that country. The volume will also be of great interest both to those who advocate orthodox economic policies and to those who are sceptical of them. For if orthodoxy succeeds in Bangladesh it probably would succeed anywhere, but if it fails in Bangladesh its claims to universality evaporate and alternative strategies of development will come into their own as equally deserving of attention.

Keith Griffin
Series Editor
Magdalen College, Oxford
January 1988

TABLE OF CONTENTS

Foreword	vii
List of Tables	xii
Acknowledgements	xvii

1	**INTRODUCTION**	**1**
	A Brief Account of Recent History	1
	The Role of the Government in Economic Development	3
	Poverty and Underdevelopment	5
	Long Term Stagnation and Decline	6
	Initial Conditions	8
	An Outline	9
	Notes and References	9
2	**GROWTH AND STRUCTURAL CHANGE**	**11**
	The Rate of Population Growth	11
	Labor Force and its Distribution	14
	Growth in GDP and Per Capita Income	19
	Macroeconomic Changes Since Independence	24
	Notes and References	29
3	**AGRICULTURAL DEVELOPMENT**	**31**
	The Resource Base and the Organization of Production	31
	The Structure and Growth of Agriculture	35
	Factors Behind Growth	45
	Implications for Income Distribution	51
	A Review of Agricultural Policies	57
	Conclusions	63
	Notes and References	64

4 INDUSTRIALIZATION — 67
Large, Small and Cottage Industries — 67
A Comparison among the Three Groups of Industries — 71
The Growth of Manufacturing Industries — 75
Modern Manufacturing Industries — 78
The Public and Private Sectors — 79
An Interpretation of Nationalization and its Aftermath — 84
The Process of Accumulation — 88
Foreign Exchange Regime and Industrial Growth — 92
Conclusions — 95
Notes and References — 96

5 TRADE, PUBLIC FINANCE AND PRICES: SOME ISSUES — 99
External Trade and Debt — 99
Public Finance and Resource Mobilization — 110
Prices, Money and Finance — 115
Notes and References — 121

6 THE DEVELOPMENT OF INFRASTRUCTURE — 123
Energy and Power — 124
Transport and Communications — 129
Flood Control — 137
The Social Infrastructure: Education and Health — 139
Conclusions — 144
Notes and References — 145

7 INCOME DISTRIBUTION AND POVERTY — 147
Main Indicators and their Limitations — 147
The Evidence — 151

Some Conclusions Based on an Interpretation of the Evidence	158
Factors Behind Inequality and Poverty	163
Discrimination Against Women	168
Notes and References	171

8 CONCLUSIONS — 175

Macroeconomic Performance	176
The Green Revolution Strategy and Rural Development	178
The Open Economy Strategy and Privatization	179
Industry and Infrastructure	180
Income Distribution and Social Development	181
Notes and References	182

Annex to Chapter 2: National Income Estimates	183
Bibliography of Works Cited	189
Index	195

LIST OF TABLES

1 Introduction

Table 1.1	Basic Facts	4
Table 1.2	Per Capita Income as a Multiple of Per Capita Income of Bangladesh	7

2 Growth and Structural Change

Table 2.1	Labor Force and Employment	15
Table 2.2	Sectoral Distribution of the Labor Force and Labor Productivity	16
Table 2.3	National Income, Population and Per Capita Income	20
Table 2.4	Trend Growth Rates	22
Table 2.5	Macroeconomic Accounts	26
Table 2.6	Macroeconomic Characteristics before Independence	28

3 Agricultural Development

Table 3.1	Changes in the Structure of Landholdings, 1960-1984	34
Table 3.2	The Composition of Agricultural Value Added, 1986/87	36
Table 3.3	Changes in the Number of Livestock and Poultry 1960 to 1983/84	38
Table 3.4	Estimates of Area, Yield and Production of Fisheries in Bangladesh, 1983/84	38
Table 3.5	Growth in Crop Production in the Pre- and Post- Independence Periods	41
Table 3.6	Recent Trends in Production and Productivity of Important Crops, 1973-87	43

Table 3.7	Changes in Yield Rates for Important Crops, 1984-87 Over 1968-71	44
Table 3.8	Trends in Cultivated Land, Cropped Area and Cropping Intensity	46
Table 3.9	Progress in the Diffusion of the Modern Agricultural Technology	47
Table 3.10	Movement in Agriculture's Terms of Trade 1973/74 to 1986/87	49
Table 3.11	Movement In Terms of Trade of Various Agricultural Sub-Sectors 1973/74 to 1985/86	50
Table 3.12	Adoption of the New Agricultural Technology by Different Farm Size and Tenurial Groups, Results of a Farm Survey in 1982	53
Table 3.13	Use of Irrigation and Modern Varieties of Rice and Wheat, Estimates of 1983/84 Aricultural Census	54
Table 3.14	Farm Size and Productivity of Land in Rice Cultivation in Technologically Advanced and Backward Villages, Results of the Farm Survey 1982	55
Table 3.15	Farm Level Prices of Major Agricultural Inputs, by Size and Tenurial Status of Farms, 1982	56
Table 3.16	Trends in Allocation and Composition of Public Development Resources for Agriculture	58
Table 3.17	Recent Estimates of Rates of Subsidy in Input Distributions and Marketing of Foodgrains	60
Table 3.18	Internal Procurement of Rice and Maintenance of Support Prices, 1975-86	62

4 Industrialization

Table 4.1	Manufacturing Industries, 1981/82	68
Table 4.2	Indices for Small and Cottage Industries with Large and Medium Industries as Base	76

List of Tables

Table 4.3	Share of Manufacturing Industries in GDP at Current Prices	77
Table 4.4	Growth and Productivity in Modern Industries	80
Table 4.5	Large-Scale Industrial Ownership Before and After Nationalization	81
Table 4.6	Ownership of Large Scale Industries, 1981/82	82
Table 4.7	Some Comparative Features of Nationalized and Private Industries	83
Table 4.8	Sectoral Real Price Deflators	92
Table 4.9	Exchange Rates	94

5 Trade, Public Finance and Prices: Some Issues

Table 5.1	Exports, Imports, Trade Balance and Remittances	100
Table 5.2	Debt and Debt Service, 1985/86	101
Table 5.3	Composition of Imports	102
Table 5.4	Merchandise Exports	105
Table 5.5	Government Revenue and Expenditure	112
Table 5.6	Composition of Public Expenditure	114
Table 5.7	Selected Price Indicators	116
Table 5.8	Money Supply	117
Table 5.9	Nominal Interest Rates on Deposits and Loans	118
Table 5.10	Annual Increase in Bank Credit	119
Table 5.11	Causative Factors Behind Increases in Money Supply	120

6 The Development Of Infrastructure

Table 6.1	Trends in the Supply and Distribution of Electrical Power System	126
Table 6.2	Installed Electric Power Generation Capacity by Type	127
Table 6.3	Consumption of Electric Energy by Type of Consumer, 1975/76 and 1984/85	129

List of Tables

Table 6.4	Growth of Traffic by Mode of Transport, 1977-85	130
Table 6.5	Capacity and Utilization of Road Transport	132
Table 6.6	Recent Expansion of Paved Roads by Types, 1980-86	133
Table 6.7	Capacity and Utilization of Rail Transport	136
Table 6.8	Development in the Communication System	136
Table 6.9	Physical Progress in the Field of Flood Control and Drainage During The Second Five-Year Plan Period (1980-85)	138
Table 6.10	Government Expenditure on Education and Health	140
Table 6.11	Literacy Rates	140
Table 6.12	Primary School Enrollment	141
Table 6.13	Selected Indicators of Health Status	143

7 Income Distribution and Poverty

Table 7.1	Percentage Shares of Income Accruing to Fractions of Population Ranked in Ascending Order of Income per Household	149
Table 7.2	Percentage Shares of Income Accruing to Fractions of Population Ranked in Ascending Order of Per Capita Income	150
Table 7.3	Rural–Urban Income Disparity	150
Table 7.4	Incidence of Poverty	154
Table 7.5	Nutritional Status of Rural Children	157
Table 7.6	Wage Rates of Male Agricultural Workers	158
Table 7.7	Real Wage Indices in Selected Non-Agricultural Sectors	160
Table 7.8	Distribution of Rural Landownership, 1977, 1978 and 1983/84	167
Table 7.9	Landless Agricultural Laborers and Related Data	168

Table 7.10   Selected Indicators of Sexual Inequality   170

Annex to Chapter 2. National Income Estimates

Annex Table 2.1   Trend Growth Rates of Sectoral Values
             Added, 1972/73-1985/86   186

ACKNOWLEDGEMENTS

We are deeply grateful to Dr. Louis Emmerij and Professor Keith Griffin for all the help we received while writing this book. Our debt to Professor Griffin is much greater than what is usually owed the General Editor of a series. Professor Griffin helped with many ideas, detailed comments on several drafts and stylistic editing.

Mr. Abdus Salam, the Director-General of the Bangladesh Bureau of Statistics, helped in many ways and gave useful comments on some of our hypotheses. Mr. Md. Azizur Rahman, a Joint Director of the Bureau, went out of his way to help resolve many statistical puzzles. Several other members of the BBS staff provided assistance.

We are grateful to Professor Rehman Sobhan, the Director-General of the Bangladesh Institute of Development Studies, for the opportunity to present some of the findings at a seminar at the Institute. Among the other members of the BIDS who helped are Dr. M. Asaduzzaman, Dr. Nuimuddin Chowdhury, Dr. Omar Haider Chowdhury, Dr. Atiq Rahman and Dr. Dilip Kumar Roy. Thanks are also due to Dr. Rizwanul Islam of the ILO's Asian Employment Program and Dr. S. Zaman Mazumder and Mr. M. R. Dhaly of the Bangladesh Planning Commission.

Dibbo Khan provided valuable assistance in preparing the manuscript. He also helped with the collection of data.

This book has been dedicated to Professor Nurul Islam to commemorate the forthcoming sixtieth anniversary of his birth (in early 1989). He has contributed to the professional development of an entire generation of Bangladeshi economists, including us. We also benefited more directly from discussions with him on some of the issues presented in this volume.

In the course of our discussions with the persons named above, it became clear that few of them shared our views fully and each of them diasagreed with some of our ideas.

A.R.K.
M.H.

1 Introduction

Bangladesh is a nation of 105 million people huddled together on a territory of 55 600 square miles (144 000 square kilometers). It is the ninth most populous country in the world, only recently pushed down from the eighth rank by Nigeria. It is also one of the poorest nations on earth. Ethiopia is the only country, among those for which estimates are available, which is consistently ranked below Bangladesh in terms of per capita income.

A BRIEF ACCOUNT OF RECENT HISTORY

The territory that constitutes Bangladesh came under British rule in the mid-eighteenth century along with the rest of eastern India. In August 1947, as a consequence of the independence and partitioning of British India, the present political boundary of Bangladesh was drawn for the first time. It emerged as the eastern wing of Pakistan, geographically separated from the western wing by more than a thousand miles of Indian territory. It consisted of the Muslim majority districts of the former province of Bengal and a part of the adjoining province of Assam.

During the quarter century of political association with Pakistan, the living standard of Bangladesh (then East Pakistan) steadily fell behind that of West Pakistan (now Pakistan). Although East Pakistan consisted of the majority of the population of the state of Pakistan, it exercised little political power – an outcome that was causally linked with the absence of political democracy in the country[1].

Almost since the inception of Pakistan, the demand for greater autonomy of East Pakistan began to be voiced. It gradually developed into a powerful movement for regional autonomy which was crystallized in 1966 in the Six Point Program of the Awami League, the main political party of East Pakistan. The Program effectively demanded a form of economic association between East Pakistan and the rest of Pakistan that in many ways would be looser than that between the members of a customs union.

In the elections held in 1970, to form an assembly for the drafting of a new constitution for Pakistan, the Awami League achieved nearly universal victory in the region and emerged as the party with an absolute majority in the country as a whole. This made it impossible to adopt a constitution that could ignore the demand for complete autonomy of East Pakistan.

Constitutional talks between the Awami League and the military rulers of Pakistan broke down in March 1971. Sheikh Mujibur Rahman, the leader of the Awami League, was imprisoned by the military rulers who resorted to a massive use of force to put down the uprising of the Bengalis. A guerrilla war of independence was started by Bengali defectors from the Pakistan army and by youth. The Awami League leadership declared independence and sought refuge in India. Towards the end of 1971 war broke out between India and Pakistan. The Indian armed forces, supported by the Bengali guerrillas, marched into Bangladesh. With the surrender of the Pakistan army in Bangladesh on 16th December, the independent Government of the People's Republic of Bangladesh was installed in Dhaka.

The nation formed itself into a parliamentary democracy following the return of Sheikh Mujibur Rahman in January 1972, on being released by Pakistan. A Westminster-type constitution was adopted in October 1972. The democratic experiment was however short-lived. In January 1975 the Awami League drastically amended the constitution to institute a presidential form of government under one-party rule. In August 1975 a group of junior army officers assassinated Sheikh Mujibur Rahman, staged a *coup d'etat* and installed a member of his cabinet as the President. This regime was soon overthrown. A series of *coups d'etat* took place in early November 1975, at the end of which General Ziaur Rahman emerged as the *de facto* ruler of Bangladesh. In April 1977 he got himself elected as President. A period of comparative stability followed until Ziaur Rahman was assassinated in May 1981. He was succeeded by his Vice-President Abdus Sattar who was elected President in November 1981. In March 1982 General Ershad, the Army Chief of Staff, staged a bloodless *coup d'etat* and became the Chief Martial Law Administrator. He appointed himself President in December 1983 and got himself elected to the same position in October 1986.

The Awami League was committed to the building of a "socialist" economy. In terms of actual action, "socialist transformation" was limited to the nationalization of most of the large-scale manufacturing industries, banking, insurance and foreign trade in jute, the main export. An overwhelming proportion of the nationalized assets had however been abandoned by the former Pakistani owners and had fallen into public hands *de facto*. The agrarian structure of this predominantly rural economy, characterized by a very unequally distributed private ownership of land, was left untouched. The Awami League also stood for secularism as a major guiding principle of the constitution in this predominantly Muslim nation. (According to the 1981 census 87 per cent of the population were Muslim.) Successive governments have steadily de-emphasized both socialism and secularism. Substantial denationalization of industry and financial institutions has taken place, especially in the early 1980s, and the commitment to Islam has grown over the years. However, public ownership – at about 40 per cent of the assets of modern manufacturing and also extensive in finance – still remains substantial and the country is by no means in the grip of the fundamentalist ideology that has come to sweep many a Muslim nation in recent times.

THE ROLE OF THE GOVERNMENT IN ECONOMIC DEVELOPMENT

The country has, however, lacked a strong and effective government. In a modern state the role of the government is a critical determinant of both the rate and the quality of economic growth. There is no unique strategy through which a government can promote growth. In the contemporary developing world successful examples of the role of government in promoting economic growth can be found under widely differing systems. The systems differ in the principle of ownership, degree of equality, concept of justice and in many other respects. Irrespective of such systemic differences, the success of a government in promoting economic growth depends on its ability to carry out certain basic functions effectively. It should be able to guarantee stability in the sense of generating confidence among the leading economic agents – the "entrepreneurs", whose composition would of course vary from one system to another – that the system is viable and durable. It should be able to create a broad coalition of the actual and potential entrepreneurs, one that transcends narrow parochial boundaries and is based on a consensus about the goals of economic policy. It should define the rules of the game that are consistent with these goals – the system of incentives, broadly defined, and the functioning of the institutions that constitute the systemic infrastructure – and enforce these rules with sufficient neutrality and effectiveness. Neutrality in this context does not mean neutrality with respect to different social classes and groups. It merely means the avoidance of overtly arbitrary deviation from the rules to favor some sub-group(s) of the coalition of the leading economic agents. The latter should be made to perceive clearly that adherence to the rules of the game is both the necessary and the sufficient condition of continuation of the enjoyment of the product of their effort and industry.

Table 1.1 Basic facts

Population (est. January 1987)		104 million
Area		55 598 square miles
		(144 000 square kilometers)
Average density (1986/87)		1 875 persons/square mile
		722 persons/square kilometer
Per capita GDP (1985/86)		4 400 Taka ($147)
Per capita food intake (1981/82)		1 925 kilocalories per day
Life expectancy (1982–84 av.):	Male	55 years
	Female	55 years
Infant mortality rate (1 year)		122 per thousand births
Adult literacy rate (1981):	Male	40 per cent
	Female	18 per cent
Primary school enrollment rate (1984)		63 per cent
Per capita commercial energy consumption (1985)		43 kg coal equivalent
Urban population as per cent of total (1985/86)		18
Villages with electricity (1985) per cent of total		8
Cultivated land per agricultural worker (c. 1985)		1.2 acre (0.49 ha)

Sectoral shares (per cent):	GDP (1985/86)	Employment (1983/84)
Agriculture	47.7	58.6
Manufacturing: "Modern"	4.5	1.4
Other	3.6	7.4
Services	44.2	32.6

Note: Sectoral shares of the GDP are based on the current price estimates. As discussed in the Annex to Chapter 2, value added in manufacturing is a little understated; its share should be about 10 per cent.

Economic growth under any system depends on the successful fulfillment of the above role by the government. Thus entrepreneurs will not commit their assets to productive investment unless they consider the system to be stable. Nor will they engage in productive enterprise if the rules of the game make it more profitable to engage in activities other than production. One of the themes of the present study (see Chapter 4 in particular) is that in Bangladesh successive governments have by and large failed to perform this important function effectively. Political stability has clearly been lacking. Lack of stability is not, however, synonymous with the periodic occurrence of *coups d'etat* or frequent changes in government through other means. Despite such occurrences, countries like Thailand and South Korea have been stable in the sense of guaranteeing the essential continuation of the rules of the game and an environment conducive to the development of the leading economic forces. In Bangladesh successive regimes have been preoccupied with setting up arrangements for their own survival. They were not strong enough to impose a coalition among the often contending economic forces – the actual and potential entrepreneurs – and subject them to the discipline of a set of rules of the game whose continuity would gradually come to be accepted.

POVERTY AND UNDERDEVELOPMENT

One might begin the quantification of the poverty of Bangladesh by citing per capita income: 4 400 Taka at current prices in 1985/86. This is equivalent to US $147 at the exchange rate (about Tk 30 = one dollar) prevailing in that year. The poorest 40 per cent of the Bangladeshis had a substantially lower per capita income: approximately Tk 2 450 or $82.

Much more telling are the specific indicators of living standards. Per capita daily consumption of food has fluctuated around 2 000 kilocalories in recent years (e.g., it was estimated to have been 1 925 kilocalories in 1981/82). This average has been significantly below the average requirement which has been variously estimated for Bangladesh to be between 2 020 and 2 150[2]. In 1983/84 an estimated 37 per cent of the Bangladeshis consumed less than 1 800 kilocalories per capita per day. Many received far less than 1 800 kilocalories and the seasonal fluctuation around this annual average was high. It is therefore clear that between a quarter and a third of the Bangladeshis have such a low consumption of food over prolonged periods that they are exposed to serious risk of health damage and (in children) permanently impaired development. Anthropometric measurements showed that in 1985/86 about 94 per cent of the Bangladeshi children suffered from some degree of malnutrition.

According to the census of 1981 only 29 per cent of the adults (those over 15) were literate in the sense of being able to write a simple letter. In 1984 only 63 per cent of the children in the relevant age group were enrolled in primary schools, which are often very rudimentary institutions. In the same year 122 of every thousand children born were expected to die before attaining age one. Average life expectancy of the

18 per cent of Bangladeshis living in urban areas is 61 years. The remaining 82 per cent, living in rural areas, have a life expectancy of 54 years.

About 60 per cent of the members of the labor force are employed in the agricultural sector and the sector accounts for 45 per cent of domestic product. Manufacturing industries account for about 9 per cent of the labor force and approximately 10 per cent of domestic product. The sector is characterized by a duality: less than a sixth of the industrial labor force, employed in the relatively capital-intensive modern industries, produce half of the sector's net output. The remaining industrial workers are engaged in different types of small-scale and cottage industrial activities with very low productivity per person.

Physical infrastructure is poor. The railway and road networks are both inadequate and in an unsatisfactory state of maintenance. Inland waterways, an important means of transport, are insufficiently developed. Commercial energy consumption, at 43 kgs of coal equivalent per head, is low even by the standards of the poor countries. Only about 8 per cent of the villages have access to electricity (in the neighboring Indian province of West Bengal the proportion is above 45 per cent). Although the supply of natural gas is substantial, its distribution has been constrained by the inability to finance the construction of a transmission pipeline across the rivers that divide the country between an eastern region (in which gas reserves are located) and a western region.

Before independence Bangladesh was self-reliant in spite of its acute poverty. Indeed, during the earlier years of the Pakistan period it was subjected to a net transfer of resources to finance the industrialization of (then West) Pakistan[3]. Ever since independence it has been heavily dependent on external assistance.

LONG-TERM STAGNATION AND DECLINE

It is reasonably clear that in some basic sense most Bangladeshis today have a lower standard of living than their ancestors a century or more ago. This view is based on historical data on the rice equivalent of the wage rate of agricultural workers about which information is available at periodic intervals since the 1830s[4]. Available historical documents suggest that the agricultural wage rate per day amounted to no less than 6 kgs of rice in the 1830s and over 5 kgs in the late 1880s. Even as recently as in the 1930s, a day's agricultural wage could buy between 5.5 and 6 kgs of coarse rice. In the early 1980s the agricultural wage per day on average bought less than 3 kgs of coarse rice. Even today rice accounts for more than half of the expenditure of the poorer half of the Bangladeshis. There is no evidence that over the long term it has become dearer relative to other goods and services[5]. It would therefore seem justified to conclude that agricultural workers today have a real income which is substantially below that of their ancestors 50, 100 and 150 years ago. The same sources also indicate that an average person in rural Bangladesh eats less today as compared to the earlier periods referred to above.

Another aspect of the underdevelopment of Bangladesh in modern times is the widening gap between its average living standard and that of other Asian countries, including the country's neighbors (Table 1.2). In spite of all difficulties of measurement (e.g., those related to the appropriateness of exchange rates as indicators of purchasing power at any given time and between the time periods under consideration), the stark conclusion is obvious[6]. In terms of economic growth, Bangladesh has fallen substantially behind its sub-continental neighbors, who themselves have grown far more slowly than the major South-East Asian countries. The latter in turn have grown at a considerably lower rate than the East Asian countries. The gap between Bangladesh and each of these three Asian regional groups has become progressively

Table 1.2 Per capita income as a multiple of per capita income of Bangladesh

	1958	1985
Bangladesh	1.00	1.00
India	1.27	1.80
Pakistan	1.36	2.53
Thailand	1.53	5.33
Indonesia	1.33	3.53
South Korea	2.00	14.33
Japan	6.16	75.33

Note: For 1958 country estimates are based on the data in the UN, *Statistical Yearbook*, 1960 while that for Bangladesh is from the same source as in Chapter 2. For 1985 the estimates are from World Bank, *The World Development Report 1987*.

wider during the last three decades (and perhaps over a much longer period).

INITIAL CONDITIONS

Several of the factors that are often cited as making poverty and underdevelopment so difficult a challenge in Bangladesh deserve attention. The first is that Bangladesh is a country with very limited natural resources. A moderate reserve of natural gas is about the only important resource apart from land. Land is naturally fertile, but extremely scarce relative to the number of those who are dependent on it for their livelihood. Net sown area of land per agricultural laborer is only 1.2 acres.

The large size of population and its relatively rapid increase constitute a very serious problem. The existing density of population – 1 875 persons per square mile in 1986/87 – is easily the highest of all countries with the exception of city states such as Hong Kong and Singapore. The annual increase in population is a staggering 2.6 million people, and the number should grow exponentially unless the rate of growth begins to decline. Expansion in the infrastructure necessary to provide the expanded population even with the existing low per capita level of facilities will claim a very high proportion of the savings this nation is able to generate.

Infrastructure in irrigation, drainage, transport, communications, power and energy distribution are under severe strain and in need of large, often indivisible, investments that are difficult to finance. The lack of adequate infrastructure is a serious obstacle to the attraction of substantial direct foreign investment which is sometimes seen as an avenue for industrialization.

These are formidable problems. There is however a need to consider them in the right perspective. As extreme or even more unfavorable land/labor ratios in agriculture have been observed in South Korea in the 1960s and 1970s and in China and Java in more recent times[7]. The population growth rate in Bangladesh is nowhere near the highest in the developing world, as a comparison with Pakistan, Kenya and most African countries would show. There are several examples of a dramatic reduction in the birth rate within short time periods in recent history, including those of South Korea and China. Infrastructure, though inadequate, is generally better in Bangladesh than in many Asian neighbors (e.g., Nepal and Burma) and African countries. Perhaps the simultaneous existence of all these negative features and the absence of some redeeming features that characterize the countries having some of these problems are the source of the pessimism that Bangladesh usually invokes.

Even so one must recognize that not all the initial conditions are unfavorable. A strongly positive factor is that this large nation is virtually unilingual and nearly homogeneous in many other ways. It is not bogged down in any significant internal or external conflict that requires large-scale commitment of resources for military purposes. There are few social taboos and forces within the country that might prove to be serious obstacles to modernization and the adoption of programs such as contraception. These very important favorable factors for development are absent in many developing countries.

AN OUTLINE

The purpose of this study is to analyze the development of the economy of Bangladesh since independence with a focus on the role of the strategy pursued by the government in promoting growth and alleviating poverty. Chapter 2 discusses the macroeconomic aspects of the country's development experience. Chapters 3 and 4 discuss the performance of agriculture and manufacturing industries. Chapter 5 is concerned with the major issues of trade, finance and inflation. Chapter 6 discusses the infrastructure, both physical and social. In Chapter 7 an attempt is made to analyze the trends in the distribution of income and the incidence of poverty and to relate their changes to structural factors and government policies. The concluding chapter summarizes the experience and evaluates the strategy in the light of the performance of the economy.

Notes and References

1. See Keith Griffin and A.R. Khan (eds), *Growth and Inequality in Pakistan*, Macmillan, London, 1972 for an account of the economic relations between the two regions and their unequal growth.
2. The first of these estimates is used by the Bangladesh Planning Commission while the second one is an earlier FAO estimate. It has been suggested by some analysts (see Michael Lipton, *Poverty, Undernutrition and Hunger*, World Bank Staff Working Papers, No. 597, 1983) that the FAO standards of average requirement are too high. It is however widely

recognized that a prolonged period of substantially lower energy intake, say below 1 800 kilocalories per day, would entail a serious risk of health damage for an average Bangladeshi with an average level of activity.
3. See Keith Griffin and A.R. Khan (eds), *op.cit.*
4. See A.R. Khan, "Real Wages of Agricultural Workers in Bangladesh" in A.R. Khan and Eddy Lee (eds), *Poverty in Rural Asia,* ILO/ARTEP, Bangkok, 1984, pp. 197-203.
5. *Ibid.*
6. It may however be mentioned that estimates of internationally comparable incomes by and large support the picture of the relative rates of growth depicted in Table 1.2. See Robert Summers and Alan Heston, "Improved International Comparisons of Real Product and Its Composition: 1950-1980", *The Review of Income and Wealth,* June 1984.
7. See A.R. Khan, "Population Growth and Access to Land: An Asian Perspective", in Ronald Lee *et al.* (eds), *Proceedings of the Seminar on Population and Rural Development,* held in New Delhi, December 1984 under the auspices of the International Union for the Scientific Study of Population, Oxford University Press (forthcoming).

2 Growth and Structural Change

This chapter provides a macroeconomic background for the analysis of the development experience in Bangladesh since independence. It begins with a discussion of the trends in population growth and changes in the size and occupational distribution of the population. Next it analyzes the trends in the growth of national income and other macroeconomic aggregates.

THE RATE OF POPULATION GROWTH

Until the middle of 1986 the Bangladesh Bureau of Statistics (BBS) used a time series on population which implied that the rate of population growth in Bangladesh had been declining since the 1970s and had fallen to as low as 2.2 per cent per year or lower in the 1980s[1]. The BBS series on population implied an annual rate of growth between January 1981 and January 1985 of 2.19 per cent. If these estimates were accurate, they would indicate that there had been a dramatic demographic transformation in Bangladesh compared to the immediate pre-independence period. For example, in the three years ending in January 1970 the population of Bangladesh was estimated to have increased at an annual rate of 3 per cent per year.

BBS estimates of population growth rates between 1974 and 1981 are based on actual counts during the censuses taken in those years (adjusted on the basis of post-enumeration surveys). The annual rate of growth between the two censuses was 2.3 per cent. Most experts appear to accept the adjusted census estimates of population as reasonably reliable in the absence of any convincing analysis to the contrary. It would therefore be justified to conclude that the growth rate had actually declined from the peak of about 3 per cent immediately before independence to about 2.3 per cent in the 1970s. Given the existing state of knowledge, there is no reason to believe that this decline could have resulted from such factors as the famine of 1974 and/or possible unrecorded emigration. Much of the decline appears to have been due to a reduction in the natural rate of growth.

The estimates for the period since the 1981 census have not however been confirmed by an actual count. The optimism of the BBS was prompted by results from the Demographic Survey and the Vital Registration System (VRS) which showed that during 1980-85 annual estimates of the crude birth rate ranged between 33.4 and 35 per thousand and that of the crude death rate ranged between 10.2 and 12.3 per thousand. In the pre-independence years the crude birth rate was estimated to have been above 45 per thousand and the crude death rate between 18 and 20 per thousand. Most well informed people agree that fertility fell somewhat between the late 1960s and the early 1980s while mortality fell less and perhaps not at all. However, demographic experts have been widely skeptical about the VRS estimates of the crude birth rates. It is widely believed that the VRS, especially in the early 1980s, suffered from a significant under-enumeration of births. Even among official agencies there has been disagreement about the actual rate of population growth. During the years when the BBS used a steadily declining rate of growth in preparing its population estimates, the Planning Commission used a consistently higher rate. Finally, in the summer of 1986 the BBS itself abandoned its optimistic assumptions and decided instead to use significantly higher rates of growth that happen to be identical to the rates that the Planning Commission uses. The BBS has not so far explained why they have changed their position, but it is clear that in effect they have agreed that the crude birth rates estimated by the VRS were indeed biased downward and seriously underestimated the number of births in the country[2].

The currently accepted official time series on population – which is yet to be verified by an actual count for the period after 1981 – contains the following features:

(a) The population growth rate peaked in the late 1960s reaching 3 per cent per year. At that time the birth rate was somewhere between 45 and 50 per thousand and the death rate was close to 20 per thousand.
(b) In the first decade after independence the population growth rate declined substantially to something like 2.3 per cent per year due to a decline in the birth rate to well below 40 per thousand and a smaller decline in the death rate to about 15 per thousand.
(c) In the early 1980s the population growth rate increased significantly to a level above 2.5 per cent per year. The reasons behind this rise are not yet adequately explained. It seems unlikely however that it is due entirely to a further decline in mortality. Available evidence suggests that there has been no trend decline in

the death rate in the 1980s. It follows therefore that implicit in the current estimates of population growth for the post-1981 census period used by the BBS and the Planning Commission is an admission that the crude birth rate in the 1980s rose significantly and is higher than it was in the 1970s.

The information on which this story is based is not definite, but if one accepts that the outlines of the story are valid, there is a problem of how to explain the erratic movements in the birth rate, *viz.*, a decline between the late 1960s and the late 1970s of as much as 10 per thousand followed by a significant rise in the early 1980s. Some decline in fertility since the 1960s can plausibly be explained by an increase in the use of contraceptives, an increase in the mean age at first marriage for women (from 13.9 years in 1961 to 16.7 in 1981), a modest increase in female education, and a response to a perception of some decline in infant mortality (though the infant mortality rate still is very high at about 122 per thousand births). However, these changes taken together are not large enough to account for the substantial decline in fertility that is thought to have taken place in the 1970s. Moreover, these changes do not enable one to understand why the downward trend in fertility was suddenly reversed in the 1980s. There is a puzzle here that calls for an explanation.

One explanation is that a good part of the sharp decline in fertility in the 1970s was a consequence of increasing poverty. That is, it was poverty-induced. A number of surveys have shown that fertility at first rises with per capita income and then falls. A similar inverted U-shaped relationship has been found between the birth rate and social status. For example, the number of children born per woman is the lowest among landless families and then rises among landholding families with the amount of land per family. Similarly, fertility is lower for families without any education than for families with primary education and, sometimes, secondary education. But then it falls off again and fertility is lowest of all for familes at the top end of the educational distribution[3]. This scattered evidence suggests the possibility that changes in the distribution of income and in particular an increase in the incidence of extreme poverty could lead to lower fertility. An economic reason for this would be a decline in the value of children to the increasing numbers of households sinking into extreme poverty and deprivation.

As will be shown in Chapter 7, available evidence strongly points to a sharp worsening of the living conditions of the poor and to an increase in the proportion of the population in poverty in the 1970s. It is possible that this tended to reduce fertility and that this was a more important cause of the observed reduction in the birth rate than the more conventional factors mentioned earlier. In the early 1980s the incidence of poverty probably declined a little as compared to the worst years of the 1970s (though it remained higher than in the late 1960s) and the real incomes of the rural poor probably improved a little. The hypothesis outlined above would lead one to expect that the decline in fertility would then go into reverse – and this is what appears to have happened. When the increase in extreme poverty came to a halt and the living standards of the very poor began to recover, the birth rate also began to rise.

LABOR FORCE AND ITS DISTRIBUTION

At first glance it appears from the data that a dramatic change has taken place in the occupational distribution of the labor force in Bangladesh since independence (Tables 2.1 and 2.2). Between the censuses of 1974 and 1981, the labor force in agriculture actually declined in absolute terms for the first time in known history. The decline was 8.3 per cent in just over seven years. Between the 1981 census and the Labor Force Survey (LFS) of 1983/84, there was some increase in the absolute size of the agricultural labor force, but there was a further decline in its ratio to the total labor force. In the decade between the 1974 census (taken at the midpoint of the fiscal year 1973/74) and the 1983/84 LFS, the agricultural labor force remained virtually unchanged while the total labor force increased by nearly a third. Thus the share of agriculture in the total labor force declined from 79 per cent to 59 per cent. Conversely, the share of manufacturing industries – in large, small and cottage enterprises together – increased by more than four-fifths and that for other sectors doubled.

How is one to interpret these apparently dramatic changes in the composition of the labor force over the decade under review? There are three possibilities, and combinations of these possibilities, that can be considered.

(a) First, it is possible to interpret the data as indicating a dynamic diversification of the economy due to rapid growth of output in industry and services both in urban and rural areas. The employment pattern shifts in response to a change in the

Table 2.1 Labor force and employment

	Census 1974 (1st January)	Census 1981 (1st March)	LFS 1983/84 (1st January)
Levels (in millions)			
Population	76.4	89.9	96.8
Labor force	21.9	25.9	29.0
Employed labor force	21.4	25.3	28.5
Male	20.5	23.9	25.9
Female	0.9	1.4	2.6
Unemployed labor force	0.5	0.6	0.5
Male	0.5	0.5	0.4
Female	—	0.1	0.1
Housewives	17.8	22.4	24.2
Inactive	9.7	11.8	12.8
Children below 10	26.9	29.9	30.8
Employment in:			
Agriculture	16.8	15.4	16.7
Non-agriculture	4.6	9.9	11.8
Percentages			
Labor force as per cent of population	28.7	28.8	29.9
Male labor force as per cent of male population	53.0	52.7	53.5
Female labor force as per cent of female population	2.5	3.4	5.4
Agricultural employment as per cent of total employment	78.5	60.9	58.6
Labor force as per cent of population 10 and above	44.2	43.2	43.9

Sources: 1974 and 1981: Census data reported in *Statistical Yearbook 1986*, pp. 192–193. 1983/84: *Final Report of the 1983/84 Labor Force Survey.* Data for 1983/84 have been adjusted upwards because the LFS population is lower than that in the latest population series of the Bangladesh Bureau of Statistics (BBS). For example, LFS shows a population of 95.2 million and a labor force of 28.5 million. Since the latest BBS population estimate is 96.8 million, the labor force is adjusted to (96.8/95.2) 28.5 = 29.0 million.

Table 2.2 Sectoral distribution of the labor force and labor productivity

	1973/74	1983/84	Change	Per cent of total change
Employed labor force: millions	21.4	28.5	7.1	100.0
Agriculture	16.8	16.7	−0.1	−1.4
Manufacturing	1.0	2.5	1.5	21.1
Trade	0.8	3.3	2.5	35.2
Transport, storage	0.4	1.1	0.7	9.9
Services	2.2	2.3	0.1	1.4
Construction	—	0.5	0.5	7.0
Others	—	0.3	0.3	4.2
Not accounted for	0.2	1.8	1.6	22.5
Urban employed labor force	2.1	3.8	1.7	23.9
Agriculture	0.3	0.3	0.0	0.0
Non-agriculture	1.8	3.5	1.7	23.9
Rural employed labor force	19.3	24.7	5.4	76.1
Agriculture	16.5	16.4	−0.1	−1.4
Non-agriculture	2.8	8.3	5.5	77.5
Value added per laborer (Taka at 1972/73 *market* prices)				
Agriculture	1 716	2 242		
Manufacturing	3 316	3 150		
Trade	6 428	2 060		
Transport	8 820	4 855		
Construction	47 583	7 357		

Note: Value added per laborer in manufacturing is based on unadjusted BBS data: with an upward adjustment for a possible underestimation, the figure for 1983/84 would be 3,793. Labor force data are from the same sources as Table 2.1. Value added figures are from BBS source shown in the annual *Statistical Yearbooks*.

composition of production. Labor is pulled out of agriculture into the rapidly growing industrial and service sectors. This would be associated with increasing labor productivity and real wages both in agriculture and in the non-agricultural sectors.

(b) A second possibility is that growth in agriculture at the margin has been labor displacing, rather than labor absorbing. This would tend to push labor out of agriculture and into various non-agricultural activities, mostly of a residual variety characterized by low labor productivity. If the "push" was strong enough, labor productivity in the non-agricultural sector might even fall further. Though labor productivity in agriculture would rise, real wages might not increase because of the downward shift in the demand for labor.

(c) A third possibility is that the actual change in sectoral labor use was not proportional to the change in sectoral labor force as recorded in the censuses and the LFS. These censuses and surveys classify the sectoral distribution of labor on the basis of the primary source of employment. For example, a person employed in agriculture for 51 per cent of the time and in handicrafts for the remainder of the time would be classified as a member of the agricultural labor force. If the allocation of his labor time were to change, so that he worked in handicrafts for just over half of his time and in agriculture for the remainder, he would cease to be classified as a member of the agricultural labor force and would instead be reclassified as a non-agricultural (manufacturing) worker. Labor use or the input of labor in agriculture would in this example decline by a little more than a fiftieth of a person-year whereas labor force in agriculture would be reported as having declined by one person.

Table 2.2 provides some information on where the new entrants to the labor force found employment and how much they contributed in the new sectors of their employment. Some of the notable features may be summarized as follows:

(a) Seventy-six per cent of the new entrants to the labor force remained in the rural areas and nearly 78 per cent of the new entrants found employment not in agriculture but in the non-agricultural sectors of the rural economy. The numbers employed in agriculture, as already mentioned, actually fell.

(b) Trade (including a small component of hotels and restaurants) accounted for by far the largest share of the growth in employment. It absorbed more than 35 per cent of the increase in the labor force, raising the sector's employment by more than 15 per cent per year. If one excludes those whose occupations could not be ascertained, it turns out that trade absorbed 46 per cent of the increase in the labor force[4]. Manufacturing, the second largest labor absorbing sector, came far behind, providing employment to 21 per cent of the increase in the labor force. Transport and construction, accounting respectively for 10 and 7 per cent of the

increase, are the next most important labor absorbing sectors.
(c) If these increments in employment are compared with changes in the sectoral composition of GDP over the same period, several highly implausible implications emerge. If one accepts the official data at face value, labor productivity in agriculture must have increased at an annual rate of 2.7 per cent per year. In manufacturing the data imply that labor productivity declined 0.5 per cent a year. Or if one accepts the upward revision in the official estimates of value added in manufacturing that are discussed in the Annex to this chapter, then labor productivity rose 1.4 per cent a year, still only half that in agriculture. In the most labor absorbing sector, namely trade, labor productivity allegedly declined at a staggering annual rate of 11 per cent. Similar rates of decline took place in transport (6 per cent per year) and construction (17 per cent per year).

One might be tempted to argue that value added in trade, transport and construction in the official GDP estimates is grossly underestimated. But this is hardly plausible. If labor productivity were to have remained unchanged, it would have been necessary for value added in trade to grow at an annual rate of 15 per cent (as compared to the estimated 2.7 per cent or less) and value added in construction to grow at an annual rate of 30 per cent (as compared to the estimated 7 to 8 per cent). These hypothetical rates are inconsistent with the well-established indicators of growth in these sectors (e.g., the volume of goods produced and traded and the volume of construction inputs) and it would be absurd to imagine that such enormous differences between official and actual growth rates over a decade could remain unrecognized by the statisticians.

Two other facts, discussed in greater detail in a later chapter, also are relevant in interpreting changes in the occupational distribution of the labor force. First, there is no evidence that real wages in agriculture increased between 1973/74 and 1983/84, as the first possibility discussed requires[5]. Secondly, the data show that most of the increase in the labor force was absorbed in rural employment. If these new entrants were productively employed, the consequent generation of income would have created a great deal of demand for mass consumption goods, notably coarse rice. In reality, the price of coarse rice fell, relative to the cost of living in general, without any evidence of increased per capita availability.

It therefore seems unlikely that a dynamic diversification of the economy was pulling labor out of agriculture in massive numbers into fast growing non-agricultural sectors. A more likely explanation of the employment data is that the reported change was largely due to the last two of the three possible factors listed above. Changes in the sectoral distribution of labor use (or labor inputs) were less dramatic than changes in the sectoral shares of the labor force which were measured by the censuses and surveys. To this might be added the possibility, suggested by the non-increasing real wages coexisting with an apparently increasing labor productivity in agriculture, that incremental labor absorption in agriculture was smaller than average. The two phenomena are related: as agricultural growth absorbed less labor at the margin, more and more people found themselves with agriculture as the secondary, rather than the primary, source of employment. Agriculture's share of labor input declined though not nearly as much as its share of the labor force as the primary source of employment. It is very likely that a good deal of the increase in non-agricultural employment was in activities with very low productivity (e.g., rudimentary trading in rural areas).

However, before leaving the topic for the moment, it is important to recall that these conclusions apply to the period roughly to 1983/84. As will be discussed later, the changes that occurred in the few following years for which at least some preliminary information is available, are more difficult to interpret.

GROWTH IN GDP AND PER CAPITA INCOME

Table 2.3 assembles time series on GDP, GNP, population and per capita GDP and GNP since 1949/50. While the basic series are the ones prepared by the BBS, the Table includes an alternative set of GDP and GNP estimates which are based on an upward adjustment in value added in manufacturing in the BBS series. It has been alleged by some critics that this component of the BBS estimates has been underestimated in recent years[6]. The details of the assumptions underlying the adjustments made in the alternative series are discussed in the Annex to this chapter. It should however be made clear that in the opinion of the authors the alternative series represents an upper bound of the estimated rate of growth of the manufacturing sector. In the discussion below the reference to growth rates, etc. is always based on the BBS series unless otherwise stated.

Table 2.3 National income, population and per capita income

Year	GDP	GNP	Population	Adjusted GDP	Adjusted GNP	Per capita GDP	Per capita GNP	Adjusted per capita GDP	Adjusted per capita GNP
1949/50	27 233	27 189	42.2	27 233	27 189	645	644	645	644
1950/51	28 696	28 655	43.2	28 696	28 655	664	663	664	663
1951/52	29 660	29 635	44.3	29 660	29 635	670	669	670	669
1952/53	30 557	30 528	45.4	30 557	30 528	673	672	673	672
1953/54	31 945	31 882	46.5	31 945	31 882	687	686	687	686
1954/55	31 232	31 224	47.6	31 232	31 224	656	656	656	656
1955/56	29 923	29 884	48.8	29 923	29 884	613	612	613	612
1956/57	33 119	33 083	50.0	33 119	33 083	662	662	662	662
1957/58	32 454	32 444	51.2	32 454	32 444	634	634	634	634
1958/59	30 641	30 617	52.5	30 641	30 617	584	583	584	583
1959/60	34 134	34 093	53.8	34 134	34 093	634	634	634	634
1960/61	35 833	35 811	55.1	35 833	35 811	650	650	650	650
1961/62	38 535	38 501	56.6	38 535	38 501	681	680	681	680
1962/63	39 222	39 142	58.1	39 222	39 142	675	674	675	674
1963/64	42 881	42 760	59.7	42 881	42 760	718	716	718	716
1964/65	43 563	43 575	61.3	43 563	43 575	711	711	711	711
1965/66	45 041	45 053	62.9	45 041	45 053	716	716	716	716
1966/67	45 482	45 494	64.6	45 482	45 494	704	704	704	704
1967/68	49 500	49 512	66.5	49 500	49 512	744	745	744	745
1968/69	50 953	50 965	68.5	50 953	50 965	744	744	744	744
1969/70	51 833	51 840	70.6	51 833	51 840	734	734	734	734
1972/73	45 300	45 300	74.2	45 300	45 300	611	611	611	611
1973/74	49 073	49 225	76.4	49 073	49 225	642	644	642	644
1974/75	51 535	51 657	78.0	51 202	51 324	661	662	656	658

1975/76	55 372	55 539	79.9	55 061	55 228	693	695	689	691
1976/77	56 369	56 609	81.8	56 146	56 386	689	692	686	689
1977/78	60 240	60 772	83.7	60 080	60 612	720	726	718	724
1978/79	62 813	63 519	85.6	62 823	63 529	734	742	734	742
1979/80	63 586	64 763	87.6	63 718	64 895	726	739	727	741
1980/81	67 514	69 299	89.6	67 840	69 625	754	773	757	777
1981/82	68 460	70 034	92.1	69 011	70 585	743	760	749	766
1982/83	70 817	73 839	94.4	71 801	74 823	750	782	761	793
1983/84	73 804	76 511	96.8	75 242	77 949	762	790	777	805
1984/85	76 679	78 349	99.2	78 629	80 299	773	790	793	809
1985/86	79 792	82 321	101.7	81 880	84 409	785	809	805	830
1986/87	83 292	86 523	104.1	85 757	88 988	800	831	824	855

Note: GDP and GNP are in millions of Taka at 1972/73 prices. Population in millions. Both are from the BBS. Adjusted GDP and GNP are based on upward adjustment in the BBS estimates for possible underestimation of industrial value added. See Annex to Chapter 2 for detailed explanation.

Table 2.4 shows the estimates of trend rates of growth in these various series for the pre-independence (1949/50 –1969/70) and post-independence (1972/73 –1986/87) periods. These rates of growth have been estimated by using a trend equation that allows both for a kink and a discontinuity at the time of independence (see note to Table 2.4). The major conclusions can be summarized as follows:

(a) During the two decades before independence, the rate of growth of GDP was about 3.2 per cent per year. Much of this growth was

Table 2.4 Trend growth rates—Per cent per year

	GDP/GNP	Per capita GDP/GNP
Pre-independence period (1949/50–1969/70)		
GDP	3.20	0.66
GNP	3.21	0.66
Post-independence period (1972/73–1986/87)		
GDP	4.05	1.64
GDP: Adjusted	4.29	1.90
GNP	4.34	1.93
GNP: Adjusted	4.58	2.18

Note: Growth rates are estimated by fitting the following trend equation:

$$\text{Log } Y_t = a_1 + a_2 Z_t + b_1 T + b_2 Z_t T$$

Where:

Y = Dependent variable (GDP/GNP or per capita GDP/GNP)

T = Time = 1 for 1949/50, ... 38 for 1986/87; subscript t denotes the same for variables; and

Z = 0 for pre-independence years and 1 for post-independence years.

The fitted equations confirm the hypotheses that income fell significantly at the time of independence (all the estimated a_2 coefficients being negative and significant at the 1 per cent level) and that the trend rate of growth in the post-independence period was significantly higher than the trend rate of growth in the pre-independence period (b_2 is positive and significant at the 1 per cent level). Note that b_1 is the pre-independence growth rate and ($b_1 + b_2$) is the post-independence growth rate. All coefficients are significant at the 1 per cent level. These equations gave the best fit among a large number of alternatives tried: R-squared is about 0.99 for GDP/GNP trend equations and about 0.8 or higher for per capita GDP/GNP trend equations. Forcing the assumption of a lack of discontinuity at independence or the assumption of identical growth rate in the periods before and after independence sharply reduces the R-squared.

offset by the increase in the population which grew at an average annual rate of over 2.5 per cent. (The rate was lower in the 1950s and higher in the 1960s.) The annual increase in per capita income averaged 0.66 per cent. Net factor income received from abroad was insignificant; so growth in GNP was the same as in GDP.

(b) During the post-independence period, GDP grew at a significantly faster trend rate, over 4 per cent per year. The corresponding annual trend rate of growth in per capita GDP was 1.64 per cent, i.e., almost two-and-a-half times as fast as in the pre-independence period.

(c) However, the significantly higher growth rate in the post-independence period is somewhat misleading because there was an initial decline in the level of GDP immediately after independence. (See the note on the trend equation in Table 2.4.) Thus the point of departure for calculating the trend was an unusually depressed level of income. The pre-independence peak per capita GDP (in 1968/69) was not equalled again until 1980/81. Had GDP continued to grow at the pre-independence trend rate (avoiding the fall immediately after independence), per capita GDP in 1986/87 would in fact have been higher than it actually was.

(d) The growth rate in GNP was about three-tenths of a percentage point higher per year than the growth rate in GDP during the post-independence period. This is due to the rapid growth in net factor income received from abroad since the late 1970s. This, in turn, reflects the new phenomena of a large emigration of workers to the oil-exporting countries of the Middle East and the remittances made by them.

(e) The peak per capita income after independence (in 1986/87) was 7.5 per cent higher than the peak per capita income before independence. Per capita annual income in the first six fiscal years of the 1980s was about 5 per cent higher than in the second half of the 1960s. In assessing the significance of these differences in income levels and growth rates before and after independence one should not overlook the fact that in the post-independence period public administration, defense and miscellaneous services have grown much faster relative to the rest of the GDP than in the pre-independence period. The share of these components in total product was about 8 per cent in the late 1960s and 12.5 per cent in the mid-1980s. It is perhaps doubtful that public administration, military expenditure and miscellaneous services contribute as much to the general well being of the population as the other components of domestic product.

MACROECONOMIC CHANGES SINCE INDEPENDENCE

It is interesting to compare the major macroeconomic variables and parameters before and after independence. For the period before independence the second half of the 1960s (fiscal years 1965/66–1969/70) will be used as the reference period. For the period after independence, the first six years of the present decade (fiscal years 1980/81 to 1985/86) have been chosen. In this section these are referred to as the "pre-independence" and "post-independence" periods respectively. Tables 2.5 and 2.6 summarize the major macroeconomic facts about these two periods.

As noted above, per capita income in the second period was about 5 per cent higher than in the first period. Per capita consumption in the second period, however, was about 12 per cent higher than in the first period. This is due to a sharp decline in the rate of domestic saving, which fell from 8 per cent of GDP in the pre-independence period to about 2 per cent in the post-independence period. That is, the rate of savings fell by three-quarters after independence was achieved.

Investment, however, increased from 12 per cent of GDP in the pre-independence period to 14 per cent in the post-independence period. But within the post-independence period there was a tendency for the rate of investment gradually to decline in recent years.

The gap between the higher rate of investment and the lower rate of domestic savings was covered by a vastly increased rate of foreign capital inflow ("foreign savings") which, measured as the difference between imports and exports, increased from 3 per cent of GDP during the pre-independence period to 11 per cent in the post-independence period. That is, the ratio of foreign savings to total product increased by 267 per cent after independence. When considered as a proportion of investment, capital inflows increased from 28 per cent before independence to 84 per cent after independence.

A part of the capital inflow consists of remittances from Bangladeshis working abroad. For the period before independence, estimates of remittances are not available because of the inadequacy of information about the triangular flow of funds among Bangladesh, Pakistan and the rest of the world. However, it is unlikely that such flows were large. In the post-independence period, in contrast, remittances averaged more than 3 per cent of GDP. Even if one excludes this source of funds, capital inflows (financed by net foreign loans and grants) were 8 per cent of

GDP as compared to a mere 3 per cent before independence.

Only 16 per cent of investment in the post-independence period was financed by domestic savings. Another 25 per cent was financed by workers' remittances. The remaining 59 per cent was financed by net external assistance. (That is, in addition to financing 59 per cent of investment, gross external assistance also financed the repayment of external debt.) As mentioned above, only 28 per cent of investment was financed by net external assistance in the pre-independence period.

Public savings in the post-independence period have been negative, on the average -1.6 per cent of GDP[7]. Private savings have also been low and generally negatively correlated with the rate of capital inflow, signifying that these have probably been seen as the residual resource to be drawn upon when foreign capital inflows are inadequate.

Continued dependence on a high inflow of foreign assistance has led to increased indebtedness. By mid-1986, the outstanding medium- and long-term (M&LT) external debt stood at $6.14 billion. This was equivalent to more than two-fifths of current GDP and nearly eight times the value of merchandise exports in 1985/86. The terms of (M&LT) external indebtedness are still very favorable, with an average repayment period of 39 years, a grace period of 9 years and an average interest rate of 1.5 per cent. Debt service payments (on M&LT loans alone) have, however, more than doubled in nominal dollar value between 1980/81 and 1985/86 and in the latter year these payments amounted to 23 per cent of the value of merchandise exports. If the servicing of the short-term commercial debt (a good part of which is allegedly transitional due to the concentration of maturities in recent years) is included, then total external debt service payments in 1985/86 amount to 61 per cent of the value of exports. (See Chapter 5 for details.)

To summarize: during the two decades before independence, the economy of what is now Bangladesh grew rather slowly, averaging about two-thirds of a percentage point per year in per capita terms. Since independence, the rate of growth has been about two and a half times as fast as in the pre-independence period. At the time of independence there was a sharp fall in income and consequently much of this higher growth represents a catching up with the pre-independence peak. If one were to extrapolate the pre-independence trend rate of growth into the post-independence period, the predicted per capita income for 1986/87 would be higher than the actual level of income.

One favorable factor during the post-independence period that would translate a given rate of growth of GDP into a higher rate of growth of per capita income was the slower rate of growth of the population.

Table 2.5 Macroeconomic accounts—Current millions of Taka

	1980/81	1981/82	1982/83	1983/84	1984/85	1985/86	Av. 80/81–85/86
GDP at market price	233 263	265 144	288 423	349 922	418 746	481 622	339 520
Consumption	225 762	264 126	287 540	345 728	405 737	461 195	331 681
Private consumption	210 122	248 215	270 772	321 716	373 325	423 061	307 868
Public consumption	15 640	15 911	16 768	24 012	32 412	38 134	23 813
Domestic savings	7 501	1 018	883	4 194	13 009	18 497	7 517
Public savings	−6 313	−1 320	−2 577	−7 395	−9 657	−11 132	−5 393
Private savings	13 814	2 338	3 460	11 589	22 666	29 629	12 910
Foreign savings	29 731	38 819	38 329	38 887	42 523	42 477	38 461
Investment	37 232	39 837	39 212	43 081	55 532	60 974	45 978
Workers' remittances	6 196	7 725	14 224	13 762	10 340	16 611	11 476
Net capital inflow	23 535	31 094	24 105	25 125	32 183	25 866	26 985

As per cent of GDP						
Domestic savings	3.22	0.38	0.31	1.20	3.11	3.84	2.21
Public savings	−2.71	−0.50	1.20	−2.11	−2.31	−2.31	−1.59
Private savings	5.92	0.88	−0.89	3.31	5.41	6.15	3.80
Foreign savings	12.75	14.64	13.29	11.11	10.15	8.82	11.33
Workers' remittances	2.66	2.91	4.93	3.93	2.47	3.45	3.38
Net capital inflow	10.09	11.73	8.36	7.18	7.69	5.37	7.95
Investment	15.96	15.02	13.60	12.31	13.26	12.66	13.54
Consumption	96.78	99.62	99.69	98.80	96.89	95.76	97.69
Private consumption	90.08	93.62	93.88	91.94	89.15	87.84	90.68
Public consumption	6.70	6.00	5.81	6.86	7.74	7.92	7.01
As per cent of investment						
Public savings	−17.0	−3.3	8.8	−17.2	−17.4	−18.3	−11.7
Private savings	37.1	5.9	−6.6	26.9	40.8	48.6	28.1
Foreign savings	79.9	97.4	97.7	90.3	76.6	69.7	83.7
Workers' remittances	16.6	19.4	36.3	31.9	18.6	27.2	25.0
Net capital inflow	63.2	78.1	61.5	58.3	58.0	42.4	58.7

Note: Public savings = current revenue of government less current expenditures in which non-investment development expenditures are included. Foreign savings = imports less exports. "Net capital inflow" = foreign savings less workers' remittances.

Source: BBS, *Statistical Yearbook, 1986*, relevant issues of *Monthly Statistical Bulletins* and Ministry of Finance, *Economic Survey, 1986/87.*

Table 2.6 Macroeconomic characteristics before independence

As per cent of GDP	
Domestic savings	8.4
Foreign savings	3.2
Investment	11.6
Consumption	91.6
Private	85.7
Public	5.9
As per cent of investment	
Domestic savings	72.0
Foreign savings	28.0

Note: The definition of foreign savings is the same as in Table 2.5. The estimates are based on the current price series in Alamgir and Berlage, *op. cit.*

During the 1970s the population increased at a significantly slower rate than in the 1960s. In more recent years however the population growth rate does not appear to have continued to decline. Indeed, recent revisions in the official estimates suggest that the population growth rate may have increased in the 1980s.

The labor force data, literally interpreted, suggest that there has been a remarkable structural change in the economy. This, however, is not supported by the available evidence on changes in the sectoral composition of GDP and other relevant aspects of the economy. It seems therefore that data on the labor force need to be interpreted with great care. Changes in the occupational composition of the labor force are a poor indicator of the changes in the composition of actual labor use or labor input.

Compared to the period before independence, Bangladesh has achieved a somewhat higher rate of investment in the post-independence period. This occurred despite a sharp decline in the domestic saving rate and a corresponding rise in the propensity to consume. Higher rates of consumption and investment have been made possible by two things: a vast increase in the flow of external assistance and a large inflow of remittances from workers overseas. Indeed, workers' remittances alone were higher than the rate of domestic savings. In per capita terms, net foreign assistance (at about $10 per year in recent years) is not nearly as high as in some extreme cases in the developing world. But instead of resulting in a large rise in the rate of investment, the increased flow of foreign assistance has been associated with a sharp reduction in domestic savings. Had the rate of domestic saving in the post-independence period been the same as in the pre-independence period, the investment rate would have risen to about 20 per cent, or nearly half as much again as the actual rate. This would have led to a higher rate of growth and a greater capacity to service the foreign debt. One of the main causes of the low domestic saving rate is chronic dissaving by the public sector. Despite very favorable terms, debt service charges have become a disturbingly high proportion of export earnings.

Notes and References

1. The reference is to the population series that is used to derive per capita income from total national income. See, for example, BBS, *Monthly Statistical Bulletin,* May 1987, Table 11.2 (row 17). To the knowledge of the present authors this is the only series showing estimates of actual population. All the others are projections based on alternative fertility and mortality assumptions.
2. Note however that the BBS continues to publish the VRS estimates.
3. The evidence for these fertility characteristics has been summarized and their sources cited in Sawon Hong, *Demographic Characteristics of Bangladesh,* Dhaka, June 1980, pp. 25-30.
4. This indicates the possibility that the definition of the sector and/or the principle of enumerating the labor force in the sector changed between the 1974 census and the 1983/84 LFS.
5. The evidence on changes in real wages in agriculture after 1983/84 is more ambiguous (see Chapter 7).
6. See, W. I. Abraham, *Manufacturing Output and the Industrial Production Index,* Industrial Statistics Improvement Unit, Dhaka, 1984 (mimeographed) and World Bank, *Bangladesh: Recent Economic Developments and Medium Term Prospects,* Vol. I, March 1986. The latter makes use of Abraham's work.
7. Public savings are estimated after adding "non-investment development expenditure" to recurrent expenditure. See Chapter 5 for details.

3 Agricultural Development

This chapter analyzes the performance of the agricultural sector since independence. It begins with a look at the resources available to the agricultural sector and the organization of agriculture. It then examines the growth of agricultural production and the factors behind it. Next the implications of growth for the distribution of income are discussed. Finally, an analysis is made of public policy towards the agricultural sector.

Agriculture is the largest and the most important sector of the Bangladesh economy. It contributes about 48 per cent of the GDP and absorbs about three-fifths of the labor force. Agricultural products – e.g., raw jute, tea, hides and skins and fish – account for nearly two-fifths of the earnings from merchandise exports. If jute manufactures are included, the share rises to more than 80 per cent. Agriculture is the main source of income for over 80 per cent of the households in the rural areas and hence is an important determinant of the market for non-farm goods and services.

Since independence the rate of growth of agricultural production has been faster than the growth of population. The progress has, however, been limited mostly to the production of cereal crops, particularly wheat and the winter season rice. The growth of cereal production was supported by heavy government involvement in the development of water resources and high rates of subsidy on modern inputs used by the farmers. The government also intervened in the foodgrains market through internal procurement at a pre-determined price and distribution to consumers through various channels in order to reduce fluctuations in domestic price and to support the farmgate price. Since there is virtually no scope for the expansion of cultivable land, future growth of agricultural production will depend on the rate of expansion of cropped area through increased irrigation, the diffusion of the new agricultural technology and diversification through the development of non-crop sectors such as fisheries and livestock.

THE RESOURCE BASE AND THE ORGANIZATION OF PRODUCTION

Land is very scarce in Bangladesh and is very intensively used. The total area of the country amounts to about 14.3 million hectares (ha) of which 15 per cent is under forests and 20 per cent is occupied by bodies of water and homesteads. Arable land is about 9 million ha, of which 8.7 million ha is currently cultivated. Under the pressure of growing population, there was some increase in cultivated land, from 8.29 million ha in 1950/51 to 8.7 million ha in 1969/70. By the end of the 1960s a kind of equilibrium had been reached in the pattern of land use which has changed little since then. In 1985/86 cultivable waste land was only 270 000 ha, about 3 per cent of the cultivated area.

The country has abundant water resources which attracted people to it in the past and turned it into a densely settled region centuries ago. Three major rivers – the Ganges (locally named the Padma), Brahmaputra (Jamuna) and Meghna – and their numerous tributaries flow through Bangladesh and discharge huge volumes of water. Heavy rainfall and a suitable geological structure produce excellent supplies of ground water which is available up to a depth of about 12 meters in most regions and at less than six meters in large parts of the country. Agricultural growth in Bangladesh now critically depends on the development of this important resource.

The recently prepared national water plan contains the following evaluation of the water resource availability in the country[1]. Surface water flows vary from a maximum of 102 000 cubic meters per second in August to a minimum of 7 030 cubic meters per second in February. The surface water available in storage during the critical dry season from January to April is about 1 115 million cubic meters, 45 per cent of which is extractable from instream storage and the remaining 55 per cent from static water bodies. The major source of the available surface water is the stream flow which originates mostly from outside the country and hence is difficult to control on a unilateral basis. Very small amounts of stream flows are currently withdrawn from the main rivers. About 26 per cent of the regional river and canal flows is withdrawn for irrigation. The ground water availability in March, the driest month, is estimated at 24 415 million cubic meters, about 29 per cent of the total seasonal volume of available recharge. Only 20 per cent of the available ground water resource is currently (1985/86) used for irrigation, and for domestic and industrial purposes. Nearly 6.9 million ha of land could be irrigated with the available water resources as compared to only about 1.9 million ha which is currently irrigated. The potential for agricultural growth through water resource development is therefore very substantial.

Land is *not* of uniform quality and elevation. The overall picture of the gently sloping alluvial plain disguises considerable variability of local relief which affects cropping patterns, the intensity of land use and crop yields. Complex local differences in elevation have important implications for the planning of drainage and irrigation as they are associated with differences in soil permeability and crop suitability. The national water plan classifies land into four major types according to flood depth. The high land areas which are flooded up to a maximum of 30 cm constitute about 36 per cent of the total land. This type of land is cropped with the low-yielding upland rice *(aus)* or jute during the rainy season, followed by pulses or oilseeds during the dry winter season. With the development of irrigation facilities, two rice crops of high yielding or modern variety (HYV or MV) can be grown on such land. The medium high land, flooded between 30 and 90 cm during the peak monsoon months, constitutes another third of the total land. This type of land is currently double cropped with pre-monsoon rice or jute, followed by transplanted monsoon rice. About one-sixth of the total land is flooded between 90 and 180 cm, which is suitable only for the high-risk, low-yielding and deep water monsoon rice. The development of flood control and drainage facilities for such land could stabilize and improve the yield of the monsoon rice and allow an additional HYV rice crop through the control of early floods. The remaining one-sixth of the area consists of extremely low land which does not permit the growing of any crop during the monsoon rice season. This area grows a single crop of rice during the winter season.

Due to the high pressure of population and limited opportunities for non-agricultural occupations, land is cultivated in very small holdings. The operation of the Islamic laws of inheritance of property has resulted in the fragmentation of holdings into a large number of scattered plots. The 1983/84 agricultural census estimated the average size of a farm holding at 0.91 ha, which represents a sharp decline from 1.43 ha in 1960 (Table 3.1). The small farm, defined as a holding under one hectare, is the dominant production unit. With traditional technology, such a farm is incapable of producing a subsistence income, so members of most of the small farm families also work as agricultural wage laborers and engage in various non-farm activities during slack agricultural seasons in order to augment incomes from farming. The proportion of small farms increased from about 52 per cent in 1960 to 70 per cent in 1983/84 and the area operated by them increased from 16 per cent to 29 per cent of the total land (Table 3.1). During the same period the proportion of large farms, holdings of more than three hectares, declined from 11 per cent to 5 per cent and the area operated by them declined from nearly two-fifths to one-fourth of the total land. The above characteristics of the landholding pattern imply that the proportion of farmers who can generate enough surplus for reinvestment, especially in indivisible assets such as irrigation facilities, is small.

Table 3.1 Changes in the structure of landholdings, 1960–84

Size of farm (in hectares)	Per cent of landholdings		Per cent of land operated	
	1960	1983–84	1960	1983–84
Up to 0.40	24.3	40.4	3.2	7.8
0.41 to 1.0	27.3	29.9	13.0	21.2
1.01 to 2.0	26.3	18.0	26.4	27.5
2.01 to 3.0	11.4	6.8	19.3	17.6
3.01 and over	10.7	4.9	38.1	25.9
All farms	100.0	100.0	100.0	100.0

Sources: Government of Pakistan, *1960 Census of Agriculture, Vol. II, East Pakistan*, Agricultural Census Organisation, Karachi, 1962; BBS, *Report of the 1983/84 Census of Agriculture and Livestock*, Dhaka, 1986.

The 1977 agricultural census reported that two-fifths of the farms had more than 10 fragments each and another one-fourth between 6 and 10 fragments each. The fragmentation of holdings facilitates the reduction of risk by diversifying the elevation and type of plots in the land portfolio of the farmer, and by allowing him to grow different crops. It however reduces the productivity of labor, makes labor management more difficult and acts as a constraint to private investment on lumpy irrigation equipment and other forms of mechanization by large farmers.

Marginal landowners tend to cling to the tiny, non-viable holdings because of the high value attached to land as a source of security due to the uncertainty of wage employment and non-farm occupations. They prefer to rent land to make their holdings viable rather than sell land and join the labor market. The 1977/78 land occupancy survey estimated that about two-fifths of the farm households cultivate land under various tenancy arrangements, of which the dominant form is sharecropping, an oral contract under which the tenant agrees to bear all costs and pays half of the gross produce to the landowner[2]. In some parts of the country the landowners share the cost of fertilizer and irrigation water with the tenants growing HYV cereals. In some areas the tenurial arrangement is changing from sharecropping to fixed rent in order to suit the needs of cultivation of modern varieties. In the coastal areas of the country, which remain technologically backward, the terms of tenancy are more stringent. For traditional rice crops tenants pay two-thirds of the gross produce as rent, or an advance cash rent negotiated every year in addition to half of the produce paid after harvest. A comprehensive tenancy reform was promulgated in 1984 providing for tenurial security for at least five years and one-third share each for land, labor and material inputs. But these provisions have not been implemented due to the absence of formal lease contracts, an excess demand for land in the tenancy market and the lack of an enforcement machinery.

The distribution of landownership is quite unequal. It has not improved significantly over time. Successive governments have done virtually nothing to promote a more egalitarian distribution of landownership. Landless agricultural laborers, as a percentage of the total agricultural labor force, have increased over time. The details of these issues are discussed in Chapter 7 below.

THE STRUCTURE AND GROWTH OF AGRICULTURE

In Bangladesh agricultural activities center around crop cultivation which accounts for over two-thirds of agricultural value added (Table 3.2)[3]. Another 15 per cent of the value added originates in livestock and poultry raising, which are activities supplementary to crop husbandry, carried out by using homestead land and surplus family labor of farm workers. Fishery and forestry, which are relatively independent activities, contribute only about a sixth of agricultural value added. The focus of the present chapter is mainly on the crop sector. It is, however, useful to provide a brief outline of the livestock and fishery sectors before turning to the main subject.

Livestock

The 1983/84 agricultural census estimates that about 7.26 million households (52 per cent of all rural families) own some cattle. Of these, 6.65 million are farm households. Only 5 per cent of the cattle population was owned by households which did not cultivate land. Ownership of animals is widespread among cultivators because: (a) animals provide the power needed for the heavy farm work such as ploughing, threshing and transportation of the harvested produce; and (b) the market for these services is either undeveloped and/or not

Table 3.2 The composition of agricultural value added, 1986/87

Subsectors	Value added in 1986/87			Annual rates of growth 1974–87
	Million Tk at current prices	As a per cent of agricultural value added	As a per cent of GDP at current market prices	
Crops	164 165	68.9	31.5	2.9
Forestry	20 272	8.6	3.9	2.7
Fisheries	18 789	7.9	3.6	2.5
Livestock	35 069	14.7	6.7	3.0
Agriculture	238 295	100.0	45.7	2.8

Note: The estimates of value added for forestry, fisheries and livestock sectors are of dubious quality and hence the estimates of growth rates may contain a wide margin of error. The information on growth rates for forestry, fisheries and livestock sectors are for the 1977–87 period.
Sources: BBS, *Monthly Statistical Bulletin of Bangladesh,* April 1987 and *Statistical Pocket Book of Bangladesh, 1981.*

dependable due to the high seasonality of demand. Livestock and poultry are major sources of animal protein, an important source of cash income and often a depository of savings to hedge against inflation and natural calamities.

The scarcity of land and fodder constitute the major obstacle to the development of a commercial livestock sector. There are only a few commercial livestock and poultry farms, mostly operated by the government as research and breeding facilities. Draft animals are sold for slaughtering at the end of their working lives and female calves are sold for rearing by others or for slaughtering if they are not required as work animals. These, along with the illegal import of live animals from across the Indian border, are the sources of supply of meat, the demand for which is concentrated in the urban areas. Like cattle, poultry is widely held by farm families and is not raised on a commercial basis. According to the 1983/84 agricultural census, 74 per cent of all rural households and 81 per cent of all farm households owned some poultry. The average size of poultry holdings was between 7 and 8 birds, ranging from 5 for the landless households to about 14 for farms operating more than three hectares of land.

Estimates of value added in the livestock sector are of doubtful quality[4]. Growth rates obtained from the time series data on value added probably contain a wide margin of error. The official time series gives a growth rate of 3 per cent per year in the decade up to 1986/87 (Table 3.2). The 1983/84 agricultural census estimated that there were 22.1 million cattle, 14.2 million goats and sheep and 73.7 million poultry and that they grew at annual rates of 0.8 per cent, 2.2 per cent and 5.9 per cent during the inter-censal period between 1960 and 1983/84. In more recent times (i.e., during the period between the 1977 and 1983/84 censuses) the annual growth rate for goats and sheep accelerated sharply to 7.4 per cent and that for poultry decelerated a little to 5 per cent. The growth rate for cattle remained unchanged. According to recent estimates, about 73 per cent of the value added in the livestock sector is due to cattle, 16 per cent to poultry and 11 per cent to goats and sheep. If these figures are taken as weights and the value added for each component is assumed to have grown at the same rate as stock, the annual growth rate in value added for the livestock sector during the period between the censuses of 1977 and 1983/84 becomes 2.2 per cent, which is significantly lower than the official estimate.

Fisheries

Fish has always been a preferred food in the Bangladeshi diet. About 6 per cent of the protein intake and more than half of the animal protein in the diet comes from fish. Fisheries contribute about 8 per cent of the agricultural value added, 3.6 per cent of the GDP and 9 per cent of the earnings from merchandise exports. The sector employs about 1.1 million commercial fishermen, nearly 7 per cent of the agricultural labor force. Also, a significant proportion of households live on trade and transport of fish and on manufacturing fishing nets and equipment.

Bangladesh has a marine fishery area of about 70 000 square kilometers in the declared exclusive zone with exploitable stocks of 360 000 to 456 000 tons of shrimp, demersal and pelagic fish[5]. The current annual harvest of marine fish is estimated at 172 000 tons, accounting for about a fifth of total production of fish.

Nearly four-fifths of the production comes from inland fishing (Table 3.4). The inland fishery area is estimated at about 4.3 million ha: 1.2 million ha of rivers and lakes, 2.8 million ha of flood plains and 153 000 ha of ponds (the remaining area is accounted for by brackish water fishing).

Official estimates show an absolute decline in fish production from about 800 000 tons in 1964/65 to 640 000 tons in 1975/76 and a moderate increase since then. The production of *inland* fisheries stagnated up to

Table 3.3 Changes in the number of livestock and poultry, 1960 to 1983/84

Type	1960 (000)	1977 (000)	1983/84 (000)	Annual rate of growth (%)	
				1960–77	1977–84
Cattle and buffalo	19 416	20 978	22 062	0.8	0.8
Goats and sheep	6 137	8 944	14 226	2.2	7.4
Chickens and ducks	20 096	53 590	73 713	5.9	5.0

Source: BBS, *Reports of Agricultural Censuses*, 1977 and 1983/84.

Table 3.4 Estimates of area, yield and production of fisheries in Bangladesh, 1983/84

	Water area (thousand ha)	Yield (kg/ha)	Production (thousand tons)
A. Inland fisheries			
Capture fisheries:			
Rivers	1 032	201	207
Lakes and depressed basins	189	298	56
Flood plains	2 833	71	201
Culture fisheries:			
Ponds	153	755	116
Brackish water fisheries	52	159	8
B. Marine fisheries:			
Commercial			19
Artisanal			153

Source: BBS, *Yearbook of Agricultural Statistics, 1985/86*, Dhaka, 1987.

1980/81 and thereafter increased at an annual rate of 2.7 per cent. The production of *marine* fisheries increased rapidly since 1974/75, at an annual rate of about 6 per cent in the late 1970s and 10 per cent in the 1980s. The annual rate of growth of *total* fish production was 0.3 per cent in the late 1970s and 4.5 per cent in the 1980s. The annual growth of value added during the last decade is estimated, on the basis of the data that are of uncertain quality, to have been about 2.5 per cent (Table 3.2). Export of fish – mostly shrimp – increased rapidly from 2 474 tons in 1975/76 to 15 000 tons in 1984/85 and accounted for 9 per cent of the value of merchandise exports in the first half of the 1980s (14 per cent in 1985/86).

Results of the national nutrition surveys indicate a secular decline in the per capita availability of fish due to stagnant domestic supply and rapid population growth. Daily per capita consumption of fish declined from 32.8 grams in 1962-64 to 24 grams in 1975/76 and 23 grams in 1981/82.

There is however a good potential for increasing fish production, particularly from aqua culture and brackish water fisheries. The estimated current yield in the flood plains is about 71 kg per hectare compared to 270 kg in the Mekong delta and 110-216 kg in other tropical regions. It may, however, be difficult to increase production from this source as additional flood plain area is reclaimed for irrigation, drainage and flood control and embankments for flood control affect the movement of fish seeds in flood plains.

Recent estimates show that only one-third of the existing ponds are used for fish culture and fish fry is stocked in about two-thirds of them. Productivity is low because of the poor condition of the fry at the time of stocking, the presence of predators in ponds and the lack of any follow-up management. Present yields in pond fishing are estimated to range from 300 kg per hectare under natural conditions to 755 kg per hectare under semi-intensive culture. Experiments in the Chandpur Irrigation Project area, practising multi-species carp culture with low quality supplementary feeds, show that these could be increased to about 3.75 tons. An important problem facing the development of pond fishery is the system of ownership. Unlike cultivated land, a pond can not be divided up at each stage of inheritance. Joint ownership is therefore widespread which makes it difficult to organize entrepreneurship for fish cultivation. This, along with other causes, have led to widespread dereliction of ponds due to years of neglect and lack of investment. Capital cost of rehabilitation is often too high to provide a reasonable market rate of return[6].

Prospects for increased brackish water fisheries are also good. Available estimates show that the suitable area is as much as 225 000 ha as compared to the actual area of 52 000 ha in 1983/84. Experiments have shown that with suitable measures the yield could be increased three times from the current level of about 160 kg per hectare.

Crop production

Agriculture in Bangladesh is overwhelmingly dominated by rice. It is grown on about 10.5 million ha which is nearly four-fifths of the total cropped area. Rice is grown in three seasons, and is harvested in July-August (*aus*), November-January (*amon*) and April-June (*boro*). On a large proportion of land two rice crops are harvested in a year. Other important crops are jute, wheat, sugarcane, potato, tobacco, tea, pulses and oilseeds. Jute is the main cash crop and is grown on about 5 per cent of the total cropped area. The area under wheat was negligible as recently as the 1970s, but a rapid growth in area under wheat over the last decade has turned it into the third most important crop after rice and jute.

Table 3.5 compares the experience of growth in crop production activity in the post-independence period with that in the two decades before independence. Gross value of production of major crops grew at almost the same rate during the two periods. There were, however, important differences in performance between the two periods. First, the post-independence period experienced a considerable deceleration in the increase in sown area under crops. Area expansion accounted for 44 per cent of the increase in output during the pre-independence period and only 32 per cent in the period since independence. The rate of growth of production was maintained through an acceleration in the growth of yield per unit of land, which increased at 1.7 per cent per year in the post-independence period compared to 1.4 per cent per year during the two preceding decades. Second, recent growth has mainly been accounted for by an increase in the production of cereal crops, rice and wheat. The annual growth rate for cereals rose from 2.6 per cent in the pre-independence period to 2.8 per cent in the post-independence period while that for non-cereal crops fell from 2.2 per cent to only 0.9 per cent[7]. Third, the rise in the growth rate of cereals was mainly due to the acceleration in the growth of yield per hectare, which increased from 1.5 per cent to 1.9 per cent per year between the two periods. For the non-cereal crops, the rate of growth in yield per hectare was only about half of that for cereals in the years since independence. Also, there was hardly any *acceleration* in the yield per hectare for non-cereal crops in the post-independence period. Fourth, the expansion of cropped land in the post-independence period was exclusively on account of the cereal crops. For non-cereal crops the growth in cropped area in the post-independence period was negative, compared to about 1.3 per cent annual increase during the two decades before independence. Thus, in all respects the growth of crop production in the post-independence period was based on cereal crops. Since some of the non-cereal crops (e.g., jute, sugarcane and tobacco) are important industrial raw materials, the pattern of agricultural growth since independence has had an adverse implication for industrial development.

Table 3.5 Growth in crop production in the pre- and post-independence periods

Crops	Period	Gross value of production (1)	Cropped land	Yield per unit of land
Rice and wheat:	1950–71	2.6	1.1	1.5
	1973–86	2.8	0.9	1.9
Other crops: (2)	1950–71	2.2	1.3	0.9
	1973–86	0.9	−0.1	1.0
Major crops:	1950–71	2.5	1.1	1.4
	1973–86	2.5	0.8	1.7

(1) The values are estimated at constant 1981–82 prices.
(2) Includes jute, sugarcane, tobacco, different varieties of pulses and oilseeds, potatoes and chilli.
Source: Estimated by fitting semi-logarithmic trend lines on time series data for gross value of production constructed from the series on land area and production of 15 major crops published by the Bangladesh Bureau of Statistics. These crops account for about 95 per cent of the total cropped area.

The two decades before independence experienced a secular decline in the per capita production of food due to a population growth rate in excess of the rate of growth of cereal production. Since independence the rate of growth in cereal production has been significantly higher than the rate of growth of population. It has, however, not been possible to prevent an upward trend in the absolute volume of cereal imports. The objective of attaining self-sufficiency in foodgrains has remained as elusive as before. Annual average imports of rice and wheat were 1.77 million tons (about 10 per cent of domestic demand) during the 1980-85 period, compared to 1.61 million tons during the late 1970s and 1.12 million tons in the late 1960s.

The increased import of cereals in spite of an increase in per capita domestic production since independence is explained by an income induced increase in the demand for food. Since independence per capita income has increased at an average annual rate of 1.6 per cent. At the currently low level of income and food consumption, the income elasticity of demand for cereals is very high, between 0.53 and 0.73 according to some estimates based on the data on cross-sectional behavior of consumers[8]. Thus with a 2.5 per cent increase in population and a 1.6 per cent increase in per capita income, the demand for cereals would increase at 3.3 per cent to 3.7 per cent per year. The rate of growth in the production of cereals since independence has been significantly below the lower limit of this range. As a consequence imports have had to increase to make up for the widening gap between demand and domestic production.

An important point to note is that between the late 1960s (the immediate pre-independence years) and the early 1980s per capita consumption of cereals fell while per capita income and consumption rose[9]. Between these two periods there is no evidence of a rise in the real price of cereals. One is led to surmise that these apparently conflicting facts are explained by a worsening of the distribution of income between these two periods.

A more disaggregated view of the developments in the crop sector in the post-independence period can be obtained from Tables 3.6 and 3.7 which show that the growth had an extremely narrow base. Increased production of cereals was mainly due to that of wheat and the winter season *(boro)* rice. Among other crops only tea and potato attained respectable rates of growth.

Rice production reached a level of about 11.5 million tons by the end of the 1960s. It went below 10 million tons in the 1971-73 period due to the disruptions caused by the war of independence but recovered quickly to the pre-independence level by 1973-74. In 1986/87 production was 15.7 million tons, the highest ever reached. The trend rate of growth during the 1973-87 period is estimated at 2.2 per cent per year. Growth was mainly due to the expansion of area (3.7 per cent per year) under irrigated *boro* rice, and an increase in yield of *boro* (2.0 per cent per year) and *amon* rice (1.3 per cent per year).

Improved performance in cereal production in the post-independence period was mostly due to an impressive increase in area (14 per cent per year) and yield (5.2 per cent per year) of wheat. Wheat area increased from only 123 000 ha in 1973/74 to 677 000 ha by 1984/85 and production from 111 000 tons to 1.46 million tons. This source of increased cereal production however seems to be drying up, as substantial deceleration in the growth of production is noted in the early 1980s.

Table 3.6 Recent trends in production and productivity of important crops 1973–87

Crops	Area under the crop as per cent of total cropped land (1986/87)	Trend rate of growth (per cent) (1)		
		Production	Area	Yield
Rice	78.4	2.2	0.5	1.7
Aus	21.5	0.0	−0.8	0.8
Amon	44.7	1.8	0.5	1.3
Boro	12.2	5.7	3.7	2.0
Wheat	4.3	19.7	14.5	5.2
Jute	5.7	1.9	0.6	1.3
Sugarcane	1.2	0.7	1.2	−0.5
Tea (1)	0.3	3.6	0.3	3.3
Tobacco (1)	0.4	0.8	1.0	−0.2
Pulses (1)	1.9	−1.4	−1.2	−0.2
Mustard seeds	1.3	1.4	−0.3	1.1
Potatoes	0.8	3.3	2.3	1.0
Chilli (1)	0.5	−0.8	−0.5	−0.3

(1) Estimates for 1986/87 crop year for these crops were not available at the time of processing the information. The land allocation figures for these crops are for 1985/86 and the growth rates are for 1973–86 period.
Source: Estimated by fitting semi-logarithmic trend lines on time series data published by the Bangladesh Bureau of Statistics.

Recent growth in cereal production was achieved partly at the expense of non-cereal food crops. The area sown under oilseeds, pulses and spices declined in absolute terms from the pre-independence levels, mainly due to the reallocation of land to wheat and *boro* rice, as expansion of irrigation facilities enabled farmers to exploit the highly profitable new technology available for rice and wheat. The decline in production has been severe for pulses, which are the major source of protein intake for the poor. The production of potatoes, a major vegetable in the Bangladesh diet, increased at about 33 per cent per annum – two-thirds from area expansion and one-third from yield improvement. The production of this crop has, however, remained stagnant at around 1.1 million tons since 1981/82 due to weak internal markets.

The production performance of the major cash crop, jute, has been erratic, and has followed the classic cobweb pattern. The highest level of

Table 3.7 Changes in yield rates for important crops, 1984–87 over 1968–71
Figures in tons per hectare

Crops	Averages for 1984–87	Averages for 1968–71	Per cent change
Rice: (1)	1.45	1.15	26
Aus	1.02	0.89	15
Amon	1.40	1.14	23
Boro	2.45	2.03	21
Wheat	2.00	0.85	135
Jute	1.49	1.29	16
Sugarcane	41.79	46.50	−10
Tobacco	0.93	0.89	5
Tea	0.95	0.69	38
Mustard seeds	0.70		
Potatoes	10.21	9.32	10

(1) The figures are in terms of milled rice. One ton of milled rice is equal to approximately 1.5 tons of paddy.
Sources: BBS, *Agricultural Production Levels in Bangladesh, 1947–72*, Dhaka, 1974; *Monthly Statistical Bulletin,* various issues.

production of jute before independence was about 1.3 million tons, in 1969/70. Production dipped to only 710 000 tons in 1974/75 and did not recover to the pre-independence level until 1984/85. In 1985/86 jute production reached the peak of 1.55 million tons due to an exceptionally high level of prices prevailing in 1984/85 (about three times higher than in the previous year). It was followed by a drastic drop in prices in 1985/86 and a poor jute harvest in 1986/87 of 1.21 million tons. The long-term trend in jute production is difficult to discern because of the fluctuation, which was due mainly to the variation in the jute-rice price ratio. The 1969-85 time series shows a downward trend in production at an annual rate of about −1.4 per cent. This happened in spite of a moderate growth in crop yield (1.3 per cent per year) achieved through the government's intensive jute cultivation program.

Among other cash crops, only tea – a plantation crop – has a respectable growth of production. The area under tea plantations remained stagnant, but production increased from 27 000 tons in 1973/74 to 43 000 tons in 1985/86. The annual rate of growth in land productivity is estimated to have been about 3.3 per cent.

FACTORS BEHIND GROWTH

Land and labor

The contribution of the traditional factors, land and labor, to agricultural growth has been shrinking for quite some time, and they can no longer be counted as major sources of future growth[10]. It has been argued that in spite of the existence of a large volume of surplus labor, it is possible to increase productive employment in individual crops by overcoming certain institutional and technological obstacles which restrict employment[11]. It is, however, unlikely that in the long run this will continue to be an important source of increased production. An increase in employment in crop production in future is likely to be dependent on the reallocation of land in favor of more labor-intensive crops.

It has also been indicated that cultivable waste land is less than 3 per cent of the cultivated area, which has started declining under pressure of urbanization and the habitation of the growing population. More intensive use of land by way of growing additional crops during a given year has been the main source of the increased effective supply of land. Easy options of increasing the intensity of cropping may largely have been exhausted. Cropped area increased by about a fifth during the decade of the 1960s (Table 3.8), and area expansion accounted for about 2 per cent annual increase in crop production during that period. Since independence cropped area has increased by only 7 per cent and the cropping intensity has increased very slowly, from 143 per cent in the late 1960s to 154 per cent in the early 1980s (Table 3.8).

Diffusion of the new technology

The major factor behind the growth of cereal production during the post-independence period was the diffusion of the new "seed-fertilizer-water" technology – popularly known as the green revolution – at a reasonably rapid rate. The area sown with modern varieties of rice and wheat was negligible at the time of independence. The coverage of the modern varieties increased to 14 per cent of the land under rice and wheat by 1976/77 and to one-third of the area by 1986/87 (Table 3.9). In the latter year modern varieties accounted for 50 per cent of the total production of rice and wheat. It has been estimated by sample surveys that the entire area under modern varieties is treated with chemical fertilizers, and that the rate of application of chemical fertilizers is about

Table 3.8 Trends in cultivated land, cropped area and cropping intensity
Figures are yearly averages

Period	Cultivated land (thousand ha)	Cropped land (thousand ha)	Cropping intensity (per cent)
1950–55	8 421	11 000	131
1955–60	8 232	10 488	127
1960–65	8 493	11 282	133
1965–71	8 719	12 441	143
1971–76	8 398	12 131	145
1976–81	8 419	12 679	151
1981–86	8 634	13 289	154

Sources: Compiled from Central Statistical Office, *Twenty-Five Years of Statistics in Pakistan,* Government of Pakistan, Karachi 1974; BBS, *Year Book of Agricultural Statistics,* various issues, Dhaka.

six to ten times (depending on the season) higher on modern varieties than on local varieties[12]. With the rapid diffusion of the modern varieties, the sale of chemical fertilizers has expanded greatly. Their consumption per hectare of cropped land increased from only about 11 kg of nutrients in 1969/70 to about 46 kg by 1986/87 (Table 3.9). The rate of increase has however slowed down considerably during the 1983-87 period, partly because of a rapid increase in fertilizer prices, due largely to the reduction of subsidies on this input.

The diffusion of modern varieties and the rapid increase in fertilizer consumption may have been led by the investment for water resource development in which the government played a major role. The area irrigated by mechanical methods increased from less than 4 per cent in 1969/70 to about 8 per cent by 1976/77 and further to about one-fifth of the cultivated land by 1985/86. The regional variation in the diffusion of modern varieties of rice and wheat shows a unique relationship with the variation in the area irrigated by modern methods. Nearly three-fourths of the regional variation in fertilizer consumption is also explained by the variation in irrigated area[13]. Using the parameters of the production functions for specific varieties of crops, it has been estimated that the increased use of modern variety seeds, fertilizer and irrigation may have contributed about two-thirds of the increase in crop output during the 1975-85 period[14].

The observed complementarity among irrigation, modern seeds, and fertilizer is very high. But whereas irrigation requires prior capital investment and institutional arrangements for the coordination of

Table 3.9 Progress in the diffusion of the modern agricultural technology

Year	Per cent of rice and wheat area covered by modern varieties	Fertilizer sales per unit of cropped land (kg of nutrients per ha)	Area irrigated by mechanical methods as a per cent of cultivated land (1)
1969/70	2.5	11.0	3.8
1976/77	14.2	19.8	8.5
1977/78	16.6	26.9	9.6
1978/79	19.4	27.4	10.0
1979/80	22.7	30.9	11.0
1980/81	25.4	31.6	12.2
1981/82	25.8	29.9	13.3
1982/83	28.2	33.8	15.3
1983/84	28.3	39.8	17.0
1984/85	31.5	45.3	19.7
1985/86	31.0	40.0	20.0
1986/87	33.2	45.8	n.a.

(1) Mechanical methods of irrigation include low lift pumps, tubewells and gravity irrigation through canals. Official statistics on area irrigated by various methods are known to be of dubious quality. The figures published by the BBS are lower than that estimated by the Planning Commission. In 1985/86, another 4 per cent of the cultivated area was irrigated by traditional methods. Ground water extraction through tubewells now accounts for about 55 per cent of the total area irrigated by mechanical methods.
Source: Compiled from figures published by the BBS in *Statistical Year Book* and *Monthly Statistical Bulletin*, various issues.

actions among many farmers because of fragmented and scattered holdings, the use of modern variety seeds and fertilizers are current production decisions taken by individual farmers. This suggests that irrigation is the leading input in the new technology package, and that the development of irrigation facilities constitutes the key constraint on the growth of crop production in the country.

In the post-independence period the growth in land productivity has been due mostly to the reallocation of land from low-yielding local varieties to higher-yielding modern varieties of crops. For given varieties of rice very little increase in yield has taken place. In fact, for the modern variety of *amon* and *aus* rice, and for sugarcane, pulses and spices declining trends in crops yields have been found. Some increase in yield could be achieved through more intensive and efficient use of fertilizer and good quality seeds and, in some cases, more intensive use of labor. For many local varieties less than a half of the land is treated with fertilizer and the rate of application on the treated land is less than 40 per cent of the rate recommended by the extension department as economically optimum. Studies on fertilizer response show that one unit of fertilizer nutrient gives a return of 9-10 units of paddy on experimental plots and 4.5 units of paddy on farmers' fields[15]. At the current levels of prices the incremental benefit-cost ratio of fertilizer use is estimated at 2:1. Still, studies on fertilizer demand show that the farmers have started reacting adversely to the increase in the fertilizer-crop price ratio[16]. A major factor behind the suboptimal level of application of the purchased inputs like fertilizer and pesticides was the high risk to cultivation from frequent occurrence of floods and droughts, and large fluctuations in prices.

Prices and terms of trade

Very little is known about the effect of the internal terms of trade on intersectoral allocation of resources in Bangladesh. It has been argued that favorable agricultural prices may not have much effect on agricultural growth due to technical constraints[17]. Since land is scarce production can only be increased through more intensive use of non-land inputs and the reallocation of land from low to high productivity crops. In Bangladesh these are largely dependent on the expansion of irrigation and flood control facilities, the provision of which has so far been the responsibility of the government. Private investment in land improvement has been very limited. Results of village studies show that agricultural surplus, inflated through favorable prices, is used more for conspicuous consumption, investment for the education of children, housing and trade than for investment in agriculture[18]. Agricultural investment per hectare of land is found to be higher in smaller farms. No measurement of the price elasticity of supply for the crop sector as a whole is available, but estimates of the price elasticity of supply of rice range between 0.12 and 0.4, indicating low response to prices[19]. Relative prices of competing crops however play an important role in making decisions about the allocation of fixed land resources among different crops. This has particularly been demonstrated for jute with the application of the price expectation and supply adjustment models. Jute competes with *aus* rice. In allocating land to jute, farmers have been highly responsive to the expected price of jute relative to the price of rice. Available estimates of the price elasticity of supply of jute range from 0.4 to 0.6 in the short run and 0.8 to 1.2 in the long run when adjustment of supply is completed[20].

Estimates of agriculture's terms of trade are not directly available. The indices in Table 3.10 are based on the BBS indices of wholesale prices of agricultural and industrial products. It is hard to say to what extent these indices reflect movements in the prices of purchases and sales of the agricultural producers in general (or of specific products). Be that as it may, a comparison of the price indices of agricultural and industrial products shows a cyclical movement of the "terms of trade" in the post-independence period. It moved against agriculture during the first three years after independence, then improved steadily to reach the pre-independence level in 1978/79. Thereafter prices moved against agriculture again and by 1982/83 the terms of trade were unfavorable by about 20 per cent compared to the levels of 1969/70. Since then prices have once again moved in favor of agriculture.

Table 3.10 Movement in agriculture's terms of trade, 1973/74 to 1986/87

Year	Wholesale price indices (1969/70 = 100)		Agriculture's terms of trade
	Agricultural products	Industrial products	(1969/70 = 100)
1973/74	228	294	78
1974/75	370	459	81
1975/76	340	401	85
1976/77	348	392	89
1977/78	397	432	92
1978/79	445	449	99
1979/80	481	544	88
1980/81	509	603	84
1981/82	581	667	87
1982/83	596	741	80
1983/84	727	788	93
1984/85	883	858	103
1985/86	919	904	102
1986/87	1014	915	111

Sources: BBS, Statistical Year Book of Bangladesh, various issues; Monthly Statistical Bulletin, April 1987.

Price movements have not been uniform for the various subsectors within agriculture. Table 3.11 presents a set of indices of terms of trade for crop and non-crop sectors[21]. It is clear that for most of the post-independence period cereal prices increased at a slower rate than the prices of industrial products. Price movements were much more favorable for non-cereal crops than for cereals. Dramatic improvements in the terms of trade were experienced by the non-crop sectors, e.g., livestock, forestry and fisheries.

Table 3.11 Movement in terms of trade of various agricultural sub-sectors 1973/74 to 1985/86
(1972/73 = 100)

Year	Crop sector (1)			Livestock (2)	Fisheries (2)	Forestry (2)
	Cereals	Non-cereals	Total			
1973/74	104	119	106	95	81	90
1974/75	140	152	142	79	72	90
1975/76	91	116	95	93	101	89
1976/77	95	128	101	101	123	92
1977/78	96	141	104	115	110	127
1978/79	110	122	112	142	146	140
1979/80	99	103	100	142	123	114
1980/81	90	125	96	120	111	114
1981/82	93	99	95	109	104	105
1982/83	92	89	93	107	94	120
1983/84	101	135	106	111	116	145
1984/85	107	145	113	160	141	167
1985/86	93	112	97	175	153	218
1986/87	n.a.	n.a.	n.a.	187	167	235

(1) Constructed from time series data on harvest prices of major crops, published by the Bureau of Statistics, using the share of these crops in the crop value added for the period 1982–84. The price indices for industrial products have been used as deflators.
(2) Compiled from information on value added in constant and current prices, as published by the BBS in the national income accounts.

The analysis of the trend of prices supports the view that the supply of most agricultural products could not keep pace with demand. If the government had not augmented the domestic supply of cereals through food aid and commercial imports, the relative prices of cereals might also have had an upward trend. As already reported, most other crop and non-crop sectors grew at a slower rate than population. Livestock, fishery and forestry products have very high income elasticities of demand, in the range between 1.0 and over 2.0 depending on the product[22]. Demand for these products probably grew at the rate of 4 to 6 per cent per year in the post-independence period, while their supply from domestic production increased at less than half these rates. Imports of these products were generally ruled out on grounds of low priority. Substantial increases in relative prices were the outcome.

By increasing profitability price increases should have induced producers to increase supply. This does not appear to have happened, especially in the non-crop sectors. It suggests that there are serious supply-side constraints to the growth of these sectors which can not be overcome merely by the provision of price incentives.

IMPLICATIONS FOR INCOME DISTRIBUTION

As shown above, the main source of agricultural growth in the post-independence period was the rapid adoption of the HYV technology based on the use of improved seed, fertilizer and controlled irrigation water. Nearly one-third of the households do not own any cultivable land. Among cultivators more than two-thirds are small farmers who operate farms less than one hectare in size. What benefits have these disadvantaged groups derived from the spread of the HYV technology?

Results of early studies of the "green revolution" in India and elsewhere showed that although the technology is scale neutral, poor farmers can not benefit from it as much as the rich because: (a) the new crop varieties need large investments in purchased inputs which the poor can not afford, (b) small farmers have little access to financial institutions from which working capital can be borrowed on reasonable terms, and (c) the new technology entails fixed costs in the form of access to information, sources of supply of new inputs and the arrangements for the marketing of additional surplus, which tend to discourage adoption by small farmers. It was argued that the impact of the growth of production would be reflected more in an increase in land and labor productivity which would be appropriated by the landowners, than in an increase in employment and augmentation of wages which would benefit the landless. It was further argued that by making agricultural enterprises more profitable the new technology would induce large landowners to evict tenants and to buy out marginal and small holdings, forcing them into landlessness. The diffusion of the new technology was thus seen as a mechanism, especially when not accompanied by countervailing measures such as land redistribution, for the widening of inequalities in income and asset distribution and the deepening of absolute poverty[23].

Available information at the national level does not permit a testing of the above hypotheses in Bangladesh. The following findings are suggested by a recent study based on a large survey completed in 1982[24].

An important factor determining the equity implications of the new technology is the extent and intensity of adoption among different size groups of farmers. Findings of the study in this regard are presented in Table 3.12. About three-fourths of the farmers adopted the new varieties, although these were grown on about one-third of the cropped land. The proportion of adopting farmers was not very different among farm size and tenurial groups. The new technology thus appears to be widely distributed among landholding farmers, irrespective of the size of holding and tenurial status.

Contrary to expectation, the intensity of adoption was higher for the small owner and tenant farmers. In the case of fertilizer the difference in use per unit of land was quite large: 60 kg of nutrients per hectare for the small farmers compared to about 45 kg for the large farmers. Tenant farmers allocated a larger proportion of land to the modern varieties and used similar amounts of fertilizer as compared to the owner farmers. This was achieved despite limited access of the small farmers to institutional credit markets. Only one-sixth of the sample farm households received loans from institutional sources, 14 per cent of the small farms compared to 24 per cent of the large ones.

The inverse relationship between the farm size and the adoption of the modern varieties was also confirmed by the 1983/84 agricultural census (Table 3.13). The census estimated that about 22 per cent of the rice and wheat area was covered by HYV during 1983/84 and that the rate of adoption was 29 per cent for the marginal farmers compared to only 19 per cent for farmers operating more than three hectares.

The higher rate of adoption of the new technology by the smaller farms may have been the result of the tendency on the part of the large landowners to cultivate new crop varieties through tenants and the provision of irrigation by the government which relieved the small farmers of the burden of costly investment. The 1982 survey found a higher proportion of tenants than owners among those adopting modern varieties. The area under tenancy was higher for modern varieties than for local varieties in all three seasons. As noted earlier, the adoption of the modern varieties is critically dependent on access to irrigation facilities. The study found that even with the privately owned tubewells and power pumps, small farmers have as much access to irrigation facilities as the large ones. This is probably because of the

Table 3.12 Adoption of the new agricultural technology by different farm size and tenurial groups, results of a farm survey in 1982

Groups of farmers	Per cent of farmers		Per cent of cropped area covered by modern varieties seeds	Amount of fertilizer used (kg of nutrients per ha)	Per cent of land irrigated
	Using modern varieties	Fertilizers			
Size of farm:					
Small (up to 1.0 ha)	75	86	43.2	60.3	32.3
Medium (1.0 to 2.0 ha)	74	92	35.8	54.2	32.9
Large (2.01 and over)	77	95	32.5	44.8	28.3
Tenurial status:					
Owner farmers	77	88	35.7	54.7	33.6
Owner-cum-tenants and pure tenants	74	91	38.1	53.3	29.6
All farms	75	89	36.8	54.1	31.7

Note: The sample consists of 640 randomly selected households from 16 villages in the country.
Source: Mahabub Hossain, *Nature and Impact of Modern Rice Technology in Bangladesh*, Research Report, International Food Policy Research Institute, Washington, D.C., 1988.

Table 3.13 Use of irrigation and modern varieties of rice and wheat, estimates of the 1983/84 agricultural census

Size of farm	Per cent of rice and wheat area under modern varieties	Per cent of cultivated land irrigated	Per cent of cultivated land under jute	Per cent of cultivated land under sugarcane
Marginal (0.01 to 0.20 ha)	28.6	23.1	10.9	1.6
Small (0.21 to 1.0 ha)	25.8	22.7	10.4	1.7
Medium (1.01 to 3.0 ha)	21.4	19.0	9.5	2.1
Large (3.01 and above)	18.7	18.3	7.4	2.4
All farms	22.3	19.9	9.2	2.1

Source: BBS, *The Bangladesh Census of Agriculture and Livestock: 1983/84*, Vol. II, Cropping Patterns, Dhaka, November 1986.

random distribution of plots belonging to different size groups of farms around the facilities. Moreover, since large landowners seem to cultivate modern varieties through tenants, who are basically small farmers, it is not surprising that the use of irrigation facilities would be high on small farms. This is confirmed by the 1983/84 agricultural census which found that about 20 per cent of the cultivated land was irrigated, 23 per cent for the marginal and small farmers compared to 18 per cent for the large ones (Table 3.13).

The income distribution effect of the new technology also depends on its impact on land productivity across different groups of farms. A large number of studies in Bangladesh have found an inverse relation between farm size and land productivity[25]. Most of the findings are, however, for areas which did not experience a significant diffusion of the modern technology and refer to time periods (mostly the late 1960s and early 1970s) when the technology was at an early stage of adoption. Some recent studies for India, where the size-productivity relation was also found to be inverse for traditional crops, argue that this relationship is unlikely to hold for the modern varieties which are much more capital intensive[26]. These studies argued that the large farmers, who have more savings and better access to financial markets, would use modern inputs more intensively than the small farmers; as a consequence, a positive size effect on land productivity may result, depending on the importance of the purchased inputs in the cultivation of crops.

Information on the relationship between farm size and land productivity in rice cultivation from the 1982 survey is reported in Table 3.14. Since productivity is likely to depend on the stage of development of the new technology, sample villages covered by the survey were classified into *advanced* and *backward* villages. In the former, two-thirds of the rice area was under HYVs, while in the latter HYVs accounted for only 7 per cent of the rice area. Paddy yields in the former group were about 60 per cent higher than in the latter. Yield was found to be inversely related to farm size for both groups of villages. The difference in yield between the small and large farms was however less pronounced for the advanced villages, suggesting a narrowing of the productivity gap between size groups due to increased diffusion of HYVs. Nevertheless land productivity for the small farmers was about a fifth higher than that for the large farmers even in the advanced villages.

Table 3.14 Farm size and productivity of land in rice cultivation in technologically advanced and backward villages, results of a farm survey, 1982
Paddy yield in tons per hectare

Farm size	Backward villages	Advanced villages	Per cent difference (advanced over backward)
Small farm	1.80	2.72	51
Medium farm	1.43	2.32	62
Large farm	1.32	2.13	61
All farms	1.59	2.55	60

Source: Mahabub Hossain, *Nature and Impact of Modern Rice Technology in Bangladesh, op. cit.*

Small farmers and tenants however paid higher prices for inputs, particularly for water and labor (Table 3.15). Privately owned irrigation facilities belong to large landowners who also control most of the irrigation cooperatives. They appropriate a sizeable mark-up on irrigation water sold by them. In some areas the owners of tubewells and power pumps take a quarter of the gross produce as rent for irrigating the land under the command area. Table 3.15 shows that fertilizer prices are invariant across farm size groups but the cost on account of irrigation was about 25 per cent higher on small farms compared to the large ones and 18 per cent higher on tenant farms compared to owners.

Small farmers also paid 14 per cent higher cost for a unit of labor, presumably because they hire labor during more busy periods of agricultural operations when wage rates are higher.

Table 3.15 Farm level prices of major agricultural inputs, by size and tenurial status of farms, 1982

Farmer groups	Fertilizer price (Tk/kg)		Irrigation charge (Tk/ha)	Wage rate (Tk/day)
	1982 *aus* and *boro* season	1982 *amon* season		
Farm size:				
Small farm	3.20	3.64	1 660	20.22
Medium farm	3.23	3.55	1 440	19.43
Large farm	3.18	3.51	1 344	17.33
Tenurial status				
Owner farm	3.20	3.58	1 455	18.91
Owner-cum-tenant farm	3.22	3.62	1 724	22.88
All farms	3.21	3.60	1 549	19.59

Source: Mahabub Hossain, *Ibid.*

To summarize: the rate of adoption of modern technology in rice and wheat appears to have been higher for the small farmers than for the large farmers. This is partly explained by the higher than average rate of adoption for the tenant farmers (through whom the owners of land were adopting modern technology and appropriating much of its benefits) and partly by the propensity of the small farmers to survive, which was facilitated somewhat by their access to irrigation provided by the government. Smaller farmers however paid much higher prices for inputs, especially irrigation, than the larger farmers who were often the recipients of the extremely high rents for irrigation water purchased by the small farmers. Overall, the distribution of income almost certainly changed for the worse.

The movement of real wages in agriculture is discussed in Chapter 7. It is clear that the increased labor demand from the adoption of modern technology would by itself have failed to prevent a continued fall in real wages. Real wages indeed fell until the early 1980s. Since 1982/83 they have been creeping upwards and in 1985/86 they rose discontinuously due to a number of special circumstances. It is too early to say if the rise in real wages since 1982/83 constitutes a reversal of the long-term declining trend since before independence. Real wages in the mid-1980s remained considerably below those in the immediate pre-independence years.

A REVIEW OF AGRICULTURAL POLICIES

The progress in the adoption of the new technology in crop production can largely be attributed to a set of government policies introduced in the early 1960s. These include direct government involvement in the procurement and distribution of modern agricultural inputs at highly subsidized prices, support for agricultural research and extension and public investment in irrigation. In the late 1970s the government began to reverse some of these policies. The impact of these policy changes on the growth and distribution of agricultural incomes remains a matter of intense controversy.

In the early 1960s the government launched a "grow more food" campaign with the package of policies outlined above. The Bangladesh (then East Pakistan) Agricultural Development Corporation (BADC) was established in 1961 and was entrusted with the monopoly of procurement and distribution of seeds, fertilizers and small-scale irrigation equipment. A master plan was prepared for water resource development and the Water Development Board (BWDB) was established for implementing it.

The BADC established fertilizer stores in *upazilla* (the basic administrative unit with approximately 220 000 people on average) centers and set up networks for fertilizer distribution through appointed dealers at highly subsidized prices. It also rented out low lift power pumps to farmers' cooperatives at nominal charges. It is estimated that in 1968/69 the average rate of subsidy was about 58 per cent for urea and phosphate, 67 per cent for potash and more than 70 per cent for the low lift pumps[27]. The BWDB took up a few large multipurpose water development projects (e.g., the Ganges-Kobadak Project and the Chandpur Irrigation Project) and began the construction of embankments along major rivers and in the coastal areas for the protection of land from floods and saline water intrusion. Costs of the BWDB activities were entirely borne by the government.

As a result of these policies, the sale of chemical fertilizers increased rapidly, from only 51 000 tons in 1962/63 to 463 000 tons in 1975/76. The number of low lift pumps increased to 36 400. The operations, however, began to put a heavy burden on the government budget (Table 3.16). By the mid-1970s these policies came under serious review.

Table 3.16 Trends in allocation and composition of public development resources for agriculture

Year	Development expenditure for agriculture (1)			Fertilizer subsidy as per cent of development expenditure for agriculture	Investment for water resource development as per cent of development expenditure for agriculture (3)
	At current prices (million Tk)	At constant 1972/73 prices (million Tk) (2)	As per cent of total public expenditure		
1975/76	3 023	1 625	22.6	28.3	44.4
1976/77	3 148	1 759	18.1	26.9	38.1
1977/78	3 604	1 767	17.3	26.2	42.7
1978/79	6 194	2 854	23.3	20.8	28.5
1979/80	8 267	3 320	24.7	16.2	32.5
1980/81	9 811	3 010	25.4	12.0	46.0
1981/82	11 101	3 017	25.9	9.8	38.0
1982/83	8 733	2 268	20.4	9.7	47.2
1983/84	11 331	2 524	22.6	12.6	29.5
1984/85	9 390	1 823	13.7	10.6	64.2
1985/86	7 751	1 425	10.5	n.a.	60.9

(1) Agriculture sector includes crops, livestock, fisheries, forestry, water resources development and cooperatives and rural institutions.
(2) Deflated by the GDP deflator.
(3) Expenditures on water resources includes investments through both BWDB and BADC. About 60 per cent of the investment is through BWDB, which is also fully subsidised.
Sources: BBS, *The Statistical Yearbook of Bangladesh 1985/86;* Planning Commission, *Annual Development Programme 1986/87,* and S. R. Osmani and M. A. Quasem, *Pricing and Subsidy Policies for Bangladesh Agriculture,* (mimeographed), BIDS, Dhaka, 1985.

Moreover, the weakness of the strategy to expand irrigation through large-scale surface water development projects became apparent. Major irrigation and flood control projects implemented by the BWDB received almost all the public funds allocated to the water sector in the 1960s and nearly 60 per cent in the mid-1970s. Although the BWDB made considerable progress in controlling floods and the intrusion of saline water in the coastal and river belt areas, less than 10 per cent of the total irrigated area in the country was covered by them. A major problem was the low implementation capacity, which led to time and cost overruns for most of the large projects. Thus the choice of technology became a major issue and it was the general consensus that small irrigation equipment was more appropriate.

Questions were also raised about the distributional effects of the agricultural subsidies. It was argued by many that the irrigation cooperatives were controlled by larger farmers who tended to use them for their own benefit. The period witnessed occasional shortages of fertilizers leading to black market sales at high prices. This was attributed partly to the local monopoly of the BADC appointed dealers who were mostly large farmers. It was argued that larger farmers benefitted more from fertilizer subsidy because of the skewed distribution of land, their easy access to capital and institutional credit with which to buy fertilizer, and the supposedly higher rates of adoption of the fertilizer-intensive modern varieties by larger farmers. As discussed above, the last hypothesis has been contradicted by the available evidence.

Several policy changes have been introduced since the mid-1970s. The government shifted its attention to the development of ground water resources through deep tubewells (mostly of two cusecs capacity) and shallow tubewells (less than 0.5 cusec capacity). The government also decided to introduce a sales program for small irrigation equipment to individuals and cooperatives, and gradually to phase out the program of renting it to the latter. The subsidy on irrigation was however retained (Table 3.17). It is estimated that in 1982/83 there was about a 73 per cent subsidy on the *sale* of tubewells and a 29 per cent subsidy on the *sale* of low lift pumps. Subsidy on *rental* amounted to 93 per cent on deep tubewells and 50 per cent on low lift pumps.

A new marketing system was introduced for fertilizer distribution beginning in 1978. The new system allows any person, group or organization to register as a fertilizer dealer and to trade in fertilizer anywhere in the country. The BADC closed its *upazilla* sales centers and consolidated its sales points at major commercial centers, known as the primary distribution points (PDP). The government also adopted a policy of gradual elimination of subsidies on fertilizer. As a result of this policy the budgetary subsidy on fertilizer was reduced from about 28 per cent of the development budget for agriculture in 1975/76 to about 10 per cent in the early 1980s and virtually nothing in 1985/86[28]. During the last decade the price of fertilizer increased by about 15 per cent per

Table 3.17 Recent estimates of rates of subsidy in input distributions and marketing of foodgrains

Type of operation	Reference year	Rate of subsidy
A. Procurement and distribution of fertilizers:		
Budgetary subsidy	1983/84	25.3
Budgetary subsidy	1986/87	−1.9
Economic subsidy	1983/84	23.1
B. Procurement and distribution of irrigation equipment:		
Deep tubewell rental program	1982/83	92.5
Deep tubewell sales program	1982/83	73.3
Low lift pump rental program	1982/83	50.1
Low lift pump sales program	1982/83	28.7
C. Marketing of foodgrains:		
Domestic procurement of rice	1983/84	16.1
Domestic procurement of wheat	1983/84	5.9

Source: S. R. Osmani and M. A. Quasem, *Pricing and Subsidy Policies for Bangladesh Agriculture* (mimeographed), BIDS, Dhaka, 1985.

year compared to about a 10 per cent annual increase in the price of rice and only a 6 per cent annual increase in the BADC's cost of procuring fertilizer.

Recognising that the policy changes would increase the cash cost of production, the government also introduced a policy of price support for rice and wheat and a rapid expansion in the supply of agricultural credit through financial institutions. In the past the primary objective of the domestic foodgrain procurement system was to secure cereals to supplement external procurement to feed the public food distribution system, aimed at providing subsidized food to urban consumers and low-income groups in rural areas. Since the mid-1970s the internal procurement system has been geared in the direction of supporting an incentive price for the farmers. The supply of agricultural credit from institutional sources increased from Tk 153 million in 1970/71 to Tk 467 million in 1975/76 and to Tk 13 452 million in 1984/85, which was 8.7 per cent of the value added in crop sector in that year.

The impact of these changes in policy on agricultural development has remained controversial. International donor agencies have claimed that these policies have been favorable for growth[29]. A number of studies conducted within the country have argued that the results are by no means unambiguous[30].

The new marketing system for fertilizer has by and large been welcomed by the farmers[31]. It has increased competition among traders. In areas well connected by paved roads fertilizer is sometimes sold at a price lower than that recommended by the government, indicating that competition among traders has resulted in the sharing of the official margin with the farmers. Traders, however, have kept inadequate stocks, leading to occasional shortages and periodic fluctuations in prices, and have generally been reluctant to move fertilizer to remote areas.

The area under irrigation has expanded very fast since the shifting of emphasis in favor of the extraction of ground water and the introduction of the sales program for minor irrigation equipment. Deep tubewells in operation increased from 3 800 in 1975/76 to nearly 17 000 in 1984/85, and shallow tubewells from 4 000 to about 170 000. The area irrigated by tubewells now accounts for about 55 per cent of the total irrigated area, compared to only 16 per cent in 1975/76. But in the absence of proper zoning of areas according to the suitability for different types of equipment, the privatization program has led to improper siting and a consequent decline in capacity utilization. Two large sample surveys carried out in 1984 showed that individually owned facilities had a smaller coverage than the ones rented from the government, and fared no better than the latter with respect to maintenance[32]. The sales program had a very limited impact on the mobilization of private resources since about three-fourths of such investment was financed with credit from the public sector financial institutions, which failed to recover a large proportion of the loans. When the government began to enforce financial discipline in the credit program in 1985, sales of irrigation equipment dropped drastically. The policy also had an adverse effect on income distribution since equipment was purchased mostly by the larger farmers who sold water to the smaller owners of adjoining plots at charges much higher than cost.

The agricultural credit program was characterized by a concentration of loans in the hands of a small number of larger farmers and by a very poor rate of repayment. It is estimated that only 15 to 20 per cent of the farm households received agricultural loans and at most a third of the loans were repaid on schedule[33]. Poor repayment reduced the availability of funds for the expansion of credit and led to the practice of loan rescheduling by the banks which wanted to show a better recovery performance on paper. Since a part of the loan disbursed each year is in fact used for the rescheduling of old loans, the impact of the vastly expanded supply of credit on the financing of the fixed and working capital needs of the farmers is not clear.

The price support program has not been particularly successful. The amount of rice procured remained a small proportion of the total harvest. In most of the good harvest years (e.g., 1975/76, 1980/81 and 1985/86), growers' price in the market remained substantially below the procurement price, despite large increases in the volume of procurement in these years (Table 3.18). In 1980/81 a record 6 per cent of the rice production (about 20 per cent of the marketed suplus) was procured by the government. Yet the growers' price was about 11 per cent below the procurement price. The limited number of purchasing centers, inadequate resources for procurement, institutional rigidities preventing speedy purchase from and payment to small farmers, and the collusion between officials and traders are cited as the main reasons for the lack of success of the program[34].

Table 3.18 Internal procurement of rice and maintenance of support prices, 1975–86

Year	Procurement price (Tk/ton)	Grower's price (1) (Tk/ton)	Ratio of growers price to procurement price	Procurement (million tons)	Size of *amon* and *boro* harvest (2) (million tons)
1975/76	3 268	2 919	0.89	0.36	9.48
1976/77	3 294	2 919	0.89	0.32	8.70
1977/78	3 562	3 482	0.98	0.56	9.82
1978/79	3 589	3 669	1.02	0.32	9.51
1979/80	4 553	5 196	1.14	0.15	9.89
1980/81	4 687	4 178	0.89	0.88	10.60
1981/82	5 089	5 196	1.02	0.29	10.36
1982/83	5 625	6 107	1.09	0.17	11.15
1983/84	6 062	6 513	1.07	0.15	11.28
1984/85	6 642	7 337	1.11	0.14	11.84
1985/86	7 098	6 671	0.94	0.23	12.22

(1) The information on grower's price is available for paddy. The price of rice is estimated by using the conversion factor of 1 unit of rice equal to 1.5 units of paddy.
(2) Rice is procured during the *amon* and *boro* harvest. So the total size of the rice harvest during these two seasons is indicated.
Source: BBS, *Statistical Yearbook of Bangladesh* and *Monthly Statistical Bulletin*, various issues.

The most controversial policy issue has been the withdrawal of subsidies on fertilizer[35]. The policy had negative effects on fertilizer sales which declined in 1981/82 (by 5.2 per cent) and 1985/86 (by 8.2 per cent) following large increases in fertilizer prices in the previous years. A number of recent studies estimated the price elasticity of fertilizer demand at current levels of prices to be between -0.6 and -0.8. It was expected that the negative effect of the price increase would be compensated by the positive effect of a reallocation of resources, savings from the withdrawal of subsidies being devoted to the development of irrigation, which has a higher rate of return. But a review of the recent trend in the composition of public expenditure shows a large decline in the allocation to agriculture (Table 3.16) which indicates that resources saved have been diverted to non-agricultural activities. Moreover, the validity of the argument that the fertilizer subsidy had mostly benefitted the larger farmers is questioned by the findings of recent surveys which showed that small farmers use more fertilizer per unit of land than large ones and that farmgate prices of fertilizer are invariant with the size of farm. On grounds of equity, fertilizer subsidy appears to have been better than the high rates of subsidy on the sale of irrigation equipment which has been retained in the present policy package.

CONCLUSIONS

Bangladesh has made some progress in agriculture during the post-independence period. The rate of growth has however been too low to enable the country to achieve self-sufficiency in foodgrains, which has been the main objective of agricultural development for a long time. Agricultural growth had an extremely narrow base. It has been due entirely to growth in wheat and *boro* rice, promoted by the diffusion of the HYV technology, supported by large volumes of public resources for water control and subsidies on agricultural inputs. In recent years the area under wheat has begun to stagnate and the demand for irrigation equipment to slacken, giving rise to the concern that it may not be possible to maintain the moderate rate of progress achieved since independence.

Water control appears to be the key technological constraint to the growth of crop production. It is the main determinant of the rate of adoption of the modern seeds, of the increase in cropping intensity and the intensity of use of yield-raising modern inputs. The potential for the development of water resources is very substantial. The irrigated area could be increased from the current level of 20 per cent to well above 60 per cent with the available surface and ground water, and the flood control and drainage facilities could be extended from the existing 15 per cent of the cultivated area to nearly 64 per cent. The pace of development in this field will depend on the ability of the government to mobilize resources and/or recoup the cost of investment from the beneficiaries; its capacity to implement the large number of projects in a timely and efficient manner; and its ability to increase the adoption of irrigation in a more equitable manner than in the past. Given its meagre domestic resources, Bangladesh has so far depended on donor assistance for such projects. Sale proceeds from food aid has been a major source of local finance. This has been a built-in disincentive to achieve self-sufficiency in foodgrains.

Efforts should be made to broaden the base of agricultural growth, through the diversification of crops and the promotion of livestock, fishery and forestry. This would require the removal of numerous constraints on the supply side through broad government support.

Notes and References

1. See, The Master Plan Organization, *National Water Plan Project – Final Report*, Ministry of Irrigation and Flood Control, Dhaka, 1986.
2. For details of the tenurial arrangements and their impact on productivity see, F.T. Jannuzi and J.T. Peach, *Agrarian Structure in Bangladesh: An Impediment to Development*, Westview Press, 1980.
3. Value added estimated at constant 1972/73 prices shows that the contribution of the crop sector is about 79 per cent. The lower share at current prices is due to a highly favorable movement in the terms of trade of the various non-crop agricultural sectors. This issue is discussed in detail below.
4. Agricultural censuses (held in 1960, 1977 and 1983/84) provided information on the stock of animals and poultry. Outputs of different animal products are estimated from these data by applying some fixed parameters established by small surveys. Value added is estimated by deducting 3 per cent as current inputs.
5. Information in this section is drawn from an unpublished working paper on fisheries prepared in 1984 for the *National Water Plan Project*.
6. See, A.R. Khan, R. Islam and M. Huq, *Employment, Income and the Mobilization of Local Resources: A Study of Two Bangladesh Villages*, ILO/ARTEP, Bangkok, 1981, pp. 92-97.
7. It should be pointed out that the cereal output declined absolutely at the time of independence, though by much less than GDP. Average annual output in the three immediate post-independence years was 3.4 per cent lower than that in the three immediate pre-independence years. Thus

Agricultural Development

"catching up" with the pre-independence peak perhaps accounts for a part of the higher growth rate in the post-independence period.

8. For various estimates of the income and expenditure elasticities of demand for food see, W. Mahmud, "Foodgrain Demand Elasticities for Rural Households in Bangladesh", *The Bangladesh Development Studies,* Vol. 7, No. 1, 1979; and R. Ahmed, *Agricultural Price Policies Under Complex Socio-Economic and Natural Constraints,* Research Report No. 27, International Food Policy Research Institute (IFPRI), Washington D.C., 1981, pp. 52-56.
9. Per capita foodgrains consumption fell at the time of independence. In the early 1980s per capita consumption of foodgrains was significantly higher than in the 1970s but still significantly lower than in the immediate pre-independence years.
10. See, Mahabub Hossain, "Agricultural Development in Bangladesh – A Historical Perspective", *The Bangladesh Development Studies,*Vol. 12, No. 4, 1984, pp. 29-57.
11. Some discussion of such factors is to be found in ILO/ARTEP, *Employment Expansion in Asian Agriculture: A Comparative Analyisis of South Asian Countries,* 1980; and A.R. Khan and Eddy Lee, *The Expansion of Productive Employment in Agriculture: The Relevance of the East Asian Experience for Developing Asian Countries,* ILO/ARTEP Occasional Paper, 1981.
12. See, International Fertilizer Development Center, *Agricultural Production, Fertilizer Use and Equity Considerations: Results and Analysis of Farm Survey Data,* 1979-80 and 1982-84, Alabama, 1982 and 1984.
13. See, J.K. Boyce, "Water Control and Agricultural Performance in Bangladesh" and Mahabub Hossain, "Irrigation and Agricultural Performance in Bangladesh: Some Further Results", in *The Bangladesh Development Studies,* Vol. 14, No. 4, 1986.
14. Mahabub Hossain, "Agricultural Development in Bangladesh: A Historical Perspective", *op. cit.*
15. Bangladesh Institute of Development Studies (BIDS) and International Food Policy Research Institute, *Fertilizer Pricing Policy and Foodgrain Production Strategy in Bangladesh,* Dhaka and Washington, D.C., 1985.
16. Mahabub Hossain, "Price Response of Fertilizer Demand in Bangladesh", *The Bangladesh Development Studies,* Vol. 13, Nos. 3&4, 1985.
17. R. Ahmed, *op. cit.*
18. Atiq Rahman, "Surplus Utilization and Capital Formation in Bangladesh Agriculture", *The Bangladesh Development Studies,* Vol. 8, No. 4, 1980.
19. For a review of studies on this see, R. Ahmed, *op. cit.*
20. J.T. Cummings, "The Supply Responsiveness of Bangalee Rice and Cash Crop Cultivation", *The Bangladesh Development Studies,* Vol. 2, No. 4, 1974; S.H. Rahman, "Supply Response in Bangladesh Agriculture", *The Bangladesh Development Studies,* Vol. 14, No. 4, 1986.
21. For crop sectors the harvest prices of the major agricultural crops, published by the BBS, have been used. It would have been better to use growers' prices, but these are available only for rice, wheat and potatoes. The shares of crops in value added for the 1982-84 period have been used as

weights for the preparation of the crop price indices. The price indices for livestock, forestry and fishery are their respective value added deflators from the national accounts. Terms of trade indices have been worked out by deflating these price indices by the wholesale price index of industrial products.

22. See, Mahabub Hossain, "Agricultural Growth Linkages – The Bangladesh Case", *The Bangladesh Development Studies,* Vol. 15, No. 1, 1987; and *Nature and Impact of Modern Rice Technology in Bangladesh,* IFPRI Research Report, Washington, D.C., 1988.
23. See, Keith Griffin, *The Political Economy of Agrarian Change,* Macmillan, London, 1974, and Andrew Pearse, *Seeds of Plenty, Seeds of Want: Social and Economic Implications of the Green Revolutions,* Clarendon Press, Oxford, 1980.
24. See, Mahabub Hossain, *Nature and Impact of Modern Rice Technology in Bangladesh, op, cit.* The study is based on data collected from 16 villages representing the major ecological zones and administrative divisions in the country.
25. See, among others, M.A.S. Mandal, "Farm Size, Tenancy and Productivity in an Area of Bangladesh", *The Bangladesh Journal of Agricultural Economics,* Vol. 3, December 1980; Mahabub Hossain, "Farm Size, Tenancy and Land Productivity: An Analysis of Farm Level Data in Bangladesh Agriculture", *The Bangladesh Development Studies,* Vol. 5, No. 3, 1977.
26. P. Roy, "Transition in Agriculture: Empirical Studies and Results", *Journal of Peasant Studies,* Vol. 8, No. 2, 1981; G.S. Bhalla and G.K. Chadha, *Green Revolution and the Small Peasant,* Concept, New Delhi, 1983.
27. F. Kahnert, *et al., Agriculture and Related Industries in Pakistan,* OECD Development Center, Paris, 1970.
28. The World Bank estimated that in 1986/87 there was in fact a tax on urea of about 9 per cent of the procurement cost and a subsidy on phosphate of 14 per cent and on potash of 6 per cent. The average rate of subsidy on all types of fertilizers was estimated at −1.9 per cent.
29. The World Bank, *The World Development Report,* 1986.
30. See, for example, S.R. Osmani and M.A. Quasem, *Pricing and Subsidy Policies for Bangladesh Agriculture* (mimeographed), Bangladesh Institute of Development Studies, Dhaka, 1985.
31. M.A. Quasem *et al., Impact of the New System of Distribution of Fertilizers and Irrigation Machines in Bangladesh,* BIDS, Dhaka 1984 (mimeo).
32. M.A. Hamid *et al., Low Lift Pumps under IDA Credit in South-East Bangladesh: A Socio-Economic Study,* Rajshahi University 1984; M.A. Quasem *et al., op. cit.*
33. Government of Bangladesh and IDA, *Joint Review of Agricultural Credit in Bangladesh,* Dhaka, 1983.
34. J.U. Ahmed *et al., Paddy Rice Procurement System,* Report to the Ministry of Agriculture, Dhaka 1980; M.A. Quasem, "Government Procurement of Paddy/Rice and Farmers' Participation in Bangladesh", *Asian Profile,* Vol. 8, No. 4, 1980.
35. See, S.R. Osmani and M.A. Quasem, *op. cit.*

4 Industrialization

This chapter is concerned with an analysis of the manufacturing industries in Bangladesh and their performance since independence. It begins with a discussion of the structure of the manufacturing industries, highlighting the heterogeneity of the processes that coexist within the sector. Attention is then focused on the modern manufacturing sector with special attention to its organizational evolution and efficiency. Next the system of incentives and accumulation, promoted by the industrial and broader economic policies of the government, are analyzed. Finally, the effects of the major policy changes in recent years, e.g., denationalization and the implementation of policies to promote greater allocative efficiency, are discussed.

LARGE, SMALL AND COTTAGE INDUSTRIES

The activities that are classified under manufacturing industries in the national accounts are far from homogeneous. They range from the sophisticated modern industries based on imported technology to household production based on traditional technology and family labor. Yet to subdivide manufacturing into various groups according to the size of enterprise, the degree of technological sophistication or some other characteristic is necessarily somewhat arbitrary. Some such classification however is essential in order to distinguish different segments of manufacturing from one another. This is important because policies affect some segments differently from others and because the behavior of some segments has a greater impact on the economy and society than others. Nonetheless, the types of classifications that are possible are limited by the sources of available data and the statistical categories used in collecting the data. Information is assembled in Table 4.1 to describe the contours of the manufacturing industries sector for the year 1981/82. This is the most recent year for which detailed information is available directly from censuses and surveys or can be obtained by updating data from censuses and surveys conducted in nearby years. Four broad groups of industries are identified which correspond to the four sources of information used.

Table 4.1 Manufacturing Industries, 1981/82
Values in millions of Taka unless otherwise stated

	Large and medium	Small	Handloom	Other cottage	All manufacturing
Value added 1981/82 Factor cost (FC)	10 363	4 011	4 962	3 330	22 666
Value added 1981/82 Market price (MP)	13 721	4 613	4 962	3 330	26 626
Per cent of GDP at MP	5.2	1.7	1.9	1.3	10.0
Value added 1972/73 MP	4 120	1 385	1 490	1 000	7 995
Employment (thousand)					
Production worker	356	346	847	917	2 466
Per cent of labor force	1.36	1.33	3.25	3.51	9.45
All workers	456	400	847	917	2 620
Per cent of labor force	1.75	1.53	3.25	3.15	10.04
Value added 1981/82 FC per production worker (Tk)	29 110	11 592	5 858	3 631	9 191
Wage cost per production worker (Tk)	9 659	3 198	4 546	1 783	
Total wage cost (of production and non-production worker) per production worker (Tk)	14 306	4 306	4 546	1 783	

Fixed asset per production worker (Tk)	78 438	8 509	1961	1619
Value added per unit of fixed asset	0.37	1.36	2.99	2.24
Surplus per unit of fixed asset	0.19	0.86	0.67	1.14
Surplus per unit of total asset	0.11	0.72	0.35	0.79
Daily wage rate of production workers (Tk)	33.7	—	14.3	11.4

Note: The CMI shows book value of fixed assets. This has been multiplied by 2 to make conservative approximations of replacement cost. Days of work per year for small industries are not known, hence the daily wage could not be calculated. Small industries and handloom survey data were updated by using relevant price indices and growth rates.

Sources: Large and medium: BBS, *Bangladesh Census of Manufacturing Industries, Detailed Report*, 1981/82, Dhaka, 1986.
Small: BSCIC, *Survey Report on Small Industries of Bangladesh*, Dhaka, 1982.
Cottage: BSCIC, *Cottage Industries of Bangladesh, A Survey*, Dhaka, 1983 and Rural Industries Study Project (RISP) data in Mahabub Hossain, *Employment Generation through Cottage Industries*, ARTEP (ILO), 1984.
Handloom: BBS, Handloom Census reported in *Statistical Yearbook*, 1983/84 and RISP data.

(a) First, there are the large and medium industries (here called large industries or modern industries for the sake of brevity) covered by the annual Census of Manufacturing Industries (CMI). This census covers all enterprises which employ 10 persons or more.
(b) Second, there are the small industries. Information on these is obtained from the 1978/79 Survey of Small Industries (SSI) and then brought up to date. The SSI covered all privately owned manufacturing enterprises (excluding handlooms) which employ 10 to 20 persons (or more than 20 persons in those cases in which no mechanical power is used) and which have a value of fixed assets of Tk 2.5 million or less.
(c) Third, there are cottage industries. The Survey of Cottage Industries (SCI) for 1980/82 defines these as non-handloom manufacturing activities which are carried out wholly or mainly by members of a family either as a full-time or as a part-time occupation and which in addition employ no more than 10 persons if mechanical power is used and no more than 20 persons if no power is used.
(d) Finally, there is the handloom industry. Information on this group of activities is obtained from a 1978 census and then brought up to date.

From the above definitions, one would expect the four sources of data to overlap. In particular one would expect the coverage of the CMI and SSI to overlap and also the SSI and SCI to overlap. A detailed examination of the sources however reveals that overlapping has been minimal and perhaps is compensated by the less than complete coverage by each individual source of data on each group of industries[1]. Despite the formal definitions used in setting the boundaries among the different categories, an implicit division of labor among the three surveys seems to have been in operation. Data on the labor force and the national accounts also are consistent with the picture presented in Table 4.1. Total employment of production workers in manufacturing industries in 1981/82, according to Table 4.1, was 2.466 million. This is close to the LFS estimate of 2.5 million for 1983/84, assuming the latter refers only to production workers. If instead one assumes that the LFS also includes non-production workers, the employment level reported in Table 4.1 would appear to be too high. Even so, this would not necessarily be inconsistent with the LFS data. The reason for this is that cottage industries – the largest group in terms of employment – include part-time family workers irrespective of the number of hours worked.

Many of these people devote more hours of work to some other activity and therefore would not be listed by the LFS as workers employed in the manufacturing sector, but they would be included in the SCI. Finally, total value added in manufacturing at current market prices is only 3.6 per cent higher than the corresponding BBS estimate in the national accounts[2]. It would therefore appear that Table 4.1 contains just about as accurate a picture of the manufacturing industries in 1981/82 as one can piece together from the available sources of data. It is also probable that in terms of relative sizes and other characteristics the picture today is not much different from what it was then.

A COMPARISON AMONG THE THREE GROUPS OF INDUSTRIES

The lower end of the large and medium industries group (which accounts for only a small share of employment, assets and output of the group) is similar to the small industries group. But apart from this, the four groups are distinct: each group is reasonably homogeneous and fundamentally different from the other groups. The cottage and handloom industries are similar in some respects but differ in one important respect: there appears to be much more part-time employment in cottage industries than in handlooms. An average cottage industry worker is employed for 156 days in the sector and another 131 days in agriculture and other activities. An average handloom worker, in contrast, is employed in weaving for an estimated 317 days per year. This is due in part to the high degree of specificity of the traditional skills of handloom weavers which encourages people to specialize on a full-time basis. But in addition, the cottage industries are distinct in that they act as a residual employment category, an activity to which people are driven when more productive employment is not available. Indeed it is this which accounts for the very low earnings per worker in cottage industries, earnings which often are much lower than wages for agricultural laborers. Despite these differences, the two groups of industries often are lumped together, under the general label of cottage industries, when making comparisons with other groups.

Large and medium industries on the average employ 106 persons, and the number would be very much larger if the tail end of smaller enterprises were excluded. The large industries generally use modern technology imported from abroad. They borrow, both for fixed investment and working capital, from organized credit institutions.

Their labor force is hired in a market which is often organized and subject to a wage and benefits structure imposed by government legislation. The skilled labor they use is generally trained in formal institutions. They are located in urban areas, or, if not originally located in an urban area, their presence soon transforms it into an urban area. While their output is in principle a substitute of that of the cottage industries, there are important differences in the final use of the products of the two groups. The products of the large industries are generally consumed by higher income groups while the products of the cottage industries tend to be consumed by relatively lower income groups. Thus textiles woven by large-scale mills typically are consumed by higher income groups than those who purchase the products of handloom industries. Sari however is an exception. Similarly, refined sugar, a product of large-scale industry, is consumed by households which are richer than those which consume *gur* (raw sugar), a product of cottage industry. Immediately after independence, the large-scale industry sector was almost entirely nationalized and even today public ownership is widespread in this sector. The products of large industries are often used as inputs into cottage and small industries while the reverse rarely occurs.

Cottage industries are the polar opposite of the large industries. On the average a cottage enterprise consists of 3.5 workers, about 70 per cent of whom are members of the family and 30 per cent are hired[3]. These industries are located within households, overwhelmingly in rural areas. Their technology is traditional and capital equipment is generally produced locally. They have little access to institutional credit. The skills employed by the workers are traditional and acquired informally.

Small industries, lying in the middle of the spectrum, are closer to the large industries in terms of technology. They are almost always privately owned and are based on hired labor, although they usually are able to remain outside the reach of government legislation and the power of organized labor. Small industries on average employ 12 persons. They have less access to institutional credit than do the large industries.

The information compiled in Table 4.1 brings out some interesting comparisons among the four different groups of industries. For the manufacturing sector as a whole, labor productivity (defined as value added per production worker per year) is about the same as for the economy as a whole. However, labor productivity in large and medium industries is more than three times that for the manufacturing sector as a whole, whereas labor productivity in the (non-handloom) cottage industries is only two-fifths of the sector average. Small industries and handlooms fall in between these extremes. Labor productivity in small industry is higher than the national average labor productivity while in handlooms it is lower.

Some of these differences in labor productivity are due to differences in the number of days worked per person per year. The average number of days worked is 287 a year in large and medium industries, 317 in handloom and 156 in other cottage industries. Thus average value added per day per worker actually is higher in other cottage industries than in handloom weaving.

The number of days a year that a small industries worker is employed in industry is not known; but it obviously is low. Assuming the wage rate in small industries were the same as for handloom workers, the number of days of employment per year would be 224. However, since the wage rate in such relatively modern, urban-based industries is almost certainly higher than in the traditional, rural-based handloom industries, the number of days of employment must be lower, perhaps substantially less than 200 days a year. The reason for this is the seasonality of employment in some of the more important small industries. In the Small Industries Survey, rice mills alone account for 51 per cent of employment. The annual wage earnings of a production worker in rice milling are less than half that of other production workers in small industries. Since the difference in the wage rate could not be large, the difference in the annual earnings must be due to the very low number of days worked in rice milling as compared to the rest of the small industries.

It is, however, clear that an adjustment for differences in the number of days of employment per year would leave the ranking of each sector in terms of labor productivity unchanged. Labor productivity would still be the highest in the large and medium industries – about 50 per cent higher than in small industries and approximately four and half times that in cottage industries.

Ranking of the different groups in terms of capital intensity (defined as the estimated current replacement value of fixed assets per production worker) is exactly the same as that in terms of productivity. The percentage differences in capital intensity are however far greater than in productivity[4]. Capital intensity in large and medium industries is nine times that in small industries and 44 times that in cottage industries. The productivity of fixed capital (defined as value added per unit of fixed asset) is thus greatest for cottage industries and lowest for large industries with small industries standing approximately halfway between the two.

The wages of *production* workers as a proportion of value added are higher for cottage industries than for large and small industries. But this is partly offset by the high employment cost of *non-production* workers as a proportion of value added in large and small industries. In cottage industries, there are no pure non-production workers. Such workers account for 22 per cent and 14 per cent respectively of all employment in large and small industries. Moreover, the unit cost of non-production workers is higher than that of production workers. Thus 32 per cent of the employment cost in large industries and 26 per cent in small industries is accounted for by non-production workers. Non-production workers are of course essential for the operation of modern enterprises, but since independence employment of non-production workers has increased much faster than industrial employment as a whole, especially in the large nationalized enterprises. The growth of non-production workers in nationalized enterprises has been much greater than necessary and this has had the effect of diverting part of potential surplus of industry into private consumption.

Surplus, defined as value added less all costs of employment, as a proportion of fixed assets has been highest for cottage industries, with small industries coming close to the average for handloom and other cottage industries. Surplus per unit of fixed assets in the large industries has been less than a quarter of the rate of surplus in the rest of manufacturing industry. Estimates of surplus per unit of total assets – the rate of return of capital – in Table 4.1 have been calculated after making an allowance for working capital in total assets[5]. Cottage industries, other than handlooms, retain the highest rank and are closely followed by small industries. The rate of return on capital for handlooms, at 35 per cent of the value of all assets, is quite high. In the case of large industries, however, the rate of return is very low and is likely to be easily absorbed by other possible claims on surplus (e.g., payment of interest on loans, taxes, fees, etc.).

The low wages in cottage industries are conspicuous. In cottage industries other than handlooms, the wage rate in 1981/82 was 26 per cent below the wages of male agricultural workers. Even in handlooms, the wage rate was about 8 per cent lower than the wages of male agricultural workers. This partly reflects the fact that all agricultural laborers (with whom the comparison is being made) are men whereas 36 per cent of the handloom workers and approximately a third of the workers in other cottage industries are female[6]. Female workers' wages in general are at least a quarter lower than the wages of male workers[7]. However, quite apart from sexual discrimination, the very low wages in cottage industries other than handlooms reflects the fact that cottage industry often is a residual employer which absorbs workers who are unable to obtain more remunerative employment in other industries, including agriculture. The dramatic reduction in the share of agriculture in total employment during the decade ending in 1983/84, as revealed by the LFS data, reflects a failure on the part of agriculture to provide employment rather than dynamic development of the non-agricultural sectors. Had other sectors been expanding rapidly, this would have led to greater demand for labor, higher real wages and a very different pattern of relative sectoral wages.

THE GROWTH OF MANUFACTURING INDUSTRIES

In 1967/68 employment in large and medium industries accounted for only 0.9 per cent of the total employment in the economy. By 1981/82 the share of large and medium industries in total employment had nearly doubled, to 1.75 per cent. Yet value added in these industries, as a proportion of GDP, showed little tendency to change (see Table 4.3). In more recent years, value added in these industries declined as a proportion of GDP according to the official (unadjusted) BBS estimates. If one makes a generous upward adjustment in value added for the recent years in order to account for the increased weight of the faster growing components of industry, value added in the sub-sector appears to have grown slightly faster than GDP as a whole since 1981/82[8]. Between 1967/68 and 1981/82 value added per worker at constant prices declined by approximately 16 per cent in large and medium industrial enterprises. Much of the growth in employment in this sector is accounted for by larger numbers of non-production workers in the work force. But even production workers, mainly in public sector enterprises, were hired in excess of requirements in response to pressure to create more employment.

The evidence for small industries is not as good as for the large industries nor are data published as frequently. Direct estimates of growth over time are based on data from the two SSI surveys, conducted in the early 1960s and late 1970s. The definition of small industry was not the same in both surveys and hence one must be very careful in drawing conclusions about trends over time. In particular, one should not attach too much significance to the apparent decline in the share in GDP of value added in small industries between the two surveys. (See the last column of Table 4.2.) Similarly the apparent decline in average

Table 4.2 Indices for Small and Cottage Industries with Large and Medium Industries as Base

	Employment of production workers	Employment of all workers	Value added per production worker	Value added per all workers	Value added
Pre-independence: 1967/68					
Large and medium	—	100	—	100	100
Small	—	100	—	47	47
Non-handloom cottage	—	—	—	—	—
Handloom	—	—	—	—	—
All cottage	—	656	—	5	35
1981/82					
Large and medium	100	100	100	100	100
Small	97	88	40	44	39
Non-handloom cottage	258	201	12	16	32
Handloom	238	186	20	26	48
All cottage	496	387	16	21	80

Source: Pre-independence: *CMI*, 1967/68, *Small Industries Survey* 1963/64 and *Cottage Industries Survey* 1962/63. Data from the last two updated to 1967/68. Post independence data sources are the same as for Table 4.1.

Table 4.3 Share of manufacturing industries in GDP at current prices

	Unadjusted		Adjusted	
	Large	Small and cottage	Large	Small and cottage
1969/70	6.0	3.3	—	—
1974/75	5.8	4.7	—	4.0
1976/77	5.7	4.6	—	—
1980/81	6.1	4.5	—	—
1981/82	6.1	4.6	—	—
1982/83	5.6	4.5	5.9	5.6
1983/84	5.6	4.5	6.1	5.8
1984/85	5.6	4.4	6.4	6.0
1985/86	5.5	4.3	6.3	6.2

Note: The unadjusted series is from the BBS. These are at market prices. The method of adjusting the BBS data has been described in the Annex to Chapter 2.

labor productivity between the two surveys is probably due to a relative increase in the number of enterprises that provide far fewer days of employment per worker per year than average, a phenomenon to which attention has already been drawn. Fragmentary evidence suggests that small industries have grown faster than the large and medium industries.

Cottage industries appear to have grown most rapidly. Table 4.2 compares the findings of the two surveys, respectively in the early 1960s and the early 1980s. There is less of a problem about the comparability of data from these two surveys though the question of the comparability of their relative coverage can not be resolved. The annual rate of growth in the labor force in cottage industries has been lower between the two surveys than according to the labor force surveys (LFS) and censuses since 1974. This may reflect a difference between the surveys of cottage industries (SCI) and the LFS in the definition of employment. The SCI counts all workers engaged in cottage industry, irrespective of the number of hours worked, while the LFS counts only those for whom cottage industries are the principal source of employment. It is probable that between the 1960s and the 1980s a fair proportion of workers changed the allocation of their labor time, ceasing to regard agriculture as the principal source of employment and instead regarding cottage industries (and other non-agricultural activities) as the main source of employment. Another possibility which helps to explain the discrepancy in employment growth rates as measured by the SCI and LFS is that the rate of growth of the labor force in cottage industries accelerated after the mid-1970s.

Although the share of cottage industries in industrial employment fell between the two surveys (though not according to LFS data), their share of value added increased sharply (Table 4.2). This implies that labor productivity in cottage industries increased rapidly. But as already noted, this may reflect an increase in the number of days worked per laborer rather than an increase in output per unit of time worked. The evidence from movements in relative wages does not suggest that there has been a significant rise in labor productivity per work day in cottage industries.

To summarize: the most organized and modern part of manufacturing – large and medium industries – has not grown rapidly. Enterprises in this group have experienced falling productivity per worker and a low rate of return on capital. Systematic information on small industries is scarce; but the evidence that is available indicates that these urban-based industries have grown relatively rapidly. Cottage industries also have grown fairly fast, partly due to an influx of labor that agriculture failed to absorb. The performance of cottage industry does not therefore reflect vigorous growth. The sub-sector, in common with small industries, received little support from the government. Little help was provided to acquire technology, training, credit; nothing was done to improve marketing or to increase access of small producers to scarce resources. Even so small producers – driven by distress and ingenuity – were able to take advantage of whatever opportunities arose and they did succeed in achieving a substantial rate of growth of output. The rewards from growth in the form of wages and earnings per worker, especially in the cottage industries, were however dismally low.

THE MODERN MANUFACTURING INDUSTRIES

The Census of Manufacturing Industries for 1981/82 reported on 3 356 enterprises. The size distribution of these large and medium industries – the modern industrial enterprises – is highly skewed. There were 254 large enterprises (7.6 per cent of the total number) each of which employed 250 persons or more. These large enterprises accounted for 76 per cent of the employment and 75 per cent of the assets of the modern manufacturing industries sector. At the other end of the spectrum, 75 per cent of the enterprises in the modern manufacturing sector employed less than 50 persons each. Together they accounted for less than 11 per cent of employment and less than 7 per cent of the assets in the sector.

Table 4.4 shows a number of indicators of growth and productivity in the modern manufacturing sector. If one uses the official BBS estimates, value added in modern manufacturing has grown less rapidly than GDP. However, if one accepts some of the recent upward adjustments suggested for the sector, then the growth in value added in modern manufacturing turns out to be higher than GDP as a whole, but even so one could hardly describe the performance as outstanding. The table also shows indices of labor productivity (per production worker) in four industries for which continuous data are available from the pre-independence period. Together these industries accounted for about a third of the value of assets in modern manufacturing according to the 1981/82 CMI. In each case productivity was lower in the mid-1980s than before independence and in jute textiles – the largest industry – productivity has declined steadily.

THE PUBLIC AND PRIVATE SECTORS

Before independence modern industrial enterprises in Bangladesh were mainly owned by Pakistani private owners and the state-owned East Pakistan Industrial Development Corporation (EPIDC). At the time of independence, these two categories of owners accounted for 81 per cent of the assets of modern industry. Bangladeshi private industrialists owned only 18 per cent of the assets of modern industry. Non-Pakistani foreign ownership was negligible[9].

In March 1972, three months after independence, the Awami League Government nationalized the major large-scale industries. In fact, the action consisted of two distinct parts, one providing the legal framework for the management of enterprises abandoned by their Pakistani owners and the other nationalizing all enterprises in the jute textiles, cotton textiles and sugar industries. As can be seen in Table 4.5, the only freedom of action available to the government was with respect to the 15 per cent of the assets in the large-scale industries owned by the Bangladeshis that were nationalized. As a result of nationalization, the government came to own 92 per cent of the fixed assets of the modern manufacturing sector after March 1972[10]. Nationalization was followed, in July 1972, by the imposition of limitations on the size of new

Table 4.4 Growth and productivity in modern industries

Year	Index of value added		Index of productivity per production worker			
	BBS	Adjusted BBS	Jute textiles	Cotton textiles	Paper	Steel
1969/70	—	—	178	270	173	119
1972/73	—	—	181	201	91	101
1973/74	100	100	100	100	100	100
1974/75	136	136	104	99	99	95
1975/76	146	146	103	93	93	90
1976/77	152	152	104	92	92	110
1977/78	168	168	109	101	100	117
1978/79	179	179	97	101	101	124
1979/80	179	179	98	90	102	120
1980/81	198	198	95	98	101	124
1981/82	199	199	92	102	97	127
1982/83	189	200	94	116	98	120
1983/84	197	219	91	122	103	105
1984/85	204	238	88	115	98	111
1985/86	211	246	—	—	—	—

Source: For indices of value added, see the Annex to Chapter 2. It should be noted that the upward adjustment of the BBS estimate of value added in recent years is probably excessive; also, the revised quantum index on which this adjustment is based probably includes some fast-growing industries which should be excluded from the modern sector as defined here. See the text. Productivity indices are from BBS, *Statistical Yearbooks,* 1981 and 1986.

private industrial enterprises. Private enterprises were not allowed to exceed an initial fixed asset value of Tk 2.5 million (approximately $0.3 million at the prevailing rate of exchange) but they were allowed to grow up to Tk 3.5 million in asset value through the reinvestment of profits. Direct foreign investment was allowed only in collaboration with the public sector and only with a minority equity participation.

In July 1974, these restrictions were eased by raising the ceiling on size to Tk 30 million. The number of industries reserved for the public sector was limited to eighteen: telegraph; telephone; cables and wireless apparatus; electricity; air and sea transport; nuclear energy; arms and

Table 4.5 Large-scale industrial ownership before and after nationalization

	Number of units	Value of fixed assets: million Tk	Per cent of fixed assets
Total industries	3 051	6 137.5	100
Before nationalization			
EPIDC	53	2 097.0	34
Private Pakistani	725	2 885.7	47
Private Bengali	20	118.8	18
Private foreign	20	36.0	1
After nationalization			
Nationalized of which:	392	5 637.5	92
Former EPIDC	53	2 097.0	34
Private Pakistani	263	2 629.7	43
Private foreign	1		
Private Bengali	75	910.8	15
Private Bengali	2 178	208.0	3
Abandoned: to be sold	462	256.0	4
With foreign participation	13	36.0	1
Total private	2 653	500.0	8

Source: See text.

ammunition; shipbuilding; heavy engineering; heavy electrical machinery; minerals; oil and gas; petrochemicals; iron and steel; cement; jute textiles; cotton textiles; and sugar. Except for the last three, all the other of these industries were exclusively in the public sector during the pre-independence period as well. This liberalization of restrictions on private investment was initiated by the same Awami League Government which had enacted the nationalization measures two years earlier.

Subsequently, after a series of violent political changes which began in August 1975, the investment ceiling for private industries was raised by the Ziaur Rahman regime in a series of steps to Tk 100 million and then was completely abolished in 1978. Between 1975 and 1978, the government sold 116 enterprises to the private sector. A number of other measures designed to promote modern private industry were implemented, e.g., the reopening of the stock market in 1976, the establishment of the Investment Corporation of Bangladesh to provide bridge financing and underwriting facilities to the private sector and the abolition of restrictions on collaboration between domestic private industries and direct foreign investment.

The reimposition of military rule in early 1982 was followed by the adoption of the New Industrial Policy in June of the same year. Under this policy large-scale denationalization occurred and in particular the jute and cotton textile mills which had been taken over from Bangladeshi industrialists in 1972 were restored to their former owners. Of the 72 jute mills in the public sector on 30th June 1982, 34 (accounting for 38 per cent of production capacity) were denationalized by June 1985. Of the 52 cotton textile mills *in operation* in the public sector on 30th June 1982, 22 were denationalized within one year of the announcement of the New Industrial Policy.

Table 4.6 shows that by 1981/82 the share of the public sector in modern industries had declined from the post-nationalization peak to about 69 per cent of the value of their fixed assets and 72 per cent of their employment. By 1985 only about 160 enterprises – accounting for about 40 per cent of assets and less than a quarter of employment – remained in the public sector. These figures are not much higher than the corresponding figures before independence.

Table 4.6 Ownership of large-scale industries, 1981/82
Per cent of total

	Nationalized	Joint	Private
Book value of fixed assets	69.1	2.5	28.4
Value added	61.5	9.3	29.2
Employment: All workers	72.1	1.5	26.4
Production workers	73.5	1.0	25.5
Wage bill	76.8	4.5	18.7

Source: CMI 1981/82, Detailed Report.

The public and private sector industries in 1981/82 are compared in Table 4.7. Since that year further denationalizations have changed the composition of each. Unfortunately, available data do not permit a comparison for a more recent date. It should also be emphasized that it is impossible to identify the extent to which the differences between the public and private sectors that are shown in the table are due to differences in the composition of industries in the two sectors or to differences in their behavior. Despite these limitations, the comparison highlights some interesting contrasts.

Table 4.7 Some comparative features of nationalized and private industries

	Nationalized	Private
Fixed assets per worker (Tk of book value)	29 339	32 962
Value added per worker (Tk)	19 387	25 125
Value added per production worker (Tk)	24 360	33 270
Wages per worker (all workers: Tk per year)	11 900	7 902
Wages as per cent of value added	61.4	31.5
Value added per unit of book value of fixed assets	0.66	0.76
Surplus per unit of book value of fixed assets	0.25	0.52

Source: CMI, 1981/82, Detailed Report.

Somewhat surprisingly, capital intensity (defined in this case as the unadjusted book value of fixed assets per employee) is higher in the private sector than in the public sector. This is surprising because the public sector enterprises are larger and include industries (e.g., fertilizer, steel, paper and petroleum refining) that are thought to use very capital-intensive technology. It is of course possible that the figures in the table are misleading because the ratio of book value to replacement value of assets is very different in the two sectors, but this is improbable. A more likely explanation is that employment in the public sector has become inflated beyond the numbers needed to operate efficiently.

Value added per worker is higher in the private sector than in the public sector. The proportionate difference in value added per worker is greater than that in the value of assets per worker. Thus value added per unit value of fixed assets is about 15 per cent higher in the private sector than in the public sector.

The average wage per worker in the public sector is 51 per cent higher than in the private sector. This combined with lower productivity of labor results in a much higher share of wages in value added in the public sector industries. Surplus (i.e., non-wage value added) per unit of book value of fixed assets is more than twice as high for private industries than for the public sector industries. In view of the many qualifications made about the comparability of data between the two sectors, one can not reach definitive conclusions as to the relative efficiency of the public and private sector, but it is clear that a high proportion of the potential surplus in the public sector has been dissipated in the form of higher cost of employment. This is due partly to employing labor in excess of requirements and partly to paying higher wages than is warranted by the opportunity cost of labor.

Has the modern industrial sector grown faster as a result of denationalization? A clear answer is not possible on the basis of the available information. Official statistics suggest a deceleration of growth since the early 1980s, especially after the 1982 denationalization program. But, as mentioned earlier, attempts have been made to show that the actual increase in industrial production was higher than that indicated by the official index[11]. But even if one accepts these revisions, it is still the case that growth was slow or negative in the sectors in which denationalization was concentrated and most rapid in small-scale steel re-rolling, food processing and certain other industries that are perhaps ordinarily not included in the CMI. While the full impact of denationalization may take more time to become apparent and while it may be difficult at present to disentangle the effects of denationalization from the effects of other policies, a preliminary analysis shows that in the first three years after denationalization private jute and cotton textile mills performed no better than the public ones. Indeed in some respects, the performance of the modern private industries, including the denationalized ones, has been extraordinarily poor. This is especially the case with respect to the servicing of loans from the public sector development finance institutions. As discussed later in Chapter 5, borrowing by the private manufacturing sector from the banking system jumped discontinuously upwards with the institution of the denationalization program. Forty-four per cent of the outstanding loans owed to the Bangladesh Shilpa Bank (Bangladesh Industrial Bank) and 70 per cent of that to the Bangladesh Shilpa Rin Sangstha (Bangladesh Industrial Credit Corporation) in June 1986 consisted of overdue loans on which the borrowers had defaulted. An overwhelming proportion of these defaults were made by the private borrowers. A survey by the Bangladesh Institute of Development Studies showed that in 1985/86 only 3.9 per cent of the private industrial borrowers repaid on schedule the entire amount due for repayment while 33.3 per cent of the borrowers defaulted on the entire amount due for repayment. (The remaining 62.8 per cent defaulted on various proportions of the amounts due to be repaid)[12].

AN INTERPRETATION OF NATIONALIZATION AND ITS AFTERMATH

The nationalizations of 1972 were widely interpreted as a major step towards effecting a socialist transformation of Bangladesh, and were acclaimed as a positive step by many who are inspired by socialist ideals and deplored almost universally by those who disapprove of socialism either as a goal or as a method of development. Socialism is of course a word that is inscribed on banners of widely differing colors. It is therefore hard to make sense of this statement without a more specific definition of the term. It was often claimed, particularly by the defenders of nationalization, that the events of 1972 represented the first stage of a program that would go far beyond social democracy and would probably evolve into some form of "orthodox" socialism.

Yet there was nothing in the history of the Awami League to suggest that it would implement a program that would bring about a socialist transformation of the economy. During much of its past existence, it was a pro-Western party without a commitment to any fundamental social change. Beginning in the middle of the 1960s, its program became staunchly nationalistic, typical of parties which combined populism with support for the interests of the emerging capitalist and middle classes against non-indigenous capitalists. It was only towards the end of the 1960s that it came to adopt moderately social democratic programs, e.g., the nationalization of banks, insurance companies and basic industries. This did not reflect a significant change in the party's constituency or leadership but only the adoption of new tactical positions and fashions by the old established leadership. It is noteworthy that virtually all of the numerous political parties that contested the 1970 elections supported the nationalization of banks and insurance companies and other radical programs.

It is often said that the Awami League became radicalized in the course of the armed struggle for independence. This again appears to be too simple a view. The leaders of the party that came to rule Bangladesh after independence were the same people who had led the party for many years. They were not a bunch of radicals who had seized power during the war of independence. Indeed, the radical elements were quickly removed from leadership positions. The Indian Government and the Indian army – which clearly had no intention of promoting revolutionary movements – gave their support to the Awami League, kept a watchful eye on the course of events and decisively influenced the final outcome.

An important test of the regime's radicalism is its agrarian program. In an overwhelmingly rural society such as Bangladesh, one would expect that any program of socialist transformation would begin with a significant program of agrarian change. Yet neither before independence nor after the Awami League assumed state power did it advance an agrarian program of any significance whatsoever.

There were, however, radical elements among the students, youth and other groups who were vocal though not well organized but who nonetheless played a role in the independence movement. These groups made radical demands which the ruling party found difficult to ignore completely, particularly during the uncertain period when it was consolidating its power. The ruling party however was never forced to make a basic compromise or to sacrifice its own goals. As will be shown below, acceptance by the Awami League of some of the radical demands did not in the least conlict with its own goals. Nor did acceptance signal the beginning of a socialist transformation of the economy.

To understand the significance of nationalization, one should consider what were the possible alternatives. Conceivably the enterprises abandoned by the Pakistanis might have been handed over to private Bangladeshi capitalists. This, however, would have raised the serious problem of how to ration them since there was no possibility of selling the firms to the "highest bidders". There were few potential bidders who possessed sufficient funds or who could raise the necessary finance without support from the state. Any Bangladeshi bidder would have had to be sponsored by the state and would have required credit from public sector financial institutions. It was not easy to devise a rationing mechanism, for the distribution of such patronage would require the selection of a small number of beneficiaries (there were only 263 large abandoned units that the government retained) from a very large number of aspirants. Moreover, to hand over the enterprises to private Bangladeshi capitalists would put the regime on the defensive *vis-à-vis* the radical elements, something that the regime – like most regimes in a similar situation – wanted to avoid.

Another possibility would be to limit nationalization to the abandoned enterprises and exclude from the program enterprises owned by private Bangladeshi capitalists. This was considered at the time and rejected. Almost certainly the rejection was prompted by the perception of the need, on the part of the regime, to prove its socialist credentials *vis-à-vis* the motley collection of radical elements. The regime had to appear to be striking at the Bangladeshi capitalists too. Otherwise nationalization of the abandoned enterprises would be seen as being forced by circumstances, not as deriving from a vision of a desirable course of action.

How significant was the takeover of the jute and cotton textile mills that were owned by the Bangladeshi industrialists? As shown above, these amounted to only 15 per cent of the fixed assets in the modern industries sector. In terms of the net worth of the private sector, the transfer was negligible. Most of the assets, as much as 80 per cent, had been acquired by borrowing from public sector lending institutions. Much of the remaining 20 per cent or so probably had been financed by the commercial banks which also were nationalized after independence. There is evidence that in the past, as at present, private capitalists often directed only a part of their borrowing from the lending agencies to the investment projects for which the funds were intended, using the rest for accumulating personal assets, e.g., luxury housing or cash balances abroad. It is therefore conceivable, even probable, that in many cases nationalization amounted to no more than taking over negative net worth in exchange for a promise of positive compensation.

To private industrialists it was the control of productive enterprises, rather than the ownership of assets, that was important, for control was a source of economic power and a vehicle for personal enrichment. The concomitant of ownership was the obligation to service the debt that originally made the acquisition of assets possible. But control of production was the key to a high salary, the direct consumption of services and benefits and an opportunity to augment earnings through a whole array of activities ranging from overinvoicing of imports and underinvoicing of exports to misappropriation of funds. One significant act that followed nationalization of these enterprises was that the former owners were appointed to manage and control them. While it is not the intention of the present analysis to suggest that the Bangladeshi capitalists were in any mood to abdicate, it is clear that the owners-turned-managers, freed from the need to earn a profit to service their debts, were given an unprecedented opportunity to pursue the goal of personal enrichment in an environment in which there was little financial and industrial discipline. Any losses incurred by the enterprises could always be blamed on the inherent inefficiency of public enterprise and socialism.

In retrospect, there were other redeeming features of the nationalization of the enterprises owned by the Bangladeshis. An example is the jute textile industry, one of the two sectors in which Bangladeshi-owned private enterprises were nationalized. In the pre-independence period the high rate of profit in this industry derived from the high protection it received. There was blatant discrimination against the peasant growers of raw jute and in favor of the (mostly Pakistani) manufacturers of jute textiles. The export exchange rate for jute textiles was much more favorable than the export exchange rate for raw jute. After independence this discrimination became politically untenable and was abolished. It was unlikely that in the predominantly agrarian

Bangladesh well understood discrimination of such a magnitude against the peasantry could be re-established in the near future. Without such discrimination, the industry was destined to – indeed did – become unprofitable. Nationalization saved the private owners from the consequence of this.

THE PROCESS OF ACCUMULATION

For the class of emerging capitalists in Bangladesh the prime concern is rapid accumulation[13]. Yet accumulation through the ordinary process of "competitive" capitalism is slow and requires much effort. A much faster and easier mechanism of accumulation could be created by using state power to distribute the nation's potential economic surplus to the powerful dominant social classes.

The potential surplus of the public sector industries – which were virtually synonymous with modern manufacturing – became a major source of private accumulation[14]. The main ways in which the surplus was appropriated can be summarized as follows:

(a) First, the output of the nationalized industries was sold to private distributors at a price that was well below the market clearing price. Administered prices applied to 76 per cent of the value of output of the domestically marketed goods produced by public enterprises[15]. For most of these products the margin between the market price and the ex-factory price was very substantial and the difference was appropriated by the private distributor. Distribution licenses were often given to intermediaries who then sold them to legitimate traders at close to the market clearing price.

(b) Second, highly paid white collar employment in public sector enterprises was allowed to increase beyond any conceivable legitimate need.

(c) Third, senior managers and bureaucrats in the ministries and corporations responsible for managing the state enterprises obtained numerous benefits in kind (e.g., transport, personal services, supplies and other consumables) from the enterprises.

(d) Fourth, a great deal of illegal enrichment occurred at the expense of enterprise profit. Examples include bribes to senior staff by suppliers who passed on the cost in the form of higher prices, overinvoicing of purchases, underinvoicing of sales, and the maintenance of ghost workers on the payroll.

(e) Fifth, a concession also was made to organized labor. This took the form of an expansion in employment in excess of requirements. There were other kinds of waste as well. For example, the jute workers succeeded in persuading management to use unnecessarily high quality of raw jute. This increased the cost of production but enabled the workers to receive higher wages under the prevalent system of piece rate payment. It was, however, not possible for the industrial workers to avoid a fall in real wages.

Another major source of private accumulation was the appropriation of the scarcity premiums in an import trade which was quantitatively controlled by licensing. During Pakistan's industrialization in the 1950s and 1960s, the appropriation of the scarcity premiums on imports was a major source of accumulation. The burden of this accumulation was borne by the producers of exportables, largely small peasant growers of raw jute in the then East Pakistan. In independent Bangladesh the practice of an overvalued currency, strict licensing of imports and the passing of the scarcity premiums to the fortunate recipients of the import licenses continued. This constituted a heavy concealed tax on those who produced goods for export, notably peasants who produced raw jute and the public sector jute textiles industry.

Over the years, the scarcity premiums on commercial imports declined. The strongest evidence of this is the convergence over time between the official exchange rate and the alternative exchange rate under the wage earners' scheme (WES). The latter is the free market price of foreign exchange remitted by Bangladeshis working overseas. The purchase of the foreign exchange remitted by them entitles the buyer to a license to import goods and services of specified categories. The convergence between the official and WES rates of exchange indicates that the supply of foreign exchange – determined by the volume of foreign aid, remittances made by the workers and export receipts – has become less scarce over time.

The scarcity premiums on WES imports could not be kept high by artifical controls. This is because if the premium were to rise very much the consequence would be that remittances would decline or else they would enter the country through illegal channels. This would be undesirable. The convergence of the two rates of exchange means that the premiums on other commercial imports also declined substantially. But the premiums on public sector imports, largely financed by foreign aid, continued to be very high, although the form taken by the premium changed to agency fees and payments received by local agents of foreign suppliers. The political connections of the local agents determined who received the supply contract. Consequently agency fees were very high. There was however no difficulty in passing this high margin on to the user of imports since the user was the public sector. The whole system was fueled by a large inflow of foreign aid used to finance public sector imports.

It is instructive to continue the comparison with the historical example of Pakistan. In Pakistan capital accumulation from the scarcity premiums on imports was channelled into investment in the domestic manufacturing sector whose profitability was ensured by the very import controls which created the scarcity premiums. Industrial growth was consequently rapid although there were serious problems of inefficiency and inequality. In Bangladesh, in contrast, the accumulated surplus has not been channelled into industrial investment. It would be interesting to know why the outcome has been so different in the two cases, but unfortunately, serious analysis is difficult because of the great scarcity of information. The nature of accumulation itself encourages an information blackout. A number of hypotheses can however be advanced.

The first important obstacle to industrial development has been political. A major industrialization effort requires a minimum degree of political stability and a coalition among the major entrepreneurial groups that assures to them the fruits of their efforts (see Chapter 1). This type of political stability does not necessarily imply continuity of regime or the absence of frequent political change, including violent change. Neither South Korea nor Thailand has been stable in that sense whereas Burma and Tanzania have experienced great continuity and little violent pressure for political change. What is needed is enough authority by the state to enforce discipline and to ensure that actual and potential entrepreneurs obey the rules of the game. The state must also be able to guarantee that changes in regime do not affect the basic rules of the game in any fundamental way. The requirement of stability is of course greater, the less mature is the class of entrepreneurs. The state in Bangladesh has amply wielded its power to create mechanisms for enriching the rich and powerful; it has however not succeeded in providing the weak and emerging capitalist entrepreneurs with the required sense of stability. The chaos and indiscipline that were tolerated as a concomitant of the process of accumulation were themselves an obstacle to the creation of confidence among the beneficiaries of the process.

A second important factor is the conflict between the process of accumulation and industrialization. In the historical case of Pakistan, accumulation of surplus on a large scale and high profitability in protected domestic manufacturing were two sides of the same coin. In the early years of independent Bangladesh this was indeed the case as far as some forms of accumulation went, e.g., that from the appropriation of the scarcity premiums on imports. But the appropriation of surplus from the nationalized industries was not consistent with industrial development. It inflicted heavy losses on the public sector industries and the political pretence that the country was going through a "socialist transformation" merely aggravated the situation by discouraging the conversion of private financial accumulation into private investment.

Later on, the process of accumulation itself changed in such a way as sharply to reduce the incentive for industrial investment. High profits in the form of agency fees, indenting and similar payments did not reflect an excess of demand for imports but merely a larger volume of imports. The result was a sharply reduced level of protection for domestic manufacturing. A recent study showed that the overall wholesale trade margin on imports into Bangladesh fell by nearly a half between 1979 and 1984[16]. A comparison of sectoral price deflators in Table 4.8 shows that the terms of trade moved sharply against manufacturing industries. Comparison between statutory protection (measured by import taxes) and observed protection (measured by the difference between border prices and domestic prices) shows that the latter is way below the former with rare exceptions. This finding suggests that tariffs have not been effective[17]. Moreover, extraordinarily high profits in foreign trade "intermediation" activities has encouraged potential entrepreneurs to pursue these activities instead of engaging in manufacturing.

Of course, some industrial development did take place. Much of this was in small-scale and cottage enterprises. Entrepreneurs in these sectors did not have the option of engaging in the profitable intermediation activities. To the extent that they were users of the products of modern manufacturing, reduced protection may have helped them.

It is also true that occasional industries in the modern sector developed under special circumstances and were able to extort massive support. Bans on imports were selectively imposed to protect some existing industries whose owners had enough power and/or the capacity to bribe. But by and large industrial protection was not great, and the reason for this is that the dominant mechanism of surplus appropriation depended upon the absorption of massive amounts of imports.

This does not imply that greater protection of industry is what is needed to accelerate industrial growth. The point is that protection

Table 4.8 Sectoral real price deflators

Year	Manufacturing	Agriculture
1972/73	100	100
1978/79	86	106
1979/80	92	102
1980/81	92	96
1981/82	91	94
1982/83	96	96
1983/84	88	101
1984/85	83	107
1985/86	79	117

Note: The real deflator for a sector is the sectoral value-added deflator (estimated by comparing the BBS estimates of sectoral value added at current and constant prices) expressed as per cent of the GDP deflator (also obtained from the BBS).

declined. The rules of the game of accumulation, the absence of political stability and poor infrastructure combined with low protection to produce few incentives for industrial investment. Had reduced protection been accompanied by changes in the rules of the game and the positive promotion of industrialization through the provision of an improved political and better infrastructural environment, growth might have been faster.

Where did the appropriated surplus go? Though little information is available, it is possible to advance some plausible hypotheses. Much of the surplus was wasted in high consumption: luxury housing, durable consumer goods, foreign travel, foreign education of children to an extent that would hardly have been considered normal before independence. It is also certain that a substantial volume of capital flight occurred. Indeed this is inherent in the mechanism of accumulation. Much of the agency fees and related payments were extralegal and naturally tended to be kept abroad.

FOREIGN EXCHANGE REGIME AND INDUSTRIAL GROWTH

One of the widely held orthodoxies of development economics is that the foreign exchange regime decisively influences the growth and efficiency of industrialization. Attention has been focused on the phenomenon of overvalued exchange rates and the quantitative restrictions on imports that usually accompany them in developing countries. Criticism of such policies has emphasized that they discriminate against exports; that they inevitably promote non-uniform protection for different products which in turn encourages a misallocation of resources; and that the multitude of controls and restrictions that are necessary features of such a system constitutes an obstacle to industrial growth and efficiency.

In Table 4.9 some important indicators of the foreign exchange regime in Bangladesh are presented. The real effective exchange rate (REER) – in takas per US dollar – has been estimated by adjusting the nominal exchange rate for: (i) price changes in Bangladesh relative to the weighted average of price changes in trading partners; (ii) export duties and receipts from export subsidy schemes, e.g., export performance licensing (XPL) and export performance benefits (XPB); and (iii) import tax and the premium paid on WES. In calculating the REER for exports adjustments have however not been made for the value of certain incentives (e.g., tax holidays, access to bonded warehouses, interest rate subsidies and several other benefits). Thus the REER for exports, especially the rate for non-traditional exports, is somewhat understated. Moreover, as noted above, the rates of observed protection have generally been much lower than the rates of statutory protection. Since the REER for imports uses the statutory duties and tax rates, it would appear that it is overstated.

Some of the main features of the foreign exchange regime can be summarized as follows:

(a) First, the comparison between the nominal and WES rates shows that the extent of overvaluation in the official exchange rate is low and has been declining over time. This is due to the relative abundance of foreign exchange compared to effective demand, a point made earlier. Compared to the pre-independence period and to most contemporary developing countries, the extent of overvaluation is low.
(b) Second, the REER for imports is still more favourable than the rate for exports. The difference is about 20-25 per cent when compared to non-traditional exports and about 25-30 per cent when compared to traditional exports. However, as explained above, the REER for exports is underestimated and the REER for imports is overestimated. The actual difference between the two

Table 4.9 Exchange rates

Year	Nominal	REER: Trad. export	REER: Non-trad. export	REER: Import	WES	WES premium (per cent of nominal)
1973/74	7.97	7.94	7.97	9.72		
1974/75	8.88	7.45	7.45	8.69		
1975/76	15.05	12.72	12.90	15.22		
1976/77	15.43	13.68	14.07	18.23		
1977/78	15.12	13.29	13.74	17.79		
1978/79	15.22	13.19	13.68	18.07		
1979/80	15.49	13.25	14.36	17.11	19.21	24.0
1980/81	16.26	13.17	14.08	17.35	20.11	23.7
1981/82	20.07	14.69	15.53	18.55	22.79	13.6
1982/83	23.80	15.61	15.85	19.88	24.12	1.4
1983/84	24.94	14.90	15.82	19.13	27.16	8.9
1984/85	25.96	12.59	13.73	16.42	29.29	12.8
1985/86	30.34	14.57	15.85	19.40	33.11	9.1
1986/87	30.54	—	—	—	33.11	8.4

Source: Joseph Stern, Richard Mallon and Thomas Hutcheson, *Foreign Exchange Regimes and Industrial Growth in Bangladesh*, HIID Development Discussion Paper No. 222, March 1986 (mimeo) for the period up to 1984/85. The 1985/86 estimate was made by the authors. The 1986/87 figures are for July–March.

must be considerably lower than the above measures based on the estimates shown in Table 4.9. Indeed, discrimination against exports, especially against non-traditional exports, is low, much lower than in the pre-independence period.

(c) Third, the REER for non-traditional exports is about 6-10 per cent more favorable than that for traditional exports. Thus traditional exports still are subject to some discrimination as compared to the non-traditional exports. But this too is far less than what it used to be before independence. To give an example, in the late 1960s, jute manufactures and other exports qualifying for bonus received an exchange rate that was more than twice as favorable as the rate for raw jute.

(d) Fourth, estimates of the rate of effective protection for Bangladesh are subject to numerous problems and the range of these measurements is often very wide for the same good[18]. It is nevertheless quite possible that a good deal of non-uniformity continues to characterize effective protection.

In conclusion, it would be possible to improve the foreign exchange regime further, e.g., by promoting greater uniformity among effective protection rates, by applying the same REER to both traditional and non-traditional exports and by removing whatever discrimination remains against exports in general and in favor of imports. It should be recognized, however, that the system has greatly improved over the years along the lines recommended by the proponents of allocative efficiency. Overvaluation of the exchange rate has become small, discrimination against exports has declined sharply and the level of protection has fallen substantially.

Unfortunately, these improved policies for allocative efficiency have not led to a rapid and efficient rate of industrial growth. The development of manufactured exports has been limited almost entirely to readymade garments and minor contributions from a few miscellaneous items. As discussed more fully in Chapter 5, it would be hard to argue that the exports of garments were developed primarily as a response by domestic entrepreneurs to opportunities created by favorable policy changes. The rapid expansion in the export of readymade garments has occurred as a result of collaboration with the sophisticated entrepreneurs from the East Asian countries who were faced with import quotas imposed by the developed countries on their exports. These foreign entrepreneurs transferred some of their actual or potential operations to Bangladesh because the country had not yet been hit by quotas. Both value added in production and the net foreign exchange content of exports are very low for readymade garments. To cite their growth as an example of export dynamism induced by policy improvements is perhaps a bit misleading.

CONCLUSIONS

State power in Bangladesh has been widely used to create a mechanism for private enrichment. This is just as true of the early period of nationalization as of the latter period of denationalization. Largely as a direct consequence of this strategy, nationalized industries came to be characterized by large losses and inefficiency.

The state has, however, failed to induce the accumulated riches to be channelled into productive industrial investment. The reasons behind this failure are varied and further research is needed for a proper understanding, but some important aspects can be identified. These are: the absence of a political framework that can enforce the right rules of the game and ensure "stability"; the divorce between production and accumulation, with the process of accumulation itself reducing the incentive to invest; and the inadequacy of the infrastructure, especially for small producers.

Industrial growth has been slow despite substantial improvements in policies for allocative efficiency. While such policies are desirable, the experience so far demonstrates that it is unrealistic to hope that these policies alone will provide a strong stimulus to growth.

Small and cottage industries have received little support from public policy. Yet these sectors appear to have grown relatively fast, demonstrating the resilience of small entrepreneurs and ordinary individuals.

A successful strategy of industrial development will have to be supported by a political framework that is able to impose discipline and assure stability. The rules of the game for accumulation clearly must be changed and incentives favoring production must be created. Improved infrastructure is essential. Finally, it is necessary to end the discrimination against small producers. They have to be provided with organization and support to enable them to improve their productivity and to gain access to markets, including external markets.

Notes and References

1. To give an example of the kind of detailed examination on which this statement is based, the 1981/82 CMI shows 12 924 workers employed in enterprises with fewer than 20 persons. This was 3.7 per cent of estimated employment in small industries in 1981/82. If all of these enterprises were counted by both the surveys – a remote possibility – the extent of overlap would be no more than 3.7 per cent. This probably is less than the percentage of firms that should have been but failed to be included within each survey's enumeration.
2. An important work that attempts to put together a consistent set of estimates for manufacturing industries is W.I. Abraham, *Features of Bangladeshi Manufacturing Industries: Some New Perspectives*, Industrial Statistics Improvement Unit, Dhaka, July 1984 (mimeo). For 1981/82 his estimates of value added are slightly higher than the ones used in this study for large and medium industries but much lower than the ones used for small and cottage industries.

Industrialization 97

3. The SCI shows that an average (non-handloom) cottage enterprise employs 2.9 persons and that 22 per cent of them are hired. A recent survey (see Mahabub Hossain, *Employment Generation through Cottage Industries – Potentials and Constraints: The Case of Bangladesh*, ILO/ARTEP, Bangkok, June 1984) shows that 37 per cent of handloom workers are hired while the handloom survey shows that an average enterprise employs 4.4 persons.
4. CMI book values have been doubled to produce what is almost certainly an underestimate of replacement cost. For small industries, it is not clear whether the SSI figures refer to book values or to replacement costs. No adjustment has been made to the published figures. Even if the published figures are book values and the same kind of adjustment as for CMI data were made, the conclusions would remain unchanged. For cottage and handloom industries the figures are estimates of replacement costs.
5. The CMI reports that working capital is 110 per cent of the book value of fixed assets. Since working capital is inevitably of much more recent purchase and subject to less depreciation than fixed assets, only a 25 per cent upward adjustment has been made in their book value to arrive at replacement cost. For small industries the figures are from the SIS (20 per cent of fixed assets) and for handloom and other cottage industries (respectively 94 per cent and 44 per cent of fixed assets) from Mahabub Hossain, *op. cit.*
6. See Mahabub Hossain, *op. cit.*, Table 9.
7. See A.R. Khan, R. Islam and M. Huq, *Employment, Income and the Mobilization of Local Resources: A Study of Two Bangladesh Villages*, ILO/ARTEP, Bangkok, 1981, pp. 30-32 and Chapter 7 below.
8. These adjustments are discussed in detail in the Annex to Chapter 2.
9. These data are from Rehman Sobhan and Muzaffer Ahmed, *Public Enterprise in an Intermediate Regime*, Bangladesh Institute of Development Studies, Dhaka, 1980, p. 192.
10. Nationalization was also extended to banking and insurance (except foreign-owned companies) and foreign trade in jute.
11. See the Annex on National Income Estimates for references to the work by W.I. Abraham and the World Bank.
12. See Rehman Sobhan and S.A. Mahmood, *The Economic Performance of Denationalized Industries in Bangladesh: The Case of the Jute and Cotton Textile Industries*, Bangladesh Institute of Development Studies, Dhaka, June 1966. The data on debt default are from Government of Bangladesh, Ministry of Finance, *Bangladesh Economic Survey*, 1986/87, Dhaka, June 1987, Chapter 5 (in Bengali), and Rehman Sobhan and Binayak Sen, *The Crisis in the Repayment of Loans to the Development Finance Institutions: A Crisis in the Development of Capitalism in Bangladesh?*, BIDS, Dhaka, June 1987 (Mimeo in Bengali).
13. The terms accumulation and capitalist have been used somewhat loosely. One might argue that gaining access to surplus by itself is not accumulation unless it gets converted into productive assets. Similarly, the rich do not become capitalists until they engage in productive enterprise.
14. Besides manufacturing industries, accumulation also took place in other

public enterprises and through the operation of the government budget (e.g., arbitrary award of construction and procurement contracts). For a graphic account of the widespread practice of appropriating surplus from public services see Rehman Sobhan, "Distributive Regimes under Public Enterprise: A Case Study of the Bangladesh Experience", in Frances Stewart (ed.), *Work, Income and Inequality,* Macmillan, London, 1983.
15. Rehman Sobhan, *op. cit.*
16. A.R. Bhuyan, A.T.M.Z. Haq and M.A. Rashid, *A Study on the Domestic Prices of Imports in Bangladesh and the Derivation of Shadow Prices of Foreign Exchange, Labor, and Some Major Inputs and Commodities,* The Planning Commission, Dhaka, February 1985.
17. J.J. Stern, R.D. Mallon and T.L. Hutcheson, *Foreign Exchange Regimes and Industrial Growth in Bangladesh,* HIID, March 1986 (Mimeo).
18. For estimates of effective protection see T.L. Hutcheson, *Effective Rates of Protection: An Input/Output Analysis,* Trade and Industries Project, Planning Commission, Dhaka, June 1985.

5 Trade, Public Finance and Prices: Some Issues

This chapter is concerned with an analysis of selected issues in external trade, public finance and inflation. It begins with a discussion of some issues of foreign trade, namely those concerning the magnitude of the trade gap and debt service, the nature of import dependence and the changing composition of exports. Next it discusses some issues of public finance, especially those related to the generation of an investible surplus in the public sector. Finally, it analyzes the rate of inflation since independence and some factors behind it.

EXTERNAL TRADE AND DEBT

Trade gap and external debt

As discussed in Chapter 2, Bangladesh has been highly dependent on foreign assistance ever since independence. This is reflected in the large trade gap that has characterized the country's external accounts. In recent years the deficit in merchandise trade as a proportion of GDP has been stable at about 10 per cent (Table 5.1). External transactions in non-factor services also have had a highly negative balance so that the gap in foreign trade in goods and non-factor services combined was higher, at more than 12 per cent of GDP. About a third of this gap was financed by remittances made by Bangladeshi workers abroad. The rest was filled by net foreign assistance.

Of the $15.4 billion of foreign assistance received by Bangladesh between independence and 30th June 1986, outright grants accounted for 51 per cent. The rest consisted of medium- and long-term (M&LT) loans on highly concessional terms: an average interest rate of 1.5 per cent, a repayment period of thirty-nine years and a grace period of nine years. Interest and repayment on M&LT debt have as a result remained a manageable burden, namely 23 per cent of the value of merchandise exports and 13 per cent of total foreign exchange earnings (consisting of merchandise exports and workers' remittances) in 1985/86 (Table 5.2).

Bangladesh has however contracted additional short-term loans from

Table 5.1 Exports, imports, trade balance and remittances

	Exports: million Tk	Imports: million Tk	Merchandise trade balance: million Tk	Trade balance in goods and non-factor service: million Tk	Remittances: million $	Exports as percentage of GDP	Merchandise trade balance as percentage of GDP
1973/74	2 983	7 320	−4 337	—	—	—	—
1974/75	3 136	10 842	−7 706	—	35	—	—
1975/76	5 552	14 703	−9 151	—	—	—	—
1976/77	6 670	13 993	−7 323	—	—	—	—
1977/78	7 178	18 216	−11 038	—	102	5.2	7.9
1978/79	9 632	22 073	−12 441	−17 074	124	5.9	7.6
1979/80	10 997	30 525	−19 528	−25 572	283	5.9	10.4
1980/81	11 484	37 288	−25 804	−29 731	381	5.2	11.7
1981/82	12 387	38 729	−26 342	−38 819	418	4.9	10.5
1982/83	18 016	45 265	−27 249	−38 329	631	6.6	10.0
1983/84	20 136	50 874	−30 738	−38 887	598	6.1	9.3
1984/85	26 225	68 263	−42 038	−45 523	444	6.6	10.6
1985/86	24 314	70 690	−46 376	—	555	5.6	10.7
1986/87	30 135	73 800	−43 665	—	620	6.2	9.0

Note: Remittances for all years and all estimates for 1986/87 are from Government of Bangladesh, Ministry of Finance, *Economic Survey*, 1986/87. The 1986/87 estimates are preliminary. Other data are from BBS (various issues of the *Statistical Yearbook* and *Monthly Statistical Bulletin*) which means comparable estimates are not available or cannot be made.

Table 5.2 Debt and debt service, 1985/86

Outstanding M&LT debt on 30th June 1986 ($ million)	6 139.6
As per cent of GDP	42
As per cent of exports	755
As per cent of foreign exchange earnings	449
Interest and repayment of M&LT debt ($ million)	183.7
As per cent of exports	22.6
As per cent of foreign exchange earnings	13.4
Interest and repayment of commercial and IMF debt ($ million)	316.0
Total debt service ($ million)	499.7
As per cent of exports	61.4
As per cent of foreign exchange earnings	36.5

Note: **M&LT** means medium and long term. Export refers to the value of merchandise exports. Foreign exchange earnings consist of the value of merchandise exports and workers' remittances. Data are from Government of Bangladesh, Ministry of Finance, *Economic Survey* 1986/87, Dhaka, 5th June 1987 (Bengali), pp. 250–260.

the IMF and from commercial sources for the purchase of foodgrains, crude oil, aircraft and ships. The repayment burden of the short-term debt has been much heavier than that of M&LT debt in recent years. As a consequence total debt service amounted to 61 per cent of the value of exports (or 37 per cent of total foreign exchange earnings) in 1985/86. It appears that there has been a high concentration of the maturity dates of short-term debt thereby making the repayment burden very high in recent years. The repayment burden should begin to ease by the late 1980s when the current obligations are discharged. The realization of such an optimistic prognosis will however depend on the government's ability to avoid contracting additional short-term loans in the future.

Imports

In the five years ending in 1986/87 food accounted for 28 per cent of imports, machines and transport equipment 19 per cent, petroleum 16 per cent and other raw materials and consumption goods 38 per cent (Table 5.3). These shares are almost exactly the same as they were during the second half of the 1970s. There has been little long-term change in the composition of imports as far as the broad categories are concerned although year to year variations in some categories have often occurred.

Table 5.3 Composition of imports
Millions of Taka

	Grain	Other food	Petroleum	Machinery and transport equipment	Other	Total
1973/74	3 209.3	388.6	583.7	1 032.0	2 106.4	7 320.0
1974/75	4 500.2	632.9	927.7	1 190.2	3 591.4	10 842.4
1975/76	3 912.8	944.0	1 854.0	2 082.2	5 910.2	14 703.2
1976/77	1 344.0	1 492.1	3 334.1	2 365.0	5 457.7	13 992.9
1977/78	3 912.9	1 818.2	2 664.6	2 911.0	6 909.6	18 216.3
1978/79	3 140.5	1 951.5	2 628.6	4 996.9	10 625.9	23 343.4
1979/80	9 650.0	2 805.8	6 050.0	6 372.8	12 850.4	37 729.0
1980/81	4 100.0	3 302.0	9 462.3	9 063.3	16 232.4	42 160.0
1981/82	6 912.9	5 120.5	10 970.0	10 147.5	19 213.1	52 364.0
1982/83	9 150.0	6 591.0	10 853.7	10 608.9	17 685.4	54 889.0
1983/84	9 930.0	7 180.6	9 965.7	10 511.2	21 105.5	58 693.0
1984/85	12 940.0	9 569.4	10 588.6	11 835.3	24 486.7	69 420.0
1985/86	6 669.3	9.804.9	12 161.2	12 652.3	29 402.3	70 690.0
1986/87	10 040.0	8 850.0	10 082.5	14 820.0	30 007.5	73 800.0
1982/83-86/87 Av.	9 745.9	8 399.2	10 730.3	12 085.5	24 537.5	65 498.4
% of Total	14.9	12.8	16.4	18.5	37.5	100.0
1975/76-79/80 Av.	4 392.0	1 802.3	3 306.3	3 745.6	8 350.8	21 597.0
% of Total	20.3	8.3	15.3	17.3	38.7	100.0

Note: These data are from Government of Bangladesh, Ministry of Finance, *Economic Survey* 1986/87, pp. 678–9. For 1978/79 to 1983/84 aggregate import figures from this source are substantially higher than the ones (from BBS source) that have been used in the macroeconomic analysis of Chapter 2 and this chapter earlier. The reasons are not clear. It may be due to the difference in the valution of food and/or commodity aid in the two sources. These data have not been used in the macroeconomic discussion because the other macroeconomic data are also from the BBS source. The BBS import data are not classified into such convenient categories which is the reason why this source is used here. It should be noted that the use of these data in the macroeconomic analysis would increase the estimated trade gap for the period for which the two sources are different. Data for 1986/87 are preliminary.

Self-sufficiency in food has remained an elusive target. Over the years the share of foodgrains (wheat and rice) in total imports has declined somewhat (from 20 per cent in the second half of the 1970s to 15 per cent during the five years ending in 1986/87). This has however been offset by a corresponding increase in the share of non-grain food imports (mainly oilseeds, edible oil, milk and sugar). This is the mirror image of the relative performance of these sub-sectors in domestic production. As noted in Chapter 3 improved agricultural peformance in Bangladesh has been concentrated almost exclusively in foodgrains relative to which other crops and livestock products have lagged behind. Even in foodgrains, the absolute levels of imports have not declined. The annual average import of wheat and rice during 1982/83 to 1986/87 was higher than that for the first five years after independence (1972/73 to 1976/77) which included the year of worst famine in recent history. Claims of rapid progress towards self-sufficiency through the successful implementation of a green revolution – periodically voiced alike by the government and the donor agencies – appears to have been greatly exaggerated.

Food should clearly be the focus of future import substitution. The other broad categories of imports are by and large non-competitive with domestic production though many individual items are not so. Petroleum is unlikely to claim a lower share of imports in future. Indeed an increase is likely if the economy continues to grow and the currently low international prices come under pressure. The same is true of the imports of machines and transport equipment. Given the extremely limited domestic capacity in these products, the income elasticity of demand for their imports is likely to be greater than 1. It has not been possible to divide the residual category (other imports in Table 5.3) into intermediate and consumption goods. But the bulk of the category consists of raw materials and current inputs for which demand will increase faster than GDP. It may be possible to substitute the import of some of the consumption goods in this category by domestic production, but this would partly be offset by an increased requirement for imported intermediate goods.

Exports

The immediate effect of independence on exports was to make them less diversified because Bangladesh lost some of its manufactured exports (e.g., matches and paper) that it used to export to Pakistan. The decline in exports was due partly to the difficulty of finding alternative markets and partly to reduced production. In the years immediately after independence jute in raw and manufactured forms accounted for 87 per cent of the value of merchandise exports. By 1985/86 its share had fallen to 51 per cent. In addition to the long-term decline in its share of total exports, jute has also been subject to sharp fluctuations in international earnings. This has been due to fluctuations both in quantities and prices of both raw jute and jute manufactures. Such fluctuations have been particularly extreme in the case of raw jute. An illustration from recent experience shows the seriousness of the problem. In 1984/85 there was a 26 per cent reduction in the quantity exported. This led to a 76 per cent increase in the nominal dollar price. The following year the quantity exported increased by 63 per cent, which led to a more than 50 per cent reduction in the nominal dollar price. In view of the predominance of Bangladesh in the world market for raw jute, a more careful policy for the stabilization of prices and quantities – through the operation of a buffer stock – should have received urgent consideration. In the foreseeable future Bangladesh is unlikely to be able to avoid depending on jute. A comprehensive policy for its preservation as a major export, including the elimination of the discrimination that continues to occur (see below), should have received priority.

The diversification of exports that led to a dramatic reduction in the share of jute was largely due to the increase in two items: shrimps and ready-made garments. The shares of these two exports increased from a negligible 1.5 per cent of total exports in the immediate post-independence years to 30 per cent in 1985/86. Increased share of these two exports was equivalent to 80 per cent of the reduction in the share of jute. The remainder of jute's reduced share was made up by the increased export of leather and leather products, naphtha and various small items. The rate of growth in the exports of these other items can not however be described as particularly dynamic.

The export of shrimps has existed since before independence but its growth in recent years has been very rapid. Growth in the export of ready-made garments has been truly remarkable. From virtually nothing in the mid- to late 1970s garments emerged as the largest merchandise export after jute by the year 1985/86. In that year garments accounted for more than 16 per cent of export earnings. Several special features of the growth of this export deserve attention. As will be shown below, improved incentives for export were a major feature of policy changes over the last decade. This clearly helped the growth of garments and other exports. However, there were other additional factors which explain why growth of garment exports was so dramatic and completely out of line with other exports. Most important was that the established exporters of garments in East Asia had reached the ceilings of import quotas imposed by the developed countries. This created an opportunity

Table 5.4 Merchandise exports
Values in millions of dollars

	1972–75 Av.	1975–80 Av.	1980–85 Av.	1984/85	1985/86
Raw jute	115.0	124.1	119.7	150.8	123.0
Jute manufacturers	193.7	253.9	344.5	389.8	291.1
Leather and products	18.8	50.8	66.7	69.8	60.3
Shrimps, fish, etc.	5.5	24.6	67.4	89.3	113.2
Tea	15.3	34.4	51.0	61.0	32.6
Readymade garments	0.0	0.2	33.8	116.2	130.6
Newsprint	2.9	4.5	5.4	8.5	7.3
Urea	0.0	0.0	6.9	4.8	n.a.
Naphtha, furnace oil, bitumen	1.3	12.5	33.6	20.8	10.4
Other	3.4	14.7	25.1	23.4	45.1
Total	356.0	519.7	753.9	934.4	813.4
Per cent shares					
Raw Jute	32.31	23.89	15.87	16.14	15.12
Jute manufacturers	54.42	48.86	45.70	41.72	35.78
Leather and products	5.28	9.78	8.84	7.47	7.41
Shrimps, fish, etc.	1.54	4.73	8.94	9.56	13.92
Tea	4.30	6.63	6.77	6.53	4.00
Readymade garments	0.00	0.03	4.48	12.44	16.05
Newsprint	0.82	0.87	0.71	0.91	0.90
Urea	0.00	0.00	0.91	0.51	n.a.
Naphtha, furnace oil, bitumen	0.38	2.40	4.46	2.22	1.27
Other	0.96	2.83	3.33	2.51	5.54
Total	100.0	100.0	100.0	100.0	100.0

Note: Data have been compiled from a variety of sources including the BBS, the Export Promotion Bureau, the Ministry of Finance publications and other official sources. For 1985/86 information on urea export was not available separately. Any urea export in that year is included in other exports.

for new entrants like Bangladesh both to enter the export market and to attract the established exporters to collaborative arrangements involving the transfer of technology and the financing of investment.

Exports of garments have been dependent on foreign sources not only for technology and capital but also for current inputs. A 1984 study showed the following relations among output value and input cost for export under the bonded warehouse system (value per 100 units)[1]:

	Men's Shirts	Men's Trousers
Output value	$267	$322
Material cost:	$187	$235
Per cent of output value	70	73
Imported material cost:	$183	$231
Per cent of output value	69	72

In the absence of more detailed information it is not possible to estimate net foreign exchange earnings per unit of export, but they are obviously quite low.

The greatest absolute increase in foreign exchange earnings has been due to the remittances sent home by Bangladeshi workers employed abroad, mainly in the oil-exporting countries of West Asia and North Africa. The number of workers going abroad began to increase rapidly in the early 1970s and reached a peak of 77 000 in 1985/86. It was to attract the remittances of these workers that the Wage Earners' Scheme (WES) was introduced in the early 1970s. Under this scheme Bangladeshi workers sending remittances of foreign exchange from abroad received an entitlement to import selected items of equivalent value in addition to the Taka equivalent of the remittance at the official exchange rate. These entitlements were transferable and commanded a price – called the premium – which was as much as 31 per cent of the value of the entitlement in 1977/78. The WES rate – defined as $(1+p)r$, where p = the rate of premium and r = Takas exchanging for a unit of foreign exchange at the official rate of exchange – became the alternative rate of exchange. The share of imports under WES increased rapidly, from 3 per cent in the mid-1970s to over 20 per cent in the mid-1980s. The premium has, however, declined steadily due to the gradual devaluation of the Taka. Remittances under WES increased from 10 per cent of the value of merchandise exports in 1974/75 to 83 per cent at its peak in 1982/83 (Table 5.1). In the latter year remittances amounted to $631 million. After 1982/83 remittances fell because of the decline in labor demand in the oil exporting countries in the wake of the sharp reduction in oil revenue. Following the rapid decline which lasted for two years, there was a modest recovery in the level of remittances beginning in 1985/86. Preliminary estimates suggest that the nominal dollar value of remittances in 1986/87 may come close to the previous peak.

It is too early to know the full consequences of the oil slump on remittances. It is even more difficult to predict the course of remittances in the future. It has been suggested that employment of Bangladeshi workers may have been less affected than that of people from other countries because of their lower supply price and their willingness to accept a reduction in wages that others found unacceptable. This is consistent with the finding that after 1982/83 the number of persons going abroad was affected far less than the volume of remittances.

An assessment of export policies and performance

The policies of the government that have resulted in a consistent improvement in the incentives to export were briefly discussed in Chapter 4. The most important element of these policies was the substantial reduction in the extent of overvaluation of the Taka. In the case of traditional exports (e.g., raw jute and tea), this was reinforced by the abolition of export taxes.

In the case of non-traditional exports a host of additional benefits were provided. A brief description of some of the important benefits follows.

(a) Under the Export Performance Benefit (XPB) scheme (called Export Performance Licensing before July 1985) an exporter of specified non-traditional items receives import entitlement certificates which are freely marketable. The value of a dollar of such exports thus becomes $(1+px)r$ where x = the amount of import entitlement per unit of export value (currently the rates in operation are 40 per cent, 70 per cent and 100 per cent). Thus in 1985/86 an exporter earning a 100 per cent entitlement received nearly 11 per cent more Taka for each dollar of export than the official rate of exchange (since p, the premium, was 10.8 per cent in that year). The reduction in the WES premium over the years has meant a reduced benefit of XPB for a given rate of import entitlement. Government policy has tried to offset this by increasing the rate of import entitlement for a given export and by making more exports eligible for XPB.

(b) A duty drawback scheme entitles the exporters of manufactured products to a refund of customs duties and sales taxes paid on the imported raw materials that are used in the production of goods exported.

(c) Under the bonded warehouse scheme exporters of manufactured goods are able to import raw materials and inputs without payment of duties and taxes. The raw materials and inputs are kept in bonded warehouses. On the submission of evidence that a given amount of materials has been used to produce goods which have been exported, an equivalent amount is released from the warehouse.

(d) There are numerous other incentives such as tax holidays for export industries, interest rate subsidies and back-to-back letters of credit (i.e., opening of a letter of credit for imports to support exports for which a letter of credit has been opened).

These policies have clearly benefitted exporters. It must however be recognized that they have not led to an all round development of exports or a broad-based expansion of manufactured exports. It is often alleged that this is because the incentives have not gone far enough[2]. First, incentives have been limited to an arbitrary list of non-traditional exports (which, for example, includes jute manufactures but excludes raw jute). As a consequence the traditional exports – notably raw jute – continue to be discriminated against. Secondly, the real effective exchange rate is probably significantly more favorable for imports than even for the non-traditional exports although comparable estimates can not be made because it is not possible to quantify the benefits of the bonded warehouse scheme, tax holidays, interest subsidies, back-to-back letters of credit and other incentives (see Chapter 4 and Table 4.9 therein). It is evident, however, that incentives to export are still less than incentives for import substitution. Thirdly, the current system is unnecessarily complex with a maze of multiple rates of benefits and administrative bottlenecks which offset some of the incentives. Finally, measures such as duty drawback, bonded warehouses and the provision of XPB on gross rather than net export receipts create a bias against using domestically produced tradeable inputs and in favor of using imported inputs[3]. This reduces net foreign exchange earnings. The simplification and improvement of the system of incentives in all these areas would be desirable.

It is, however, difficult to visualize a massive expension of exports, led by manufactured items, simply by effecting these further adjustments in the incentive system. A prior requirement for the expansion of exports is an expansion of domestic production and this often implies the *development* of new products and the creation of production capacities in goods for which current output is negligible or non-existent.

Examples will help clarify issues. In ready-made garments it is of critical importance to increase the use of domestically produced fabrics, interlining, packaging materials, buttons and threads. Yet domestic capacity of an appropriate quality exists for few of these things. The capacity will have to be created. Garments alone can hardly be the basis of a sustained export-led industrialization. Additional products will have to be developed. Significant possibilities exist in leather products and possibly in the development of new products from jute. A further increase in exports may come from the expansion of the production and processing of non-grain agricultural goods. Some observers have even envisaged the possibility of attracting enterprises producing technologically advanced products for export (e.g., electronics) by inducing foreign investors to relocate their activities to low-wage Bangladesh, possibly in collaboration with local entrepreneurs.

None of these possibilities is inconceivable or even unrealistic. What is required, however, is not merely a finely tuned system of appropriate incentives to export as compared to incentives for import substitution, but an appropriate system of incentives for *industrialization*. As described in Chapter 4 this is negated by the existing mechanism for accumulation and by the lack of an adequate infrastructure and an appropriate political environment. Without changes in these areas it may still be possible for a few activities to develop, especially if favorable circumstances exist as in the case of garments. A broadly based development of export-led industrialization will however remain elusive.

To summarize: a substantial improvement in export incentives has taken place in Bangladesh during the last decade. Exports have increased and certain non-traditional exports, receiving an additional impetus from special external circumstances, grew very rapidly. It would, however, be an exaggeration to describe the experience in the recent past as one of dynamic export growth. Exports as a proportion of GDP (when both are estimated in domestic currency) were marginally higher in the mid-1980s as compared to the late 1970s. In view of the declining overvaluation of the exchange rate and the consequent rise in the domestic relative price of tradeables, it appears that the ratio of exports to GDP (when both are measured at appropriate prices) has probably shown no change, or even registered a decline during the period under consideration. The development of non-traditional exports has been very narrowly based so far. The rate of export expansion has been only moderate and when this is combined with an inability to substitute food imports by domestic production, the result has been a larger external trade gap when expressed as a proportion of GDP. A large increase in workers' remittances helped bridge about a third of the gap. In recent years this source of foreign exchange earnings has faced much uncertainty. A large inflow of external resources was needed to finance the remainder of the gap in the foreign trade accounts. Most of the required resources were available as grants or as loans under very favorable terms. And yet the burden of servicing the medium- and long-term debt has become substantial. The additional need to service (the admittedly heavily clustered) short-term loans has led to a dangerously high overall debt service burden in recent years.

PUBLIC FINANCE AND RESOURCE MOBILIZATION

Inadequate domestic savings have been a serious obstacle to the development of Bangladesh. While private savings have been low, public savings, correctly defined, have been negative. Unless this changes, the problem of an inadequate domestic surplus for investment can not be addressed. It is therefore important to analyze the circumstances that underlie the present situation.

Public revenue

The first important fact to note is that the Government of Bangladesh collects a very small proportion of GDP in the form of taxes and non-tax revenues. Tax revenue has amounted to only about 7 per cent of GDP in recent years. Total current revenue (tax and non-tax revenues together) has amounted to less than 9 per cent of GDP. These are about the lowest documented rates among the developing countries. In 1985 average tax revenue and total current revenue were respectively 13 per cent and 16 per cent of GDP in the 13 low income countries for which information was available[4]. Sierra Leone was the only country among these 13 countries with rates comparable to those in Bangladesh.

Neither taxes nor current revenue have proved to be elastic with respect to GDP. There has been no trend in the recent past either in the ratio of taxes to GDP or in the ratio of current revenue to GDP.

Public revenue is overwhelmingly dependent on indirect taxes. Customs duties have accounted for 40 per cent or more of tax revenue depending on the year. Sales and excise taxes, much of which are collected on imported goods, have accounted for another 40 per cent or so of tax revenue in recent years. Together customs duties and sales taxes on imports have probably contributed about two-thirds of tax revenue.

Direct income and corporation taxes together contribute less than 15 per cent of tax revenue compared to an average of more than 25 per cent for the 13 low income countries for which information is available for 1985[4]. Clearly the government has failed to tax the rapidly rising incomes of the very rich, especially in the urban areas. This is not surprising in view of the nature of the process through which these incomes are accumulated. (See Chapter 4.) Since direct taxes are the major revenue-raising vehicles for fiscal redistribution, it would appear that fiscal policy in Bangladesh has little redistributive role on the revenue side.

Land revenue has been equivalent to one-fifth of one per cent of the value added in crop production. (The slightly higher proportions for the last two years in Table 5.5 are respectively a preliminary estimate and a projection which have yet to be confirmed.) There is no other instrument for mobilizing resources from agricultural incomes. As a result incomes in this growing sector – with a highly skewed distribution at the margin – have gone untaxed.

Because of extensive (though declining from the peak level of the early 1970s) government ownership of enterprises, a potentially major source of non-tax revenue is the profits earned by public enterprises and public utilities. In reality the contribution to the public exchequer from these sources has been very low. Telecommunications and the financial institutions are the only public sector entities which have earned a profit. Railways and postal services have always incurred losses because of their inefficiencies and the inappropriateness of the pricing policies adopted.

In 1981/82 the book value of assets of the public sector manufacturing industries was about Tk 10 billion. At current replacement value it was certainly more than Tk 20 billion. A 10 per cent return on these assets would have added Tk 2 billion to public revenue which would be nearly four times the dissaving made by the government in that year. In reality, the nationalized industries have almost always incurred losses which were financed by credit granted by public sector financial institutions.

Public expenditure

Government budgets divide public expenditure into revenue expenditure and development expenditure. The revenue surplus of the government is calculated by subtracting revenue expenditure from current revenue. According to this definition the government budget usually has a surplus. There is a temptation to equate this revenue surplus with positive public savings of an equivalent amount.

Table 5.5 Government revenue and expenditure
All values in millions of Taka

	1980/81	1981/82	1982/83	1983/84	1984/85 revised estimate	1985/86 budget estimate
1. Tax revenue	13 935	20 405	23 487	22 025	28 071	30 761
of which:						
Income tax	743	3 103	4 324	3 703	3 890	4 290
Land revenue	197	223	196	228	400	400
Customs duty	6 425	8 277	10 386	10 591	11 200	11 600
Excise and sales tax	5 700	7 762	7 690	6 288	11 150	12 870
2. Non-tax revenue	3 616	5 320	5 179	2 263	6 699	6 779
3. Current revenue (1+2)	17 551	25 725	28 666	24 288	34 770	37 540
4. Net revenue expenditure	13 254	16 531	17 933	19 712	29 300	33 130
5. Non-investment development expenditure	9 905	9 746	6 848	11 226	14 450	14 935
6. Public savings (3-4-5)	−5 608	−552	−3 885	−6 650	−8 980	−10 525
Tax as per cent of GDP	6.3	8.1	8.6	6.7	7.1	7.1
Current revenue as per cent of GDP	8.0	10.2	10.5	7.3	8.8	8.6
Customs, excise and sales tax as per cent of tax revenue	87.0	78.6	77.0	76.6	79.6	79.5
Land revenue as per cent of value added in crop production	0.2	0.2	0.2	0.2	0.3	0.3

(*) Means preliminary estimate.

Source: BBS, *Statistical Yearbook,* 1986, pp. 601-6.

Development expenditure however includes a large component of non-investment expenditure. The BBS has estimated this component on the basis of a detailed analysis of development budgets since the late 1970s. Adding the non-investment component of the development budget to revenue expenditure completely alters the picture (Table 5.5). Public savings, defined as the difference between current revenue and current expenditure (the sum of net revenue expenditure in the budget and the non-investment component of development expenditure as estimated by the BBS), turn out to be highly negative for all the years under review[5]. During 1980/81-1985/86 public savings amounted to −1.6 per cent of GDP.

Public administration and defense claim the largest share of current government expenditure. Although there was a reduction in their share between the 1970s and 1980s, they accounted for nearly one-half of current expenditure in the latter period. Defense expenditure alone accounts for 17 per cent of public expenditure. There is, however, reason to believe that a part of defense expenditure is shown under other, non-defense, budgetary heads. The most notable is the heavy subsidy on rationed food and consumables for the armed forces which is shown with other consumer subsidies[6]. Without access to confidential information, it is not possible to make an adjustment for these hidden military subsidies. It appears, however, that the share of defense in current expenditure would not rise to a qualitatively higher level even if it were possible to include the omitted items. Moreover, military expenditure still would be lower than in most countries of the region. The point however is that the country could readily have allocated even fewer resources to defense if decisions had been based on real needs.

On public administration the relevant question is not whether the level of expenditure and its increase over time are justified, but whether the composition and content of expenditure have been appropriate to the country's needs. Since independence the government has allowed employment in public administration to rise far beyond what would be warranted by efficiency considerations. At the same time the real wages and salaries of public employees have been allowed to decline far below the pre-independence levels with consequent adverse effects on morale, efficiency, morality and discipline.

Education, health, housing, labor and social welfare – the so-called social sectors – have a lower share of current expenditure than in most developing countries. Their shares also declined between the 1970s and 1980s. The shares of the economic services – agriculture, industry, power, transport, water resource and flood control – have increased almost two and a half times during the period under consideration. Food and other subsidies (not separately shown in Table 5.6) declined as a proportion of current expenditure.

Table 5.6 Composition of public expenditure

	Average for 1975/76–1977/78	Average for 1982/83–1984/85
A. Percentage shares of current expenditure		
Public administration and defense	54.9	48.0
Education and training	20.6	11.2
Health and population	6.5	6.3
Housing, labor and social welfare	5.2	4.4
Economic services	12.8	30.1
B. Percentage shares of the acquisition of capital assets		
Agriculture, rural development, water, etc.	20.3	24.9
Power and natural resources	7.0	29.2
Transport and communication	30.6	19.0
Physical planning and housing	15.2	4.9
Industry	11.1	7.4
Other	15.8	14.6

Source: BBS, *Statistical Yearbook* 1986, pp. 607–11.

The composition of public investment (financed by external and domestic borrowing) also changed substantially between the 1970s and 1980s. In the latter period power and energy development claimed close to 30 per cent of public investment, a sharp rise over their 7 per cent share in the 1970s. Agriculture (including flood control, water resources and rural development) received a quarter of investment in the 1980s as compared to a fifth in the 1970s. (However, as noted in Chapter 3, in very recent years expenditure on these sectors has tended to decline as a proportion of public expenditure.) The share of transport and communications declined from 31 per cent of public investment in the 1970s to 19 per cent in the 1980s. The share of housing and urban development declined sharply while that of industries declined moderately.

To summarize: both tax and non-tax revenues have accounted for too small a proportion of GDP. Their growth rates over time have been low. The inability to tax high incomes, the inefficiency of the public enterprises and the failure to price public services appropriately are the factors responsible for the low level and slow growth of current revenue. The level and growth of current expenditure, correctly defined, have been too high to be financed by current revenue. The result has been a high rate of public dissaving, i.e., a negative contribution of the public sector to the investable surplus. Current public expenditure has been dominated by public administration and defense. There has been a decline in the share of education, health, housing and social welfare in current expenditure while the share of economic services has increased sharply. The emphasis of public investment has shifted away from transport, housing and industries in the 1970s to power, energy and agriculture in the 1980s. In very recent years, however, public expenditure in agriculture and irrigation has tended to decline as a proportion of total public expenditure.

PRICES, MONEY AND FINANCE

Since independence the general price level has increased at an annual rate of 10 to 13 per cent (see the different indicators in Table 5.7). Immediately after independence the rate of inflation reached a very high level, averaging more than 40 per cent per year until the famine year of 1974/75. The high initial inflation was caused by a number of things: (a) a general decline in production in the aftermath of the disruptions caused by the war of independence; (b) crop failures; (c) the rise in international commodity prices, especially foodgrains and oil; and (d) the failure of the government to limit monetary demand. For two years after the famine, the price level declined in absolute terms, due largely to an easing of all the above factors. Since 1977/78 the rate of inflation has been more or less steady at about 12 per cent per year. It fell significantly below the double digit level in only one year, 1982/83. While factors such as fluctuations in crop production have had an effect on the rate of price change from time to time, the rise in the level of monetary demand has been the dominant factor behind the steady rate of inflation during the last decade. The general price level increased more than ten-fold in the seventeen years after 1969/70, the last complete fiscal year before the war of independence. For the territory now comprising Bangladesh this has been an unprecedented historical experience.

Table 5.8 shows the trend in money supply, which has been broadly similar to that in the price level. Narrow money (currency in circulation and demand deposits) increased at an annual average rate of more than

Table 5.7 Selected price indicators

		Consumer price indices		
	GDP Deflator	Dhaka: middle income	Industrial workers	Rural
1972/73	100	72	193	70
1973/74	—	100	268	100
1974/75	—	167	447	170
1975/76	—	153	365	124
1976/77	—	157	354	122
1977/78	231	177	419	147
1978/79	261	191	458	169
1979/80	295	227	525	201
1980/81	326	255	568	214
1981/82	367	297	656	262
1982/83	385	326	684	278
1983/84	449	357	761	312
1984/85	516	397	855	353
1985/86	564	436	941	368
Trend growth rate	12.8	12.1	10.3	11.4

Note: The GDP deflator has been estimated by dividing the BBS estimates of GDP at current prices by those at constant prices of 1972/73, which is the base year of the index. Estimates for 1973/74 to 1976/77 have not been made because of the unreliability of data. Consumer price indices for Dhaka middle class and rural areas both have 1973/74 as the base. The former for 1972/73 has been estimated by splicing in the BBS index for Dhaka middle–income government employees. Dhaka middle class consumer price index is from the BBS. For the rural consumer price index the method of estimation and source are discussed in Chapter 7. Price index for industrial workers has 1969/70 as the base year. It is the average of the BBS indices for Narayanganj, Chittagong and Khulna. The trend growth rates are based on the least squares fit of semi-logarithmic functions all of which are significant at a one per cent level.

40 per cent until the end of 1974, declined slightly in absolute terms during 1975, and has increased at an average rate of 17 per cent per year thereafter[7]. Broad money (narrow money plus time deposits) has increased faster than narrow money, especially since the mid-1970s. During the last decade, the annual rate of increase in broad money has been about a third higher than that in narrow money. This indicates that

time deposits have increased much faster than narrow money. The acceleration in the rate of growth in time deposits since the mid-1970s was helped by the upward adjustment in interest rate on such deposits in several steps starting in July 1974. It was only in the early 1980s that interest rates on time deposits of three months and longer durations became higher than the trend rate of inflation. Prior to that date, interest rates remained lower than the trend rate of inflation, though gradually approaching it over time (Table 5.9).

Tables 5.10 and 5.11 shed light on the sources of expansion in monetary demand. A major transition seems to have taken place between 1982 and 1983. Until 1982 the public sector was a major source of demand for bank credit. In the seven years ending in 1982 the public sector accounted for 40 per cent of the *increase* in bank credit. The

Table 5.8 Money supply
In millions of Taka

Date	Narrow money	Broad money
December 1971	3 333	5 460
December 1972	5 626	9 341
December 1973	6 961	11 526
December 1974	9 269	13 423
December 1975	9 064	13 891
December 1976	10 193	16 704
December 1977	11 927	20 808
December 1978	15 210	26 050
June 1979	15 248	27 600
December 1979	17 073	31 232
December 1980	18 651	38 639
December 1981	21 065	44 663
December 1982	23 336	52 779
December 1983	31 634	73 896
December 1984	42 268	100 582
June 1985	42 318	105 342
December 1985	45 955	114 276
December 1986	49 996	132 790

Note: Data have been taken from various issues of the *Bangladesh Bank Bulletin*. These are for the last working day of the month except in 1971 when the date is 17th December.

Table 5.9 Nominal interest rates on deposits and loans

	Up to June 1974	July 1974 to March 1976	April 1976 to April 1977	May 1977 to October 1980	October 1980 to June 1986	Since July 1986
Deposit rates:						
Savings accounts	4.5	6.0	7.0	7.0–7.75	10.0	10.0
3-month fixed deposits	4.5	6.0	7.0	7.0–8.5	12.0	12.0
3-year fixed deposits	6.0	9.25	10.25	10.25	15.0	14.25
Lending rates:						
General lending	9.0–10.0	12.0–13.0	12.0–13.0	11.0–12.0	16.0–20.0	18.0
Agricultural lending	7.0–8.0	11.0–11.5	11.0–11.5	11.0–12.0	12.0	16.0
Industrial lending	7.0–8.0	11.0–11.5	11.0–11.5	11.0–11.5	9.0–14.5	9.0–14.5

Note: Ranges shown in the table capture only the major rates. There are numerous rates, usually for relatively minor purposes, which fall outside the ranges shown. For example, the deposit rate on savings accounts was raised to 11 per cent for the rural areas beginning January 1985. For certain agricultural purposes, e.g., tea growing, the rate has been substantially lower. Savings accounts refer to the accounts without checking facilities. The lower limit on industrial lending since October 1980 has applied to the working capital loans for the jute textiles industry. Data have been compiled from the relevant issues of the *Bangladesh Bank Bulletin*.

remaining 60 per cent was accounted for by the private sector. Between June 1982 and March 1987 the share of the public sector declined sharply to less than 5 per cent while the share of the private sector jumped dramatically to more than 95 per cent of the *increase* in bank credit. In the four years since June 1982 the net increase in credit to the private sector was about 2.4 times that in the preceding four years in *real terms*.

Table 5.10 Annual increase in bank credit
In millions of Taka

	Total	To public sector	To private sector
1976	1 255.0	719.9	535.1
1977	2 161.3	562.5	1 598.8
1978	3 358.7	1 111.8	2 246.9
1979	3 565.8	90.7	3 475.1
1980	7 180.7	4 503.9	2 676.8
1981	7 607.5	1 905.2	5 702.3
1982	9 124.0	4 539.3	4 584.7
1983	7 836.0	272.1	7 561.9
1984	15 385.0	−2 080.0	17 467.0
1985	23 734.9	3 159.9	20 575.0
1986	19 655.3	3 553.8	16 101.5

Note: Figures refer to *increases* in total credit in the year preceding 30th June of the year shown in the row. Data have been taken from the monthly statistical bulletins of the BBS which quotes Bangladesh Bank sources.

The increase in credit has been particularly large for private manufacturing and agriculture. Indeed, for agriculture the volume of bank credit began to rise sharply much earlier, with the introduction of the policy of promoting the private ownership of irrigation equipment in the mid-1970s, and averaged more than a 47 per cent annual increase in nominal terms between 1977 and 1985. For manufacturing industries the increase was very rapid following the institution of the New Industrial Policy and accelerated privatization in 1982. During the following four years net credit for private manufacturing increased at an annual rate of 46 per cent in nominal terms. Credit for private commerce also increased at about the same rate. Together these three sources claimed 88 per cent of the *increased* credit to the private sector after June 1982.

The causative factors behind the change in the money supply, shown

Table 5.11 Causative factors behind increases in money supply
In millions of Taka

	Total	Public sector	Private sector	Foreign sector	Other
1979/80	2 093.4	6 899.4	3 362.6	−3 536.8	−4 631.8
1980/81	4 707.5	9 350.7	5 436.8	−3 997.5	−6 082.5
1981/82	8.0	5 660.7	4 155.8	−6 425.8	−3 382.7
1982/83	5 046.4	143.0	7 784.2	4 151.8	−7 032.6
1983/84	9 156.6	9 816.0	18 170.0	2 437.0	−21 266.4
1984/85	6 818.4	1 456.0	19 761.0	1 447.0	−15 845.6

Note: Estimates are made by the Bangladesh Bank and published in its Bulletin. Public sector includes both the government and public sector agencies and enterprises. "Other" sources include changes in time deposits and "miscellaneous" sources shown in the estimates of the Bangladesh Bank. These estimates are not available for periods before 1979/80. These are frequently revised and revised estimates often differ substantially from the preliminary ones. Some of the estimates in the above are preliminary and may have been or will probably be revised. Note that the change in aggregate money supply between June 1979 and June 1985 according to these estimates is slightly higher than those according to the estimates shown in Table 5.8.

in Table 5.11, indicate that until 1981/82 the public sector contributed about as much to the expansion of money supply as did the private sector. Since 1982/83 there has been a drastic change: in the three years starting 1982/83 the contribution of the private sector towards the increase in money supply was four times as much as that of the public sector.

As discussed in Chapters 3 and 4, non-repayment of agricultural and industrial credit to the private sector has become a serious problem. As a result of large-scale default, the expansion of private credit in these sectors has ground to a virtual halt in recent years. There was no increase in bank credit for private agriculture between June 1985 and March 1987. Bank credit for private manufacturing also encountered an abrupt and dramatic slowdown after December 1985.

The periodic upward adjustments in interest rates on bank loans and advances made most of these rates positive in real terms by October 1980 (Table 5.9). It is often suggested that this has promoted efficiency in the allocation of investment funds. The argument must however be considered invalid because the private investors have been allowed not merely to avoid paying the interest but also to default on the repayment of the principal. To the extent that private investors knew that they would be able to behave in this manner, the upward adjustments in interest rates had little effect in promoting greater allocative efficiency.

Notes and References

1. Lloyd McKay, *Report on Readymade Garments Industry,* Trade and Industry Reform Program, Government of Bangladesh, Dhaka, 1984 (mimeo), pp. 35 and 39. The data refer to the "unassisted situation".
2. See J.J. Stern, R.D. Mallon and T.L. Hutcheson, *op. cit.* and A. Rab, *Export Performance and Prospects and Government Policy to Promote Exports in Bangladesh,* Trade and Industry Reform Project, Government of Bangladesh, Working Paper (mimeo).
3. Some recent measures have tried to correct this bias. An example is the provision in the 1987/88 budget of a higher rate of XPB on garments using domestically produced fabric than on garments using imported fabric.
4. The World Bank, *The World Development Report 1987*, p. 248.
5. BBS estimates of non-investment development expenditure are shown in the *Statistical Yearbook* 1986, p. 606. What is included in it is not known. One can not rule out the possibility that it includes items that do not represent current consumption or transfer (e.g., repayment of loan of some agency carrying out an investment project). If so the method would overstate public dissaving. It however appears unlikely that there would be much scope for this. The confidence in the present estimates of current expenditure is enhanced by the closeness of these estimates with those made by the BBS on the basis of detailed economic-cum-functional classification of government budgets. See *ibid.*, pp. 607-611.
6. It is not clear where it features in the BBS classification on which Table 5.6 is based.
7. Thus, over the last decade, the trend rate of increase in narrow money has almost exactly equalled the sum of the trend rates of inflation and GDP growth.

6 The Development of Infrastructure

The subject matter of this chapter is infrastructure, both physical and social. The former includes facilities such as energy and transport while the latter includes services such as education and health. These activities are usually characterized by lumpy investment and economies of large scale. The efficient expansion of these actvities, by reducing unit costs, generates substantial external economies of a "pecuniary" character. That is, the availability of cheaper and more extensive energy and transport services increases the profitability of other activities by reducing their costs of production and widening the market for their products. These characteristics of investment in infrastructure underline the fact that one of the essential functions of government in promoting economic development is to ensure an adequate provision and efficient expansion of infrastructural facilities. It may sometimes be possible to obtain the cooperation of local communities, private individuals and groups in developing some segments of the systems, e.g., local communities may be persuaded to contribute to, or take responsibility for, the construction of feeder roads and local schools. The basic responsibility for the provision of these facilities and their expansion in step with the needs of economic development must however remain with the government.

The case is not being put for the free or nearly free provision of these services. Because of substantial economies of scale, these services should be produced on a large and efficient scale and sold at cost to users. Large and indiscriminate subsidies would limit the services because of budgetary constraints.

There are clear exceptions to the rule of charging the user full price. For some services, notably primary education and health, benefits to the society as a whole exceed the benefits to the consumer. It is therefore desirable in such cases to expand consumption beyond the level dictated by calculations of private benefit alone. The sensible policy here is to price services below their cost of production and make up the difference through public subsidies.

The focus of this chapter is on physical infrastructure, mainly energy, transport and flood protection. The last is important because of the overwhelmingly dominant physical characteristic of the country:

frequent severe flooding and the incursion of saline water. The chapter concludes with a brief discussion of education and health.

ENERGY AND POWER

Sources of energy

Total energy consumption in Bangladesh in 1984/85 is estimated to have been 364 trillion BTU, equivalent to 13.2 million tons of coal. Nearly two-thirds of the energy is supplied by traditional fuels: cow dung, firewood, leaves, and the by-products of rice, jute and sugarcane. Total energy supply has grown at only 1.9 per cent per year between 1977/78 and 1984/85. This indicates a decline in per capita energy consumption and an increase in unmet demand, especially in rural areas. This is reflected in the felling of trees in village forests and around homesteads at an alarmingly high rate, with a consequent danger to the ecological balance. The supply of energy from traditional sources increased at less than one per cent per year during the last decade. As a result, the pressure on commercial sources of energy has increased rapidly despite a decline in overall energy consumption per person. The share of commercial energy has increased from 26 per cent of the total in 1977/78 to 33 per cent in 1984/85. During the same period the consumption of commercial energy increased at an annual rate of 5.4 per cent, or 2.8 per cent in per capita terms[1].

Natural gas

Bangladesh has a substantial reserve of natural gas which is the major source of commercial energy. As of June 1985, Bangladesh had a proven gas reserve of 12.17 TCF (trillion cubic feet) compared with the total of 1.07 TCF exploited by 1985/86. There are very few proven reserves of coal and petroleum, which are mostly imported[2]. During the first half of the 1980s average annual imports of petroleum and petroleum products were 1.6 million tons, accounting for about 16 per cent of the value of merchandise imports. Coal is a minor and declining source of energy. Imports declined from an annual average of 195 000 tons during 1975-80 to only 165 000 tons during 1980-85. More than 90 per cent of the coal is used as fuel for manufacturing fire bricks, an important construction material.

The Development of Infrastructure

One of the main elements of energy policy in Bangladesh has been the accelerated use of natural gas. A major problem in the exploitation of natural gas is that all the gas fields discovered so far are located in the eastern zone which is separated from the western zone by the river Jamuna. Nearly half the population live in the western zone and natural gas remains inaccessible to them. The development of an integrated gas transmission and distribution network in this riverine country would be highly capital intensive and is likely to remain beyond the country's means for the near future. It is, however, possible to convert gas into electric power for distribution in areas that do not have direct access to gas. An east-west electricity interconnector, transporting power from east to west, began to operate in 1983.

In 1984/85 some 94.6 billion cft of natural gas (equivalent to 0.8 per cent of the proven reserves) were consumed. The use of gas for different purposes was as follows (in per cent of total):

Power generation	40.3
Direct consumption	23.2
of which:	
(domestic)	(6.7)
(industrial)	(14.1)
(commercial)	(2.3)
Loss and own use	4.0
Non-energy use (fertilizer)	32.6

The current pattern of use appears sensible, especially in view of the low ratio of exploitation to reserves. Once the rate of exploitation increases to a higher level, the question of the relative priorities in the use of gas will have to be looked at more closely.

Electrical power

The electrical power system is administered by two government corporations. The responsibility for generating, transmitting and distributing electricity is entrusted to the Bangladesh Power Development Board (PDB). The Rural Electrification Board (REB) was established in 1977 to develop distribution facilities in rural areas. The power system is divided into an eastern grid, which feeds mainly Dhaka and Chittagong divisions, and a western grid, which services Rajshahi and Khulna divisions. They are separated by the Jamuna-Padma-lower

Meghna rivers. Most of the generation capacity is located in the eastern zone because of the availability of cheap natural gas.

Total generating capacity in 1985 was 1 141 MW, an increase of 6 per cent per year over the 475 MW capacity available in 1970. The expansion in capacity, however, could not keep pace with the increase in the number of consumers (Table 6.1). The maximum demand is estimated to have increased from 213 MW in 1970 to 887 in 1985, an increase of about 10 per cent per year. The actual generation of electricity through the total system increased by about 12 per cent per year, from 1 086 million kilowatt hours (MKWH) in 1972/73 to 4 800 MKWH in 1985/86.

Table 6.1 Trends in the supply and distribution of electrical power system

Items	1960	1965	1970	1980	1985
Generation capacity (MW)	88	202	475	822	1 140
Maximum demand (MW)	42	103	213	544	887
Number of villages electrified	n.a.	n.a.	250	2 887	6 507
Number of consumers (in thousands)	n.a.	104	220	522	964

Sources: Bangladesh Bureau of Statistics, *1986 Statistical Yearbook of Bangladesh,* Dhaka, 1986 and Pakistan Central Statistical Office (CSO) documents.

Bangladesh has very little unexploited hydroelectric potential. The choice in power generation is largely limited to thermal plants based on a limited range of fuels. Indeed, 90 per cent of the installed capacity is based on thermal generation (Table 6.2). The remaining 10 per cent is supplied by the Kaptai hydroelectric plant in the Chittagong Hill Tracts. Nearly two-thirds of the thermal power generation uses gas as fuel, and all of these gas powered thermal stations are located in the eastern zone. Power generation in the western zone is based on imported petroleum, at a unit cost five times higher than in the eastern zone.

Despite the impressive increase in power generation, the supply of electric power lags behind the country's needs. The existing generating capacity is only about 10 KW per thousand population, and the amount of power available for distribution is only about 40 kilowatt hours per person. Shortages are widespread in most areas, especially during periods of peak use, particularly in the western zone. Demand for

Table 6.2 Installed electric power generation capacity by type

Type	1975/76 MW	Per cent	1984/85 MW	Per cent
Hydro	80	10.4	130	11.4
Thermal:	689	89.6	1 010	88.6
Steam turbine with furnace oil	85	11.1	182	16.0
Steam turbine with natural gas	318	41.4	408	35.8
Internal combustion with diesel	92	12.0	86	7.5
Gas turbine with shell gas	108	14.0	156	13.7
Gas turbine with naphtha and diesel	86	11.2	178	15.6

Source: BBS, *1986 Statistical Yearbook of Bangladesh*, Dhaka, 1986.

domestic use has been increasing at about 20 per cent per year and this has reduced the growth of power available for industrial and commercial use. Over the years, expensive electric power has been one of the major factors behind the relatively high cost of manufacturing, and the uncertain supply of power has been a major cause of the underutilization of industrial capacity. As an insurance against uncertain supply, many manufacturing units have set up their own generating plants. These plants are of uneconomic size and this results in a very high cost of power for these enterprises. In rural areas most of the rice mills and irrigation equipment are run by diesel operated generators.

The electric power supply system also suffers from operational and managerial deficiencies which are reflected in a very high and increasing system loss, estimated to be 35 per cent of the generated output in 1984/85[3]. The high rate of loss is attributed largely to illegal connections, theft and under-reporting of actual use through the manipulation of meter reading[4]. These irregularities are partly responsible for the fact that the system operates at a loss. In 1980/81 the net loss amounted to Tk 362 million, and this was in addition to the Tk 100 million subsidy received from the government[5].

Much of the cost of inefficient management of the system is passed on to the legitimate users through higher prices. The price of electricity increased about 19 per cent per year during the 1973-86 period, compared to a 13 per cent annual increase in the price of natural gas and petroleum products and a 15 per cent annual increase in the price of domestically produced manufactured goods. During the 1980-85 period, the average power tariff increased from Tk 0.66 to Tk 1.44 per kilowatt hour.

The supply of electric power is limited to the urban areas and industrial units. During the last ten years the Rural Electrification Board has made very limited progress in extending electricity to villages, where 80 per cent of the country's population live. By June 1985 only 6 507 villages, i.e., 8 per cent of the total (83 666 according to the 1981 census), had access to electricity, 5 per cent through the REB and 3 per cent through the PDB. Only about 8 500 irrigation pumps (about 4 per cent of the estimated number of machines in the country) and 5 600 industrial units had received electricity connections through the REB by June 1987[6].

The cost of taking electricity to rural areas is high. At a price recovering full cost, the demand for electricity in rural areas would be insignificant. One must therefore base the decision of whether to take power to the rural areas on a careful evaluation of the externalities of power supply (e.g., the reduction in the cost of irrigation and small-scale industries and the benefits of having access to services whose dissemination depends on the availability of power) and a comparison with the rate of return on alternative public investments intended to raise productivity in rural areas.

A number of issues for future energy planning are indicated by the brief analysis outlined above. First, it is essential to plan how the energy demand of the rural sector will be met in the future. The high capital cost of transporting commercial energy and the need to conserve the limited indigenous reserves of the latter suggest that it is unrealistic to plan for a massive substitution of traditional sources of fuel by gas or power. In the past little was done to improve traditional sources of energy, to economize on fuel or increase the efficiency of energy using technology (e.g., by improving traditional cooking methods). As a result, the supply of traditional sources of energy has become seriously depleted to the point of causing environmental degradation. Carefully planned action on a broad front is of high priority to prevent a further deterioration. Second, it is important to ascertain how large are the reserves of alternative sources of commercial energy and to understand the economics of using them. Further exploration and the evaluation of reserves of petroleum and of the recently discovered coal deposits, which are closer to the surface than the previously found reserves, should be undertaken. Third, there is a need to plan carefully the use of natural gas. The proven reserves are substantial, but by no means inexhaustible if one extrapolates past trends in consumption. In the eight years to 1985 the use of natural gas increased at an annual rate of more than 14 per cent. If this rate of increase continues, annual use in the year 2000 will become close to 6 per cent of the current proven reserve. It is therefore important to conserve this resource, regulate its use in the light of future changes in proven reserves, and determine the most profitable direction of future use.

TRANSPORT AND COMMUNICATIONS

The transport and communications sector accounts for only about 7 per cent of GDP. Fifty-six per cent of the sector's contribution to GDP is accounted for by road transport, 35 per cent by water transport and 3 per cent each by railways, civil aviation and communications. About 70 per cent of the sector's value added reportedly originates in the unorganized road and water transport sector, for which information is very sparse. One must therefore be careful in interpreting the above numbers.

Today's transport network reflects the influence of the colonial economy prior to the partition of India in 1947. At that time the present territory of Bangladesh – then East Bengal – was the hinterland of the industrial city of Calcutta, a source of supply of raw materials and food and a market for industrial goods. Railways and ports were located and developed to facilitate the movement of jute and rice and the reverse

Table 6.3 Consumption of electric energy by type of consumer 1975/76 and 1984/85

Type of consumers	1975/76		1984/85		Annual rate of increase 1975/76 to 1984/85 (per cent)
	Million KWH	Per cent	Million KWH	Per cent	
Domestic	135	14.5	633	22.3	18.7
Industrial	658	70.6	1,607	56.6	10.4
Commercial	88	9.4	250	8.8	12.3
Others	51	5.5	351	12.3	23.9
Total	932	100.0	2,841	100.0	13.1

Source: Bangladesh Bureau of Statistics.

movement of industrial goods. The Governments of Pakistan and Bangladesh initiated a number of improvements, mainly by way of expanding the road network. The railway system has undergone little change.

There is considerable private sector participation in road and water transport, but railways have always been in the public sector. The air transport system, operating a network of domestic intercity connections as well as some international routes, is also in the public sector.

Freight traffic is estimated to have been growing at the rate of 5 per cent per year and passenger traffic at about 7 per cent (Table 6.4). It is estimated that in 1985 about 54 per cent of the freight traffic was moved by roads, 30 per cent by waterways and 16 per cent by railways. The percentage shares of the passenger traffic of the three modes were 51, 28 and 21 respectively.

Table 6.4 Growth of traffic by mode of transport, 1977–85

Mode of transport	1977 Volume of traffic	Per cent	1985 Volume of traffic	Per cent	Annual rate of growth, 1977–85 (per cent)
Freight traffic (million ton/miles)					
Road	851	44.1	1 529	53.6	7.6
Water	638	33.0	858	30.1	3.8
Rail	443	22.9	465	16.3	0.6
Total	1 932	100.0	2 852	100.0	5.0
Passenger traffic (million person/miles)					
Road	5 564	50.4	9 608	51.4	7.1
Water	3 206	29.1	5 238	28.0	6.3
Rail	2 266	20.5	3 856	20.6	6.8
Total	11 037	100.0	18 702	100.0	6.8

Source: Planning Commission, *Inter-modal Transport Study—Final Report,* Transport Survey Wing, Dhaka, 1985.

Road transport

The road transport network is conditioned by the river system and the drainage pattern. The natural drainage of the country is from north to south. Major roads run in the same direction. Construction of east-west roads is expensive as numerous rivers impede travel in that direction. Heavy flooding requires high road embankments and good drainage, which increase the cost of construction and maintenance. Local inhabitants are unwilling to surrender scarce land for new embankments or for the extension of the existing ones. Acquisition of land normally takes a long time, often involving court cases to settle disputes and leading to time and cost over-runs in most road development projects.

Bangladesh made good progress in the development of road transport during the 1960s (Table 6.5). The mileage of paved roads more than doubled during the decade. However, during the war of independence more than 300 bridges of different size were damaged and in addition there was widespread damage to other parts of the road system. The decade of the 1970s was largely a period of rehabilitation; only 156 miles of new paved roads were constructed during this period. The Second Five-Year Plan (1980-85) placed renewed emphasis on expanding the road system. A total of 1 360 miles of new roads were added during the 1980-86 period, bringing the total length of paved roads to 3 914 miles in June 1986. The overall rate of increase in road mileage during the post-independence period was 3.1 per cent per year, and in the 1980s the rate of expansion was nearly three times faster than this.

In spite of the progress outlined above, Bangladesh has a poor road system by the standards of South and South-east Asian countries. It has only seven miles of metalled road per 100 square miles of area compared to about 10.5 miles in the Asian region as a whole. Road mileage has lagged far behind the growth of the number of vehicles using the road system. During the post-independence period buses and trucks increased at an annual rate of 18 per cent. During the Second Five-Year Plan period the volume of freight traffic increased at the rate of 7 per cent per year. Passenger traffic increased at a slightly faster rate.

Road development in the 1980s has also been unbalanced. Effort was concentrated on the development of national highways, connecting regional headquarters with the major cities (Dhaka, Chittagong, Rajshahi and Khulna) and on the construction of roads to connect *upozilla* centers with the existing network of paved roads, which became necessary after the decentralization of administration to the *upazillas* in 1983. Very little attention was given to the development of feeder roads,

Table 6.5 Capacity and utilization of road transport

	1960	1970	1980	1985	Annual rate of increase 1980-85 (per cent)
Length of metalled roads (miles)	995	2 398	2 554	3 914 (1)	8.9
Number of buses and trucks	5 564	14 386	33 665	77 758	18.2
Freight traffic (million ton/miles)	n.a.	n.a.	6 786	9 608	7.2
Passenger traffic (million person/miles)	n.a.	n.a.	6 786	9 608	7.2

(1) The figure is for June 1986

Sources: BBS, *1986 Statistical Yearbook of Bangladesh* and Pakistan CSO sources.

which connect rural markets with the road network to facilitate the movement of goods into and out of the rural areas. In 1986 about 46 per cent of the total length of paved roads consisted of national highways, while 17 per cent were regional highways and 21 per cent were feeder roads (Table 6.6). During the 1980-86 period the mileage of national highways and roads connecting *upazillas* increased by 12 and 9 per cent per year respectively, while the mileage of feeder roads increased by only 2.3 per cent per year.

The rural areas are mostly served by unpaved earthen roads which are not suitable for year-round motorized transport. There are an estimated 25 000 miles of major earthen roads and 33 000 miles of minor earthen roads[7]. These roads require frequent reconstruction and heavy maintenance, which are mostly carried out through the rural public works program. Animal driven carts are the major mode of transport on these roads. In areas with a sandy soil and good drainage manually operated rickshaws and rickshaw vans are also used on the earthen roads.

The imbalance between highways and feeder roads in the road construction program has led to inefficiency in the road system. At present the volume of import cargo transported by the trucking system to the rural areas is significantly higher than the export cargo. As a result

Table 6.6 Recent expansion of paved roads by types, 1980–86

Type of roads	1980		1986		Annual rate of expansion
	Road mileage	Per cent	Road mileage	Per cent	
National highways	854	33.4	1 679	42.9	11.9
Regional highways	535	21.0	670	17.1	3.8
Feeder roads	700	27.4	803	20.5	2.3
Upazilla connecting road	465	18.2	762	19.5	8.5
Total	2 554	100.0	3 914	100.0	7.4

Source: S. F. Rahman, "Road Development in Bangladesh under Roads and Highway Department", *The Bangladesh Times,* Dhaka, 14th april 1987.

many trucks, which haul to district and *upazilla* centers from the sea ports or major cities, return without a full backhaul load. This of course increases the average cost of transport. The small backhaul cargoes are partly due to the inadequacy of rural feeder roads. Most of the demand for motorized transport comes from arterial movement and very little from areas off the major roads, which have a large unmet demand for transport. Farmers in the interior areas engage in much greater subsistence production than would otherwise be the case, producing almost everything for the family rather than for the market which remains out of reach due to the lack of access to the commercial transport network. Larger landowners in interior villages invest in their own means of transport (animal driven carts) to market their surplus and transport passengers. These means of transport remain highly under-utilized during much of the year. The 1977 agricultural census estimated that there were about 530 000 bullock carts in rural areas with an estimated total capacity of 260 000 tons.

Water transport

The extensive river system in Bangladesh serves as a good network of waterways which plays an important part in the marketing of goods, especially of agricultural produce. For the relatively low-lying regions in the south (Barisal, Patuakhali, Noakhali, Faridpur and Khulna) boats and launches are often the only mode of transport available. In many other parts of the country they are often the most efficient means of transport.

The waterways in Bangladesh consist of about 3 250 miles of routes navigable throughout the year and another 2 000 miles navigable during the rainy season. About 3 300 launches and ferry boats, both public and private, operate in the waterways. In addition, a large number of manually operated country boats are used to transport people and products. The 1977 agricultural census estimated that rural households owned 721 000 country boats with a carrying capacity of approximately 1.02 million tons of freight. One of the consequences of the expansion of the private ownership of irrigation equipment in recent years is the use of the machinery of shallow tubewells and power pumps to "mechanize" country boats during the rainy season for commercial operations.

Water routes connect with road transport in places where large gaps in the roads require ferry services. In 1983 there were 52 major gaps of this kind, eight on national highways, seven on regional highways and 37 on district and feeder roads[8]. An estimated 8.2 million households used ferry services annually on the national and regional highways. This represents an average use of 450 vehicles per day per crossing. The number of ferries and facilities are inadequate to cope with demand. On the two major crossings on the rivers Jamuna and Padma, which respectively connect the eastern zone with the north and the south-west, trucks often have to wait for several days before crossing. This increases the cost of transport and acts as a hindrance to the movement of perishable agricultural produce, e.g., fruits, vegetables and eggs, from the agriculturally progressive northern region to the major cities of Dhaka and Chittagong, located in the east.

Inland waterways appear to be one of the cheaper modes of transport. Transport cost per ton mile by a country boat was estimated to be Tk 55 in 1984/85 compared to Tk 86 for bullock carts. During the 1975-86 period the cost of transporting by country boats increased at an annual rate of only 2.6 per cent compared to 6.1 per cent for push carts and 11 per cent for bullock carts. With the existing technology the movement of goods by country boats is extremely time consuming, so that they are mostly used for short distance haulage except for non-perishable goods like jute. To make better use of the waterways for transportation, large investments will be needed both for the dredging of the rivers and for the mechanization of boats.

Railways

The railway system consists of two major north-south routes with a total of 1 797 miles. The system in the west, representing about one-third of the route, is broad gauged. It extends from the port city of Khulna in the south-west to Rangpur in the extreme north. Throughout the eastern and south-eastern regions the rail line is meter gauged. The eastern system is linked with the western system by two ferry crossings on the Jamuna river. The system is mainly single tracked.

There has been little growth in the rail network for a long time. The route increased by only 62 miles in the 1960s and by another 21 miles since independence. Since independence the number of locomotives has declined while the number of coaches and wagons has changed little. In contrast passenger traffic has increased by 55 per cent since independence. At the time of independence the system did not have any excess capacity. Increased passenger traffic therefore appears to be more a reflection of increased overcrowding and strain than of improved efficiency of operation. The system is badly in need of investment for increased capacity. Even the critically important lines between the ports and the major urban centers are single tracked and this causes a great deal of delay in moving commodities and people.

Communications

The state of the communications systems is shown in Table 6.8. The network of post offices was extensive even before independence. In 1985 there were 7 583 post offices, which means that every post office served on average about 11 villages and an area of seven square miles. Given the low investment in transport and the inadequacy of transport services, postal communication is fairly efficient. Rural mail carriers use bicycles or walk. A letter reaches any part of the country within a week.

A telegraph service is available at most *upazilla* headquarters. In 1985, there were 601 telegraph offices in the country. Seventy-eight per cent of them were located in rural areas.

The telephone service is inadequately developed and there is a large unmet demand, particularly in urban areas. In 1973/74 there were only 60 000 telephone connections in the country. By 1984/85, the total number of connections increased to 181 400, about 85 per cent of them located in urban areas. Though the telephone service is available in all municipal areas, it is heavily concentrated in a few large cities. About 95 per cent of the telephone sets in urban areas are located in the cities of Dhaka, Chittagong and Khulna and are used mainly in government offices and commercial establishments. Residential connections, except for high level government officials and priority personnel (e.g., medical practitioners) are difficult to get. International communications, though

Table 6.7 Capacity and utilization of rail transport

	1960	1970	1975/76	1980/81	1984/85
Route mileage	1 714	1 776	1 786	1 792	1 797
Track mileage	n.a.	n.a.	2 810	2 822	2 828
Number of locomotives	472	482	450	410	288
Number of coaches	1 621	1 674	1 531	1 682	1 637
Number of wagons	15 860	19 756	18 903	19 366	19 719
Passenger traffic (million person-miles)	1 816	2 425	2 773	3 230	3 749
Freight traffic (million ton-miles)	872	921	446	489	505
Transport charge:					
Tk per passenger mile	n.a.	n.a.	0.10	0.13	0.20
Tk per ton-mile for freight	n.a.	0.24	0.50	1.12	1.69

Source: BBS, *Statistical Yearbook*, 1986, Bangladesh Railway and Pakistan CSO sources.

Table 6.8 Development in the communication system

	1974	1980	1985
Number of post offices	6 680	7 292	7 583
Population served per post office (in thousands)	11.4	12.0	13.1
Number of telephones:	60 000	119 400	181 400
Rural areas	6 000	10 000	26 000
Urban areas	54 000	109 400	155 400
Population served per telephone	1 268	747	545
Telegraph offices:	n.a.	488	601
Rural areas	n.a.	360	471
Urban areas	n.a.	128	130

Source: Ministry of Planning, *Third Five-Year Plan, 1985-90*. Planning Commission, Dhaka, December 1985.

still inadequate, have improved over the years, especially after the facilities provided by the earth satellite station came into operation in 1975.

FLOOD CONTROL

The frequent occurrence of heavy flooding has been a major source of uncertainty for farmers in Bangladesh. Almost the entire country lies in the delta of three mighty rivers, the Padma, the Jamuna and the Meghna. The three rivers are estimated to drain an approximate area of 600 000 square miles, only about 8 per cent of which lies in Bangladesh. The control of flooding can not therefore be attempted without the cooperation of the upstream riparian countries, India and Nepal. There are hardly any storage sites within Bangladesh that could be used for flood regulation. In addition, the technical problems involved in flood control are enormous. The combined total flow of the rivers amounts to about 5 million cusecs during the peak of the rainy season and the sediment load is estimated to be about 2.4 billion tons a year.

About 18 per cent of the country is flooded each year. During severe floods the affected area exceeds 36 per cent of the country and nearly 60 per cent of the net cultivated area[9]. Floods are caused by the overflow of the main river system, heavy rainfall and congestion of the drainage system. Some flash flooding is caused by overflowing tributaries, draining hilly areas along the Indo-Bangladesh border in the south-eastern and central-northern parts of the country. About 1.2 million ha in the coastal belt is subject to the intrusion of saline water during high tides.

The cropping pattern in Bangladesh has adjusted to normal flooding. On the 16 per cent of land which normally is flooded to a depth between 90 and 180 cm, farmers grow a low yielding deep water rice, which is sown in March, when the land is dry, and harvested in November, when the flood waters recede. Normal floods do not affect the crop as the plants grow as the water rises. Another 12 per cent of the land, which is flooded more than 180 cm deep, is kept fallow during the rainy season and is cropped in the dry (winter) season with a local variety of rice. Abnormally high floods however damage crops on low land, including the land that is normally flooded 30 to 90 cm deep. The frequency of severe flooding has been increasing over time due to the siltation of the river beds. Since independence the country has experienced three unusually severe floods, in 1974, 1984 and 1987. The loss of rice production due to the floods of 1974 and 1984 was estimated to be 1.2 million tons each time and the loss from the 1987 flood is provisionally forecast to be 2.8 million tons[10]. Floods and the risk of production loss that they imply discourage farmers from applying modern agricultural inputs, e.g., fertilizer, at economically optimal rates. In addition to crop damage, floods also cause other losses: deaths of cattle, destruction of homes and damage to the transportation system.

Flood control and drainage have been the responsibility of the Bangladesh Water Development Board. The Board has implemented a large number of projects since the early 1960s including the construction of flood embankments along the banks of the major rivers and coastal areas and the excavation of drainage channels. Of the 5.76 million ha which is estimated to be vulnerable to flooding, flood control and drainage facilities had been extended to 2.59 million ha by 1984/85. About 2 517 miles of embankments have been constructed in the coastal area alone to provide protection from the intrusion of saline water. The physical progress in flood control and drainage in the early 1980s is shown in Table 6.9.

Table 6.9 Physical progress in the field of flood control and drainage during the Second Five-Year Plan period (1980-85)

Items	Unit	1980	1985	Annual rate of increase (per cent)
Flood embankments	miles	3 084	3 810	4.3
Irrigation canals	miles	1 707	2 363	6.7
Drainage channels	miles	1 408	1 853	5.6
Hydraulic structures (sluice gates)	number	3 589	4 521	4.7
Bridges and culverts	number	3 203	3 565	2.2
Pump houses	number	58	89	8.9

Source: Planning Commission, *The Third Five-Year Plan, 1985-90,* Ministry of Planning, Dhaka, December 1985.

As a result of the construction of flood embankments along the rivers, the area under deep water *amon* rice fell from 2.08 million ha before independence to 1.23 million ha in 1985/86 and the land thus released has presumably been reallocated to grow transplanted *amon* and HYV *boro* rice, in which yields are respectively 50 per cent and 150 per cent higher than deep water *amon*. The coastal embankment project however has made a very limited contribution to the growth of food production. The area remains single cropped with saline-resistant local varieties of rice. The average yield increased only marginally, from 1.2 tons of paddy per hectare in the early 1950s to 1.3 tons in the early 1980s. Moreover, the coastal embankment has adversely affected the highly profitable seafood production in the area by prohibiting the breaching of embankments to obtain saline water for shrimp culture.

THE SOCIAL INFRASTRUCTURE: EDUCATION AND HEALTH

In recent years the Government of Bangladesh has allocated to education and health an average of 11.6 per cent of its total expenditure, 15 per cent of current expenditure and 7 per cent of capital expenditure (Table 6.10). This is a low ratio even in comparison with poor Asian neighbors such as Burma and Nepal, which spend respectively 19 and 17 per cent of their budgets on these sectors[11]. The shares of these sectors in capital expenditure remained unchanged between 1975/76-1977/78 and 1982/83-1984/85, while their shares in current expenditure have declined. It is therefore not surprising that these sectors, particularly education, have performed poorly in the period since independence.

Education

A comparison of the change in literacy, estimated by the population censuses of 1974 and 1981, is a little difficult because of a change in the definition of literacy between the two censuses. It has been argued that the criterion of literacy used in 1981 ("the ability to write a letter in any language") is stricter than the one used in 1974 ("the ability to read and write in any language"). If this is indeed the case, the difference between the two standards is unlikely to have been large, and it seems improbable that the result would have been substantially different if identical standards of literacy had been applied in the two years.

Estimates from the two censuses show that the adult literacy rate (per cent of population 15 years and older who are literate) improved while the "total" literacy rate (per cent of population 5 years and older who are literate) deteriorated for the male and for both sexes taken together. For the female the improvement in the adult literacy rate was greater than the improvement in the total literacy rate between the two dates. Thus the literacy rate for children between 5 and 14 declined (drastically so for male children) between 1974 and 1981[12].

Between 1973 and 1985 the number of boys enrolled in primary schools increased at an annual rate of 1.4 per cent (Table 6.12) compared to an increase in the population of the relevant age group of about 2.5 per cent, indicating that the enrollment *rate* for boys declined at the rate of 1.1 per cent per year. For girls the enrollment *rate* improved by nearly 1 per cent per year. Overall the enrollment *rate* declined by three-tenths of 1 per cent per year. The decline in the male enrollment rate was particularly steep between 1974 and 1981, suggesting that there was indeed a decline in the literacy rate for male children between the two censuses, although the extent of the decline may have been exaggerated by the change in the definition of literacy.

The asymmetry between the two sexes with respect to the performance in literacy and primary education is difficult to explain. It is notable that primary school enrollment for female children increased

Table 6.10 Government expenditure on education and health
Per cent of total

	Current expenditure		Capital expenditure	
	Av. 1975/76 to 1977/78	Av. 1982/83 to 1984/85	Av. 1975/76 to 1977/78	Av. 1982/83 to 1984/85
Education	13.5	11.2	3.6	3.5
Health	4.3	3.8	3.6	3.6

Source: BBS, *Statistical Yearbook*, 1986.

Table 6.11
Literacy rates

	1974	1981
Total literacy rates:		
Both sexes	24.3	23.8
Male	32.9	31.0
Female	14.8	16.0
Adult literacy rates:		
Both sexes	25.8	29.2
Male	37.2	39.7
Female	13.2	18.0

Source: Population censuses of 1974 and 1981 quoted in BBS, *Socio-Economic Indicators of Bangladesh*, July 1986.

two and a half times as fast as that for male children without the provision of any special facility. Indeed, there was a drastic reduction in the number of exclusively girls' schools during this period. Perhaps the opportunity cost of attending primary schools is far greater for boys, who can take up casual employment or unpaid family work outside the homestead, than for girls for whom such employment opportunities are far less readily obtained.

The rate of expansion in education has been faster, the higher the level of education. That is, primary education expanded at the lowest rate

Table 6.12 Primary school enrollment
Thousands of students

	Boys	Girls	Total
1973	5 060	2 698	7 758
1974	5 186	2 662	7 848
1978	4 612	2 945	7 557
1980	4 924	3 103	8 027
1981	5 059	3 201	8 260
1983	5 358	3 597	8 955
1985	6 002	4 080	10 082
Annual compound growth rate between 1973 and 1985	1.4	3.5	2.2

Source: BBS, *Statistical Yearbook*, 1986.

while university education expanded at the highest rate. Secondary schools and colleges expanded at rates close to that of primary schools. The ranking of the different levels of education in terms of the rate of expansion has been exactly opposite their ranking according to the rate of return. The latter is highest for primary education and lowest for general university education[13].

This pattern of growth is largely the result of the allocation of resources among the different levels of education. University education has not only received a much higher share of resources – twice as much as primary education in the first decade after independence – but its share has also grown over time. Government expenditure and the subsidy per student at the primary level have been less than 2 per cent of the corresponding amounts at the university level.

A few points about university education should be highlighted. First, one should make a clear distinction between general university education and higher technical education (producing, for example, medical, engineering and agricultural graduates and post-graduates). One of the redeeming features of the expansion of higher education is that higher technical education has also expanded very fast, even faster than general university education. The supply of technically trained specialists is by and large adequate to meet the current demand for them. The quality of technical and professional education has been maintained reasonably well while the quality and efficiency of general university education have declined disastrously. An overwhelming majority of the graduates of general university faculties (as well as the colleges) acquire no usable or employable skill, and they constitute a strong pressure group favoring the expansion of unproductive public sector employment, which adds nothing to society's welfare. Second, over the years the subsidy to higher education has increased sharply. In 1965/66 student fees were equivalent to 27 per cent of current expenditure of Dhaka University. By 1979/80 the proportion had fallen to 8 per cent. Third, the opportunity for poorer students to receive a university education has declined as a result of a decline in scholarship funds. Scholarships declined from 19 per cent of recurrent expenditure in higher education in 1969/70 to only 4 per cent in 1979/80.

The slow growth of primary school enrollment has been due to a very high drop out rate, estimated to be 50 per cent of the entrants after the first year and 25 per cent in subsequent years. This is a manifestation of a low effective demand for primary education, which appears to be rather paradoxical given the high (social) rate of return to primary education. Among the factors that explain a low demand for primary education are the following: (a) Although social returns to primary education are very high, much of the gains (including some of the private ones) may not be immediately perceived by the recipients. As a result, the direct and indirect costs of education may outweigh the perceived private benefits. (b) The content of courses and the quality of teaching often reduce the practical relevance of such education, making private benefits appear to be low. While the estimates of rates of return are based on typical institutions (outside Bangladesh in the case of primary education), the neglect and paucity of resources often make the quality of education in the majority of institutions less than that of a "typical" school.

Health

Table 6.13 contains some of the basic indicators of health status and the relative size of the health service. Life expectancy at birth in the 1980s is estimated to be about 55 years compared to about 48 years in the 1960s. Methodologies used to obtain the two estimates are different and there is a significant variability in the estimates made for the early 1980s. As a result, it is difficult to have much confidence in the precise figures for the increase in life expectancy although there is little doubt that it has improved. Infant mortality rates, though still very high (twice the rate in Burma) have also declined significantly.

No serious analysis is available of the factors responsible for these

Table 6.13 Selected indicators of health status

	1960s	1982-1984 Average Rural	Urban
Life expectancy at birth (years)			
Male	49.2	54.0	59.6
Female	46.9	53.4	61.5
Infant mortality (per thousand births)			
	1960s	1984	
Male	153	134	
Female	128	109	

	Hospital beds per thousand persons	Registered medical graduates per thousand persons
1976	0.19	0.07
1977	0.19	0.08
1978	0.20	0.08
1983	0.21	0.12
1984	0.23	0.14
1985	0.23	0.15

Sources: For the source of life expectancy and infant mortality data in the 1960s, see A. R. Khan, *The Economy of Bangladesh*, Macmillan, London, 1972, p. 27. All other data are from BBS, *Statistical Yearbook*, 1986. Infant mortality refers to deaths in the first year after birth. Hospital beds refer to government hospitals and health centers only.

changes. An improvement in the level of nutrition – the most common factor – has to be ruled out as a possible explanation since average nutrition in the early 1980s was probably lower than in the 1960s. Greater access to safe drinking water and, largely as a consequence, the eradication of epidemic diseases have probably made a major contribution.

Other indicators of health status, e.g., the morbidity rate, are not available. Trends in the availability of basic services can not be ascertained with any confidence. Hospital beds per person have increased a little, but this probably reflects a relative increase in beds in health centers, which are much more rudimentary institutions than most hospitals. The number of graduate doctors per capita has more than doubled in a decade, but there has been no corresponding increase in the capacity of the majority of the population to purchase their services. Much of the increase in the number of doctors has probably been directed to profit making private hospitals and clinics. These institutions represent a completely new phenomenon for Bangladesh. Their clientele is limited to a very thin layer of people at the top of the income distribution scale. During the last decade these private medical institutions grew at an extraordinarily high rate. The rapid expansion in the demand for their sevices is an indication of the increasing inequality in the distribution of income. Some expansion of health services in rural areas has taken place, partly as a by-product of the family planning program. It is not possible to judge the extent of improvement however, although it is hard to imagine that it has made a significant difference to the health status of the masses.

The government is officially committed to a family planning program. Current public expenditure on family planning (which accounts for almost the entire public expenditure on the program), as a proportion of the total current expenditure of the government, reveals no steady trend; it declined in the late 1970s and increased again after 1981/82. In the mid-1980s it accounted for about 2.3 per cent of total current public expenditure, about the same as that in the mid-1970s. Official surveys show that the rate of contraceptive use has increased much faster than public expenditure on the program, from about 14 per cent of the women of child bearing age in 1979 to 19 per cent in 1981 and 28 per cent in 1986[14]. Presumably these acceptance rates include traditional methods (safe period, withdrawal and abstinence) as well as modern methods. In 1979 traditional methods of contraception accounted for more than 40 per cent of the techniques used. A breakdown into the two methods is not available for more recent years. It is hard to judge what effect the increased acceptance has had on fertility rates. The account of demographic trends in Chapter 2 does not indicate a significant reduction in birth rates during the period over which the rate of contraceptive practice is estimated to have doubled.

CONCLUSIONS

Inadequate infrastructural facilities constitute a serious obstacle to the economic and social development of Bangladesh. The depletion of traditional energy sources has created a severe shortage of energy in the rural areas and led to considerable environmental degradation. Expansion in the use of gas and in the supply of electricity, generated largely from gas, have not relieved the shortage. The reason for this is that it has not been possible to take these commercial sources of energy to rural areas because of the high cost of transmission. Even in the urban and industrial areas the supply of power and energy have neither been adequate nor reliable. Transport bottlenecks have seriously affected economic development, especially in rural areas which have suffered from the inadequacy of feeder roads. Road transport has in general expanded quite rapidly, but continues to be characterized by serious imbalances, e.g., a very slow growth of feeder roads and major bottlenecks on the arterial highways because of inadequate ferry capacity. Waterways and railways are in need of large-scale investment. Some progress has been made in harnessing the rivers and controlling floods and in reducing the intrusion of saline water, but coastal embankments have been an obstacle to the growth of fisheries.

Education and health have suffered from comparative neglect. Their shares of public expenditure are low and have declined over time. Within education the allocation of resources has been characterized by inequity: higher education has received most of the funds while primary education has suffered from a serious lack of resources. The primary school enrollment rate has been declining. One redeeming feature of educational development is the rapid growth of higher technical education with its standards reasonably maintained. General university education has deteriorated sharply in quality. Access to all forms of higher education has become more unequal. There has been some improvement in life expectancy, especially for women, and in infant mortality. Although the reasons behind these improvements are not fully understood, much of the credit is probably due to increased access to safe drinking water and to better control of epidemics and diseases.

Notes and References

1. These data are from BBS, *Statistical Yearbook*, 1986, Chapter 6. Data shown below without specific reference are from the same source.
2. It is estimated that there is a reserve of about one billion tons of coal at a depth of about 1 000 meters, which presumably is uneconomic to extract. Recently a thick deposit of gondwana coal has been discovered at a depth of 190 to 350 meters, but the volume of reserve has not yet been determined. Recently crude oil has also been found in areas of gas fields. Ascertained reserves are small. Efforts for further exploration are being made.
3. The Second Five-Year Plan set the target of reducing the system loss from

40 per cent in 1979/80 to 23 per cent in 1984/85. It was reduced to 30 per cent in 1982/83, but increased again in later years. See, Planning Commission, *The Third Five-Year Plan,* 1985-90, Dhaka, 1985, pp. 255-6.
4. After allowing for technical loss and station use, the net loss is estimated at Tk 1 110 million which is about 13 per cent of the annual allocation of development funds to the power sector during the Third Five-Year Plan.
5. E.B. Wennergren, *An Assessment of the Agricultural Sector in Bangladesh,* US Agency for International Development, Dhaka, August 1983, p. 119.
6. Planning Commission, *op. cit.,* and Ministry of Finance, *Bangladesh Economic Survey,* 1986/87, Dhaka, 1987.
7. E.B. Wennergren, *op. cit.,* p. 192.
8. *Ibid.,* p. 192.
9. Master Plan Organization, *National Water Plan, Vol. II, Resources,* Ministry of Irrigation, Water Development and Flood Control, Dhaka, December 1986, pp. 10-55.
10. BBS, *Yearbook of Agricultural Statistics,* (various issues), and Planning and Monitoring Unit, Ministry of Food, *Food Situation Report,* August 1987. The estimated loss for 1987 must be regarded as a provisional forecast. The estimate was made long before the harvest of the main affected (*amon*) crop.
11. The World Bank, *The World Development Report,* 1987.
12. The total literacy rate is the weighted average of the rates for children (5-14) and adults (15 and above) the weights being the relative proportions of children (36 per cent in 1981) and adults (64 per cent) in the combined population of those five years or older. Assuming that the weights were the same in 1974, one finds that the literacy rates for children declined for the female from 17.6 per cent in 1974 to 12.4 per cent in 1981 and for the male from 25.3 per cent to 15.5 per cent! It is possible that the change of definition affected the measurement for children more drastically. While "the ability to read and write" differs little between a literate child and a literate adult, "the ability to write a letter" implies experience that may be more lacking among children than among adults.
13. This part of the chapter draws heavily on ILO/ARTEP, *Manpower Planning in Bangladesh,* Bangkok, October 1981 (jointly authored by one of the authors of the present book). Estimates of social rates of return for general university and college education are reported in the document. They are low – between 6 and 7 per cent – and substantially lower than private rates of return. For primary education rates of return estimates are not available for Bangladesh, but estimates for other developing countries show that they are very high, much higher than that for secondary and higher levels of education. See, *ibid.,* for details and for the sources of other data cited below.
14. The estimate for 1979 appears in BBS, *Statistical Yearbook,* 1986, p.886. For other years the estimates are from unpublished Planning Commission sources.

7 Income Distribution and Poverty

It was shown in Chapter 2 that compared to the pre-independence period, the average standard of living fell sharply immediately after independence, but subsequently living standards grew significantly faster than in the period prior to independence. The average levels of real income per capita and real consumption per capita were respectively 5 per cent and 12 per cent higher in the first six years of the 1980s than in the second half of the 1960s. The reason for the higher increase in per capita consumption than in per capita income was the massive increase in external aid between the two periods. Compared to the depressed levels in the immediate post-independence years, the improvement in average living standards has been impressive: per capita income and consumption increased at annual rates of at least one and two-thirds per cent. To what extent were these improvements shared by the poor and low income groups?

MAIN INDICATORS AND THEIR LIMITATIONS

As is true in most developing countries, changes in the distribution of income are harder to document than changes in average income. Greater uncertainties surround individual indicators of change in distribution than indicators of growth. Moreover, a single indicator can at best shed light on one or a few of the multiple dimensions of distributive issues. This chapter therefore begins by presenting all the available major indicators of change in income distribution and poverty. These are:

(a) Income shares of fractile groups of the population and Gini coefficients of the distribution of income in rural and urban Bangladesh for 1963/64, 1973/74, 1981/82 and 1983/84 (Tables 7.1 and 7.2);
(b) Proportions of households in different intensities of poverty (defined as different degrees of nutritional deficiency) in 1973/74, 1981/82, 1983/84 and 1985/86 (Table 7.4);

(c) Anthropometric measures of the nutritional status of children in 1975/76, 1981/82 and 1985/86 (Table 7.5); and

(d) Real wages of agricultural workers from 1949 to 1986/87 (Table 7.6) and of different categories of non-agricultural workers for the post-independence period (Table 7.7).

In addition to these measurements aimed at establishing changes in the overall income distribution and the incidence of poverty in rural and urban areas, the chapter also contains a discussion of some additional dimensions of income distribution, notably sexual inequality (Table 7.10) and the rural-urban disparity in the standard of living (Table 7.3).

The first two measurements are based on the data reported by the Household Expenditure Surveys (HES) carried out by the BBS. (The 1963/64 survey was called the Quarterly Survey of Current Economic Conditions and carried out by the Pakistan Central Statistical Office.) The main difficulty about drawing inferences from these indicators is that major methodological changes took place in the expenditure surveys beginning in 1983/84. Both the number of sampling areas and the sample size were reduced by about two-thirds, thereby sharply increasing the sampling error. Also the method of estimating food consumption was substantially changed. Prior to 1983/84, information on food consumption was collected by a single interview in which households were asked to recall consumption over the preceding seven days. Since 1983/84 information has been based on daily interviews over a thirty-day period. Moreover, the checklist of food items used since 1983/84 has been more comprehensive than the ones used before. The effect of the changed method of estimating food consumption has been to capture more items, especially items in the self-consumption category – a category that is far more important for poor households than for an average household. A comparison of the 1983/84 HES data with those from the 1981/82 HES shows that minor, non-cereal food items as a proportion of total food consumption is greater in the former than in the latter. This provides support for the above argument.

To summarize: in making inferences on the basis of the HES data, one should recognize that, compared to the earlier years, the surveys since 1983/84 have a much larger sampling error and in addition have a built-in bias which overstates food consumption generally and that of the poor as compared to the average household. It should also be noted that the greater sampling error is not offset by a reduced enumeration error in making estimates of income and expenditure since the method used to collect information on items of income and expenditure has not changed.

Table 7.1 Percentage shares of income accruing to fractions of population ranked in ascending order of income per household

	Rural				Urban				National			
	1963/64	1973/74	1981/82	1983/84	1963/64	1973/74	1981/82	1983/84	1963/64	1973/74	1981/82	1983/84
Quintile 1	8.5	7.2	7.1	7.3	6.4	6.8	6.2	6.9	7.7	7.0	6.6	9.0
Quintile 2	11.1	11.9	11.7	12.0	10.3	11.0	9.9	11.0	10.7	11.3	10.7	13.3
Quintile 3	16.6	15.1	16.2	16.2	13.4	16.0	14.3	15.4	14.6	15.1	15.2	18.0
Quintile 4	21.8	23.3	22.6	21.9	20.4	22.0	21.7	22.6	21.3	22.8	22.1	23.7
Quintile 5	42.0	42.5	42.4	42.7	49.5	45.2	47.9	44.2	45.7	44.8	45.3	36.1
Top 10%	27.0	26.4	26.7	27.8	33.0	29.2	32.1	27.7	31.0	28.4	29.5	21.8
Top 5%	17.2	16.0	16.8	19.0	21.0	18.6	20.9	17.2	20.4	16.4	18.9	14.0
Gini coefficient	0.33	0.36	0.36	0.35	0.41	0.38	0.41	0.37	0.36	0.36	0.39	0.35

Source: For 1963/64 to 1981/82, BBS, *Household Expenditure Survey 1981/82*, 1983/84 from unpublished BBS data.

Table 7.2 Percentage shares of income accruing to fractions of population ranked in ascending order of per capita income

	Rural			Urban		
	1973/74	1981/82	1983/84	1973/74	1981/82	1983/84
Bottom 40%	22.9	23.5	23.2	22.2	19.3	21.5
Top 10%	25.4	22.7	22.5	24.8	25.3	21.5
Top 5%	17.0	13.8	13.7	15.9	16.3	13.1

Source: Same as for Table 7.1.

Table 7.3 Rural–urban income disparity
Rural income per household as per cent of urban income per household

Year	Current prices	Constant prices of 1983/84
1963/64	71	—
1966/67	67	—
1968/69	63	—
1973/74	74	70
1976/77	68	68
1978/79	75	76
1981/82	54	54
1983/84	74	74

Note: Current price estimates are based on data shown in (Pakistan) Central Statistical Office, *Twenty Years of Pakistan* (quoting from the *Quarterly Surveys of Current Economic Conditions*) and BBS, *Household Expenditure Survey 1981/82* and unpublished HES for 1983/84. Constant price estimates are derived by deflating current price incomes by urban and rural cost of living indices of BBS adjusted for weights of major consumption groups which have been adopted from the 1983/84 HES.

Anthropometric measures of the nutritional status of children are based on Nutrition Surveys carried out by the Institute of Nutrition and Food Sciences (INFS) in 1975/76 and 1981/82 and the nutrition module of the 1985/86 HES. Once again, one must be careful in drawing inferences because of the vastly different sample sizes (respectively 430 and 510 children in the two Nutrition Surveys and 3 283 children in the HES) and differences in reference standards used in the two types of surveys[1].

Real wages of agricultural workers, estimated by the authors, is the longest time series of all the indicators of real incomes of the poor. In spite of the imperfections of measurement – especially those related to the cost-of-living index underlying it – this is one of the most important indicators of change in the condition of the poor. The time series of non-agricultural wages are shorter and subject to some degree of inconsistency among the alternative measurements made by the BBS.

THE EVIDENCE

Income shares of fractile groups and Gini coefficients

Table 7.1 shows the income shares of fractions of the population ranked in ascending order of income *per household* for 1963/64, 1973/74, 1981/82 and 1983/84. Table 7.2 shows the income shares of fractions of the population ranked in ascending order of household income *per capita* for 1973/74, 1981/82 and 1983/84. For 1963/64, the distribution of income based on the ranking of households according to per capita income is not available. The tables also show Gini coefficients of the respective distributions in different years.

According to the ranking by household income, there has been no significant change in the distribution of rural income over the two decades. According to the per capita income ranking, where the comparison is limited to a shorter period of a decade, inequality appears to have been slightly lower in the early 1980s than in the depressed year of 1973/74 which ended in a famine.

The distribution of income in urban areas has fluctuated considerably according to both types of measures. Inequality reached a peak in 1981/82. In 1983/84 inequality declined and the income shares of the highest groups fell.

Several observations should be made. First, inequality in the distribution of income is somewhat lower in Bangladesh than in most developing countries, including the neighboring countries of the sub-continent. Second, inequality in the distribution of per capita income is much lower than inequality in the distribution of household income. This is to be expected as the size of households is positively correlated with household income[2]. It is however highly probable that the distribution based on a per capita income ranking understates inequality because richer households have a higher proportion of "non-family" members (ranging from distant dependents to servants) who have a much lower living standard than the family members proper. In estimating per capita household income, no distinction is made between family and non-family members. Third, it is widely recognized that household surveys under-represent high income households. In Bangladesh the likelihood of capturing very high incomes is further reduced by the way such incomes have been obtained, as discussed in Chapter 4. One reason however for the increase in the income share of the top quintile of the urban population and consequently for the increase in urban inequality in 1981/82 is that in 1981 government wages and salaries were adjusted sharply upwards. Urban public employees are likely to belong to the higher income groups. The lower income shares estimated for the top urban fractile groups in 1983/84 should be discounted because of the drastically reduced sample size of the HES in that year and the consequent increase in the probability of missing out extreme values. As will be argued later, there is unmistakable, though not quantifiable, evidence of a much faster than average increase in the income of the rich in the post-independence period, especially in the urban areas.

An aspect of income distribution that often features in the development literature is that between urban and rural areas. Given the distributions of income in urban and rural areas, a reduction in income inequality between the two areas would reduce inequality in the overall income distribution.

Table 7.3 shows the disparity between rural and urban incomes *per household* from HES and comparable surveys in pre-independence years. The disparity in rural and urban incomes *per capita* would differ insignificantly from these estimates as household sizes in the two areas are roughly the same. Estimates at current prices are available for selected years over two decades between 1963/64 and 1983/84. Estimates at 1983/84 constant prices are available only for selected post-independence years.

The year 1981/82 is completely out of line. The urban-rural disparity in that year was much greater than in any other year. This is probably due to the discontinuous upward adjustment in government and public sector wages and salaries in 1981 to which reference has already been made. Since most government employees, including all the highly paid ones, are residents of urban areas, this led to an increase in disparity. If 1981/82 is excluded from consideration, it would appear that the rural-urban disparity in the post-independence period has been lower than in the pre-independence period. The reduction in disparity during the post-independence period has been greater at constant prices than at current prices due to a faster increase in the cost of living in urban areas than in rural areas.

It is useful to note, however, that HES is not always a reliable source

The incidence of poverty

Direct estimates of the nutrition status of the sample households are available from the HES for 1981/82 and 1983/84. For these measures the HES identifies three degrees of intensity of poverty. First, there are those families which have less than 1 600 kilocalories (kcalories) per person per day. Their members are subject to drastically lower than average life expectancy and (in children) permanently impaired mental and physical capacities. Second, there are those who have less than 1 800 kcalories. If they are forced to face these conditions for prolonged periods, the risk of infection, delayed recovery from illness and premature death increases and stunting occurs in children. Finally there are those who have less than 2 200 kcalories. Their deprivation, though unpleasant, would not entail serious health risk.

Direct estimates of nutrition status are not available for 1973/74 and 1985/86. (At the time of preparing the present study access to the 1985/86 HES was limited to the preliminary tabulation of data on only a few characteristics. These did not include direct estimates of the intake of kcalories.) Since direct estimates are available from only two surveys representing a very short period of time, indirect estimates of the proportion of people in poverty were made according to the following method. First, a bundle of food providing the specified level of nutrition (2 112 kcalories and 58 grams of protein per capita per day) has been identified, based on a compromise between cost and consumer preference, and its cost for the rural areas estimated. Next, the rural families with a per capita income below 1.25 times the cost of the specified food bundle have been classified as moderately poor (implying an assumption that 80 per cent of the threshold household's income is spent on food). Families with a per capita income below 85 per cent of the threshold income for moderate poverty are classified as extremely poor. Poverty thresholds over time have been adjusted by using the index of rural cost of living. Indirect estimates were made for the rural areas only.

The incidence of poverty estimated in this way is not comparable with poverty estimates based on the direct measurement of the population in nutrition deficient families[3]. The indirect measurements over time are particularly sensitive to the cost-of-living index. Since the cost of living index based on the prices implicit in the HES is not available, the likelihood of error is quite high. Moreover, the HES is not designed to measure incomes properly. Their preoccupation is with the estimation of the consumption of individual goods and services. The income estimate is almost a secondary by-product. It is quite risky to use the estimates as the basis for the indirect measurement of the incidence of poverty.

According to the direct measurements, all types of urban poverty increased (or remained unchanged) between 1981/82 and 1983/84 and all types of rural poverty declined over the same period (Table 7.4). It is, however, important to remember that the methodology of the HES was changed between 1981/82 and 1983/84 in such a way as to overstate food consumption in the latter year relative to the former year, especially for the low income groups in rural areas. One can not rule out the possibility that the improvement shown by the HES in the incidence of rural poverty between 1981/82 and 1983/84 was partly or wholly due to the bias arising out of the changed methodology.

Table 7.4 Incidence of poverty
Per cent of population

A. A comparison of direct estimates for 1981/82 and 1983/84			
		1981/82	1983/84
Rural			
Below 2 200 kcalories		74	62
Below 1 800 kcalories		47	37
Below 1 600 kcalories		31	25
Urban			
Below 2 200 kcalories		67	68
Below 1 800 kcalories		37	37
Below 1 600 kcalories		21	24
B. A comparison of indirect estimates for rural areas 1973/74–1985/86			
	1973/74	1981/82	1983/84	1985/85
Moderate and extreme poverty	56	70	39	35
Extreme poverty	43	57	24	21

Note: Data for Table A are from the Household Expenditure Survey (unpublished BBS sources for 1983/84). For Table B the background data on household per capita income distribution are from the HES (unpublished BBS sources for 1983/84 and 1985/86). The methodology of estimating the indirect measures has been described in the text.

The direct estimates from the HES of 1983/84 – a year in which food consumption of the poor appears to have been covered more comprehensively than before – show that a quarter of the population suffered from extreme nutritional deficiency. They received less than 1 600 kcalories per person per day. As discussed above, their life expectancy is drastically lower than average, and the children among them are exposed to a very high risk of permanent physical and mental damage.

The indirect estimates for the rural areas show that both moderate and extreme poverty (a) increased between 1973/74 and 1981/82; (b) declined sharply between 1981/82 and 1983/84; and (c) registered a further small decline between 1983/84 and 1985/86. Changes estimated by the HES between 1973/74 and 1981/82 and between 1983/84 and 1985/86 do not appear to be unacceptable. It is the change between 1981/82 and 1983/84 that appears to be far more dramatic than what one is led to expect on the basis of the other indicators (e.g., changes in real wages discussed below). As discussed above, the methodology of the HES was altered so drastically between 1981/82 and 1983/84 that the measurement of the change in the incidence of poverty based on a comparison of the HES of those years can not be considered reliable.

Once the improvement between 1981/82 and 1983/84 is largely discounted, there would be no basis to conclude from the indirect estimates based on the HES data that the incidence of rural poverty declined in the post-independence period: poverty increased quite sharply between 1973/74 and 1981/82 and declined moderately between 1983/84 and 1985/86. If there was no more than a moderate decline between 1981/82 and 1983/84 then the incidence of rural poverty between 1973/74 and 1985/86 could not have changed significantly. This would be a remarkable finding since 1973/74 was a depressed year, which led to a severe famine.

A final point about the indirect measures is that they are clearly inconsistent with the direct measures. The indirect measures show that the extreme poor – those below the level of income that would enable them to have 1 800 kcalories per person per day – were approximately 24 per cent of the rural population in 1983/84. The direct measure of the HES shows that 37 per cent of the rural population in that year had less than 1 800 kcalories per capita per day.

This may be the place to deal with the HES finding that nutritional inadequacy is not always due to low income. That a proportion of the very rich households would consume less than 2 200 kcalories per person per day is perhaps not so surprising; their calorie requirements are less than average due to the low incidence of physical labor. But a small proportion of them reportedly consume less than 1 600 kcalories per capita per day[4]. One can not rule out the possibility of error as the main explanation of this phenomenon since the ability of these surveys to enumerate income accurately is questionable. Apart from this, it is possible that the phenomenon reflects a combination of lower calorie requirement, a larger share of food eaten outside the home (which appears not to be caught by the HES enumeration of household consumption of food) and possible bi-modality of consumption between "members proper" and "distant dependents" in the rich households. Whatever the explanation behind this, the presence of the phenomenon clearly renders invalid any comparison of indirect estimates of nutritional inadequacy, of which the inadequacy of income is the sole determinant, with the direct estimates.

Anthropometric data on the nutritional status of children

In rural Bangladesh the incidence of mild malnutrition increased between 1975/76 and 1981/82 while that of moderate and severe malnutrition declined according to the anthropometric data from the sources cited above (Table 7.5). Between 1981/82 and 1985/86 mild and moderate malnutrition increased while severe malnutrition declined further. Over the decade the incidence of mild malnutrition nearly doubled, moderate malnutrition remained unchanged and severe malnutrition sharply declined. As noted before, differences in sample sizes and methodologies between the 1975/76 and 1981/82 Nutrition Surveys on the one hand, and the 1985/86 Survey on the other, raise serious questions concerning the comparability of these measurements over time.

Information on the nutritional status of children in urban areas is available only for the year 1985/86. While the incidence of mild malnutrition is higher for urban children (42.2 per cent) than for rural children, moderate and severe malnutrition among them (respectively 44.2 per cent and 6.0 per cent) are lower.

Real wages of agricultural laborers

The importance of real wages of agricultural laborers as an indicator of income distribution and poverty in rural Bangladesh derives from: (a) wages being a higher proportion of income of the poorer households; and (b) the increase over time in the proportion of rural households

Table 7.5 Nutritional status of rural children
Per cent of rural children suffering from malnutrition

	1975/76	1981/82	1985/86
Mild malnutrition	17.7	28.8	33.1
Moderate malnutrition	53.0	46.1	52.0
Severe malnutrition	25.8	15.1	9.6

Note: 1975/76 and 1981/82 data from INFS Nutrition Surveys and 1985/86 data from BBS, Nutrition Status Module of the 1985/86 HES. Severe malnutrition is defined as less than 60 per cent of reference median weight-for-age. Moderate malnutrition is at least 60 per cent but less than 75 per cent of reference median weight-for-age. Mild malnutrition is at least 75 per cent but less than 90 per cent of reference median weight-for-age. INFS surveys used samples of respectively 430 and 510 children of age up to five years. The BBS survey used a sample of 1 872 children between six months and six years.

dependent on wages as the main source of income. According to the 1973/74 HES, the bottom 37 per cent of the rural households, ranked according to household income, derived 31 per cent of their income from wages. According to the 1978/79 HES, wages accounted for 44 per cent of the income of the bottom 55 per cent of rural households. In the 1960s about a quarter of those who reported cultivation as their principal occupation were completely or substantially dependent on wages as a source of income; by 1979, 37 per cent of those employed in farming activities were reported to be day laborers or other types of wage earners[5].

Table 7.6 shows the course of real wages of agricultural laborers and some related indicators over nearly four decades. Two separate indices of real wages are presented: wages at 1973/74 purchasing power (money wages deflated by the index of the cost of living of agricultural workers with 1973/74 as the base); and the coarse rice equivalent of wages (money wages deflated by the price per kg of coarse rice). The two indices generally move in step; but in periods of pronounced change the second index moves more sharply because rice prices generally are more volatile than average during such periods. The discussion of trends in real wages in this section is based on the first measure unless specifically stated otherwise. Some of the major facts may be summarized:

(a) Over the entire period between 1949 and 1987/88, the estimated trend rate of decline in real wages is a statistically highly significant −1.7 per cent per year[6].

(b) There have been periodic fluctuations around this long-term declining trend. Thus, for example, there was an upward "trend" sustained over a decade from the mid-1950s to the mid-1960s. This was followed by a sharper than average declining trend for over a decade starting in the mid-1960s. In recent years some increase in real wages was observed between 1982/83 and 1985/86, much of it in the latter year.

(c) Average real wages in the five years ending in 1987/88 were about 25 per cent lower than in the second half of the 1960s. Between the same two periods, per capita real consumption in the country as a whole increased substantially and consumption in the rural sector probably increased even more. Between the depressed half decade immediately after independence and the half decade ending in 1987/88, real wages recovered by only about 9 per cent. Per capita income between the two periods increased by nearly a fifth.

Real wages in non-agricultural sectors

Table 7.7 shows indices of real wages in some non-agricultural activities: manufacturing industries as a whole, jute textiles (the largest manufacturing industry), and unskilled construction workers in three industrial centers[7]. Compared to 1969/70, real wages in manufacturing dropped by more than a third immediately after independence. Since then real wages have crept upwards but they have not succeeded so far in regaining the pre-independence level. Since the late 1970s, there has been no trend in the movement of real wages in manufacturing industries.

For the wages of unskilled construction workers no estimate is available for the pre-independence period. If one assumes – as would appear to be justified – that there was a decline between the immediate pre-independence and post-independence periods of the same order of magnitude as in manufacturing, then the pattern in the movement in real wages of construction workers would be about the same as that for workers in manufacturing industries.

SOME CONCLUSIONS BASED ON AN INTERPRETATION OF THE EVIDENCE

The evidence presented above is not always unambiguous. It is however possible to draw some broad conclusions about the direction of change

Table 7.6 Wage rates of male agricultural workers

Year	Money wages Taka per person per day	Coarse rice equivalent of money wages (kg)	Real wages 1972/74 purchasing power	Year	Money wages Taka per person per day	Coarse rice equivalent of money wages (kg)	Real wages 1973/74 purchasing power
1949	1.92	n.a.	11.29	1971/72	3.38	2.56	7.43
1950	1.62	3.24	10.17	1972/73	4.72	2.26	6.71
1951	1.56	3.06	9.55	1973/74	6.69	2.36	6.69
1952	1.52	2.71	9.42	1974/75	9.05	1.57	5.33
1953	1.38	2.71	8.19	1975/76	8.82	2.43	7.09
1955	1.32	3.22	9.21	1976/77	8.93	2.63	7.32
1957	1.70	2.46	9.52	1977/78	9.44	2.26	6.41
1958	1.85	2.64	9.21	1978/79	10.88	2.41	6.43
1959	1.85	2.61	9.27	1979/80	12.46	2.07	6.19
1960	1.95	2.83	9.83	1980/81	13.97	2.85	6.54
1961	2.18	3.16	10.88	1981/82	15.48	2.33	5.92
1962	2.25	2.96	10.55	1982/83	17.05	2.35	6.13
1963	2.41	3.17	11.28	1983/84	19.58	2.45	6.28
1964	2.65	3.63	12.72	1984/85	24.54	2.79	6.95
1965	2.34	2.93	10.62	1985/86	29.83	3.51	8.09
1966	2.40	2.38	9.10	1986/87	32.56	3.24	7.70
1967	2.60	2.39	9.19	1987/88	32.30	—	7.08
1968	2.75	2.64	9.78				
1969/70	2.96	2.82	9.40				
1970/71	3.13	3.16	9.42				

Note: Money wages for the period before 1969/70 from Khan's data collected from government gazettes and reported in his paper in ILO, *Poverty and Landlessness in Rural Asia*, Geneva, 1977; since 1969/70, BBS has been publishing wage data in its *Monthly Statistical Bulletins*. Cost-of-living index (not shown in the above table) up to 1977/78 from Khan's index in Khan and Lee, (eds) *Poverty in Rural Asia*, ILO/ARTEP, Bangkok, 1984; since 1978/70, the BBS cost-of-living index in rural areas has been used. Price of coarse rice (not shown) from (Pakistan) CSO, *Twenty Five Years of Pakistan* for pre-independence years and from BBS, *Monthly Statistical Bulletins* for post-independence years (for a few years around independence, unpublished data from the BBS have been used.

Table 7.7 Real wage indices in selected non-agricultural sectors

Year	All manu-facturing	Jute textiles	Unskilled construction workers Narayanganj	Chittagong	Khulna
1969/70	100	100	n.a.	n.a.	n.a.
1973/74	66	66	n.a.	n.a.	n.a.
1974/75	46	48	n.a.	n.a.	n.a.
1975/76	58	59	100	100	100
1976/77	63	59	108	103	96
1977/78	75	79	114	106	100
1978/79	81	84	133	127	122
1979/80	82	87	117	119	97
1980/81	85	90	138	143	126
1981/82	77	78	116	121	110
1982/83	83	75	118	131	98
1983/84	81	76	125	103	107
1984/85	n.a.	69	126	113	96
1985/86	n.a.	86	135	129	105

Source: For manufacturing industries, real wage rates for all employees from the BBS, *Statistical Yearbook* (SYB), 1983/84, for the years up to 1976/77; from SYB, 1986 for the years 1977/78 to 1983/84 (note that the estimates shown in the two yearbooks for the years 1977/78 and 1978/79 differ). For 1985/86, indices for unskilled workers and jute textiles are calculated from the information in *Monthly Statistical Bulletin*, August 1986, and deflated by the Bangladesh average of the BBS cost-of-living index for working class (ibid.) For construction workers, nominal wages (from various issues of the SYB and *Monthly Statistical Bulletins*) deflated by the BBS cost-of-living index for working class of the respective areas.

in the distribution of income and the incidence of poverty with varying degrees of confidence.

Compared to the immediate pre-independence period, the distribution of income in the early 1980s is more unequal in both rural and urban areas. The strongest evidence for this is the clearly established fact that real wages – the major determinant of the incomes of the poorer classes – are far lower today than they were twenty-five years ago. Compared to the early years after independence, the distribution of income in the rural areas in the early 1980s is again worse, the main evidence being the slower recovery in real wages than in average income and consumption. Income distribution data from the HES do not reflect this deterioration. This is almost certainly because of the inability of such surveys to measure income accurately, and the reason for this in turn is that these surveys – focusing on specific types of expenditure – are not primarily designed to measure total income. Moreover, the large reduction in the size of the HES sample in recent years has increased the probability of missing out the very rich and the very poor in addition to rendering intertemporal comparisons of their results subject to increasing sampling error with the passage of time.

In urban areas real wages in the early 1980s were lower than in the pre-independence period though recovery in urban wages since the early years after independence was faster than in rural wages. Corresponding increases in the incomes of the richer urban groups, though impossible to quantify, have clearly been greater. That the real consumption and income of the urban rich have increased at an unprecedented rate in the post-independence period is amply demonstrated by the phenomenal increase in the supply of luxury goods and services. Luxury housing (and sky-rocketing prices of urban land in high-income residential areas), foreign travel, privately financed overseas education of children, durable consumer goods, luxury consumer electronics, shops retailing precious jewelry and personal service outlets catering to the rich are the things that have expanded to a degree that would indicate an extraordinarily rapid increase in the income of the rich. The extent of increase in the volume of these goods and services can not be quantified; but the phenomenon is too obvious to leave any observer in doubt as to the reality.

Comparable measurements of the incidence of poverty, defined as income too low to permit adequate nutrition, are not available for the pre-independence period. It is however likely that between that period and the early 1980s, poverty did increase. Between these periods the average levels of grain consumption and nutrition declined. For example, the per capita daily energy intake in the 1960s was about 2 200 kcalories while estimates for recent years have fluctuated around 2 000 kcalories. Given the fall in the real income of the poor and a worsening of the distribution of income, it appears virtually certain that a higher proportion of the people, at the lower end of the income scale, have come to be afflicted with poverty.

For the post-independence period the HES data do not provide any convincing evidence of improvement in the incidence of rural poverty. There is no serious problem with its finding that the incidence of poverty increased sharply between 1973/74 and 1981/82 and decreased moderately between 1983/84 and 1985/86. The reported decline in the incidence of rural poverty between 1981/82 and 1983/84 can not however be trusted in view of the changes in the HES methodology discussed earlier. Anthropometric data on the nutritional status of children – themselves subject to uncertainties due to changes in methods between surveys – suggest an increased incidence of mild poverty and unchanged incidence of moderate poverty in the decade up to the mid-1980s. Only the severest kind of poverty appears to have declined according to this data.

The incidence of urban poverty is less easy to document because there are fewer indicators available, but urban poverty appears to have followed the same course in the post-independence period.

Two issues associated with the recovery in real wages in agriculture since 1982/83 deserve comment. The first concerns the question whether the improvement can be taken as indicative of a reversal of the long-term downward trend. The second issue is the explanation for the sharp increase in real wages in 1985/86, partly reversed in the following two years.

On the first point it would be wise to reserve one's judgement. There have been other periods of improvement and at present improvement has not been sustained as long as some of the earlier ones (e.g., mid-1950s to mid-1960s). In 1985/86 real wages in agriculture increased by 16 per cent compared to the previous year. Although real wages at constant purchasing power were still less than two-thirds of the peak level in the mid-1960s, the coarse rice equivalent of wages came close to the all-time peak since 1949. These increases are puzzling given the decline in 1985/86 in aggregate grain output and in the terms of trade for agriculture. Grain yield per unit of land and per capita consumption of rice and foodgrains also declined. Nevertheless, the price of coarse rice fell absolutely, thereby leading to a sharper increase in the coarse rice equivalent of wages than in the constant purchasing power value measure of real wages. These movements imply a fall in demand for coarse rice, a phenomenon inconsistent with the rise in the real income of the poor. To try to explain this by arguing that the (wage-earning) poor were so much better off that they shifted to better quality rice is not convincing. The price of medium quality rice increased modestly, but per capita consumption of rice as a whole and of all cereals fell.

While much of the puzzle must remain unresolved given the current state of information, there are at least two clear explanations for the increased demand for agricultural labor in 1985/86. The first is the very sharp increase in the size of the Food-For-Work (FFW) program. The amount of grain available for the program reached an all time peak of 515,000 tons (13 per cent higher than the previous year) and the cash allocation for the program was an unprecedented Tk 691 million (three and a half times the previous peak)[8]. As a result, employment under this program probably accounted for as much as 13 per cent of total wage employment (as compared to less than 10 per cent in each of the previous two years). The second source of increased demand for labor was the shift in cropped area in favor of jute. In the preceeding year the growers' price of jute reached a record high level. This led to a 37 per cent increase in jute acreage in 1985/86, at the cost of reduced acreage of (rain-fed) *aus* rice and other *aus* season crops. An acre of jute employs more than twice as much labor than an acre of *aus* rice (in absolute terms 43 person days more). The shift from rice to jute led to a 5-6 per cent increase in labor use; together with the effect of the shift from other crops to jute, the total increase in labor demand in the *aus* season in 1985/86 may have been of the order of 7-8 per cent[9]. It appears that the expectation of high jute prices led to a large increase in jute area. This, along with the increased size of the FFW program, resulted in a much increased demand for labor and higher real wages than would otherwise have occurred, especially in the *aus* season. In the event, the expectation of a high jute price was not fulfilled: there was a drastic decline in jute prices and in agriculture's terms of trade, causing a decline in the non-wage components of incomes of rural families, including the poor. This may have contributed to the reduction in demand for foodgrains and to a fall in the price of coarse rice. Had the original price expectations of farmers been realized, prices (including that of rice) would have been higher and ex-post real wages lower. But in fact ex-post real wages were much higher than anticipated by farmers and this could not be sustained. In 1986/87 and 1987/88 real wages declined by 5 per cent and 8 per cent respectively.

FACTORS BEHIND INEQUALITY AND POVERTY

Changes in the distribution of income and the incidence of poverty derive both from the operation of the forces inherent in the structure of the economy and society and from government policies tending to moderate or aggravate those forces. In the urban areas of Bangladesh government policies and actions have been the more important determinant of the distribution of income and the incidence of poverty. The effect of government policies has been to aggravate (i.e., make more unequal) the outcome that might have resulted from a freer operation of economic forces. It should be emphasized, however, that it is not government intervention *per se* but the *nature* of intervention that produced such an outcome.

In the rural areas structural economic forces were the major determinants of income distribution and poverty. Government policies (unless they are broadly defined to include the absence of action to alter the structure of the economy and society) played a secondary role. Some government policies exerted a moderating effect while others had an aggravating effect; it is hard to tell which effect was dominant on balance.

In the urban areas of Bangladesh the main determinant of the distribution of income at the top end of the spectrum was the strategy of accumulation as described in Chapter 4. The strategy succeeded in quickly enriching a thin layer of the society at the top of the pyramid at an unpredented rate without simultaneously creating a system of incentives to channel their resources into productive investment. Concessions were given to organized labor in the form of expanded employment at reduced intensity and productivity. Public sector wage rates were maintained at a higher level than those in the private sector, but not to the extent of preventing a fall in the real wage rate. Welfare measures targetted to benefit the poor were very limited. The subsidy on food distribution through statutory rationing – which was allowed to decline in recent years – had at best an uncertain effect on income distribution. Many and perhaps most of its benefits went to the public sector employees and the urban middle class. The expansion of employment in public administration and defense similarly benefitted the non-poor more than the poor. Allocation of public expenditure in education was highly inequitable. Resources were mostly channelled into higher education while primary education stagnated. The opportunity for entry into higher education became more unequal.

In rural areas the most noticeable feature of the strategy of every successive government was inaction on land reform. Government policies have instead emphasized the distribution of inputs – including those required for the adoption of modern technology – at a heavy subsidy. Most of the benefits of the subsidies on irrigation equipment accrued to the rich farmers while the benefits of the subsidy on fertilizer appears to have been more widely distributed. In recent years subsidies on fertilizer have been drastically reduced while the subsidies on irrigation equipment have been retained. Thus the policies for greater allocative efficiency have been adopted selectively, accepting those that appear to take away benefits that are widely distributed while rejecting those that would take away benefits from the rich. In recent years the richer farmers have emerged as the major suppliers of water to the smaller farmers at a very high price, often equivalent to about a quarter of the value of the crop.

Income Distribution and Poverty

Some government action, however, has helped to moderate the forces of inequality in rural Bangladesh. Reference has already been made to one of them in Chapter 4, namely, reducing discrimination against jute. This helped to improve the terms of trade for rural areas and reduce rural/urban inequality. This probably also helped to reduce rural income inequality since increased jute acreage results in increased demand for labor. In addition, jute is grown and marketed by all size groups of farmers. The policy of reducing discrimination against jute has however not been supported by a policy of stabilizing its price, which continues to be subject to violent fluctuations.

A second important program that helped increase employment and the income of the poor was the Food-For-Work program. Employment under this program increased from 56 million person days in 1975/76 to 107 million person days in 1983/84 and 1984/85. These schemes have accounted for approximately 3 per cent of all person days of rural employment and close to 10 per cent of rural wage employment. In the absence of the FFW program, real wages in agriculture and other rural activities would have fallen even more over the years and recovered less in some of the recent years.

A third important program is government support in the provision of credit specially targetted to reach the poor. The most outstanding program is the Grameen Bank (Rural Bank) which provides credit to the landless and near-landless, who have no collateral, for non-crop production activities. The program has so far achieved a near 100 per cent rate of recovery and significantly contributed to the well-being of the recipients[10]. However, in the decade since its creation the Bank has covered only 6 per cent of the villages in Bangladesh and has made a relatively small contribution compared to the resources needed by the poor. The volume of credit disbursed through this program is still small in comparison with the total credit made available to the agricultural sector. The cost of credit, at a 16 per cent rate of interest (neglecting additional hidden costs arising from a compulsory contribution to a group fund), is high, but perhaps necessary to prevent these funds from falling into the hands of the rich who have access to cheaper sources of credit.

A program of feeding the disadvantaged groups (DGF) has been in operation for some years. The purpose of the program is to supplement the food consumption of rural mothers and children who suffer from malnutrition. In 1985/86 the program distributed a total of 144 000 tons of grain. At 50 per cent of requirements, this amount would have provided supplementary nutrition to about 1.5 million mothers and children – approximately 7.5 per cent of the rural population who, according to the estimates of the 1983/84 HES, were consuming less than 1 600 kcalories of energy per day. Nothing is however known about how the program has operated and who the program has benefited.

Against this package of government policies – the sum total of whose effects on income distribution and poverty is somewhat uncertain – must be juxtaposed the following long-term forces tending to increase inequality and aggravate poverty:

(a) The supply of labor in agriculture has increased rapidly due to demographic factors and the very slow growth of non-agricultural employment.

(b) The land frontier has not expanded at all and the increase in cropping intensity has been modest because of inadequate investment in irrigation and water management. The land-man ratio declined by 50 per cent in the three decades between 1951 and 1981. The worsening land-labor ratio in agriculture has not been accompanied by a significant improvement in the distribution of landownership (see Table 7.8)[11]. Increased scarcity of land relative to labor has contributed to a rise in the share of net output accruing to the owners of land. The continued inequality in the distribution of landownership thus ensured an unequal distribution of an increasing share of net output. The continued concentration of landownership, in the face of a declining land/labor ratio, has also meant an increased proletarianization in agriculture, further expanding the supply of wage labor (Table 7.9).

(c) Within agriculture the demand for labor has increased at a very slow rate. Employment per unit of land has remained lower than what is feasible and desirable because of the prevalence of inappropiate institutions and the absence of appropiate technological advances[12]. The spread of high yielding varieties has probably contributed to some increase in demand for labor, but not enough to counter the negative factors listed above, nor as much as would have been possible with appropriate policies. Unemployed person-days, as a proportion of the total available person-days of agricultural labor, is estimated to have increased from 20 per cent in 1974 to 23 per cent in 1983/84 (Table 7.9).

Income Distribution and Poverty

Table 7.8 Distribution of rural landownership 1977, 1978 and 1983/84

A. Size distribution in 1978 and 1983/84

Size group (acres)	1978 Number of households (thousand)	1978 Per cent of households	1983/84 Number of households (thousand)	1983/84 Per cent of households
Nil	1 979	15.4	1 198	8.7
0.01– 0.49	4 286	33.3	5 201	37.6
0.50– 0.99	1 516	11.8	1 660	12.0
1.00– 2.49	2 660	20.7	2 979	21.6
2.50– 4.99	1 436	11.1	1 598	11.6
5.00– 7.49	501	3.9	650	4.7
7.50–14.99	374	2.9	415	3.0
15.00–24.99	84	0.7	89	0.6
25.00 and above	30	0.2	28	0.2
Total	12 866	100.0	13 818	100.0
Gini coefficient		0.69		0.67

B. Shares of land (per cent) owned by fractile groups of households

Fractile Groups	1977	1983/84
Bottom 20 per cent	2.7	3.7
Second quintile	5.7	6.8
Third quintile	10.8	11.5
Fourth quintile	18.6	20.5
Ninth decile	16.8	17.5
Top decile	45.4	40.1

Note: 1977 and 1978 data are from the Land Occupancy Surveys of the BBS covering 137 sample villages from each of which 30 households were selected for enumeration. 1983/84 data are from the Agricultural Census. The latter report attributes the large decline in the number of households with no land between 1978 and 1983/84 to the fact that "LOS was a very small sample (0.3%) and therefore contains a high sampling error". Others have tried to attribute it to the migration of landless households out of the rural areas. It is worth noting that the proportion of landless households varies between 11 per cent in 1977 (Table 7.9) and 15 per cent in 1978 according to the LOS. Such a large variation in one year lends support to the possibility of high sampling error in the LOS.

Table 7.9 Landless agricultural laborers and related data

Year	Landless agricultural labor		Per cent of landless rural households	Unemployment & underemployment as % of person days of agricultural workers
	Million	Per cent of total		
1951	1.51	14.3	—	—
1961	2.47	17.5	—	—
1963/64	2.71	17.8	—	—
1964/65	2.75	17.5	—	—
1966	—	—	6.97	—
1967/68	3.40	19.8	—	—
1974	—	—	—	20.4
1977	4.54	26.1	11.07	—
1978/79	—	—	7.05	—
1981	5.11	31.2	—	—
1983/84	5.11	30.6	8.70	23.1

Note: The derivation of the data on landless agricultural workers up to 1977 is explained in Ghai, Khan, Lee & Radwan, (eds) *Agrarian Systems and Rural Development,* p. 149, Macmillan, 1979, London. For 1981, the estimate is from BBS, *Socio-Economic Indicators of Bangladesh,* July 1986. For 1983/84 agricultural laborers are those who are described by the LFS as day laborers among the agricultural workers in rural areas. Data on landless rural families are from the rural credit survey for 1986, LOS for 1977, HES for 1978/79 and agricultural census for 1983/84. Unemployment and underemployment estimates are from BBS, *Socio-Economic Indicators of Bangladesh,* July 1986. Since definitions differ from one source to another, small changes can not be considered significant; strong trends over time do not appear to be affected, however.

DISCRIMINATION AGAINST WOMEN

According to the 1983/84 Labor Force Survey (LFS) only 8 per cent of the women of working age were in the labor force while 75 per cent were reported to be housewives or to be engaged in household work. (The remaining 17 per cent were students, disabled or otherwise inactive.) Numerous micro studies have established that in reality "household work" includes a great deal of unpaid economic work. The total hours of economic and household work done by women usually is far in excess of all normal standards. It is ironical that in spite of long hours of unpleasant work, very few women are counted by the LFS and other surveys as members of the labor force. It seems that in order to qualify as members of the labor force, women need to appear to be engaged in market-oriented activities, e.g., as wage earners. Clearly women in Bangladesh have much less access to paid employment than men. This probably constitutes the most significant discrimination to which women are subject.

When they have access to paid employment, women are frequently paid less than their male counterparts (Table 7.10). According to the 1983/84 LFS a female worker in agriculture in that year was paid 48 per cent of the wage paid to a male agricultural worker. This difference is so large that it is impossible to account for it by such things as differences in the nature or intensity of work done by men and women. A number of micro studies confirm that agricultural wages are lower for women than for men[13]. An exception to this is employment in tea gardens, where the differential – still positive in favor of men – is very small.

In recent years female wage employment has expanded substantially in certain manufacturing activities. The most notable among them is the export-oriented garment industry. A comparison of wages in this industry with the average industrial wage is difficult because of the lack of reliable information. It is however widely known that the female workers in the garment industry are subject to very harsh working conditions and long hours, conditions far worse than in an average urban industry.

According to the 1975/76 Nutrition Survey female children in most age groups received a lower proportion of calorie requirements than male children of the corresponding age group. The only exceptions are the lowest age group (1-3 years) and the highest age group (13-15). For the latter the result is probably due to an underestimation of the energy requirement of girls (2 226 kcalories) as compared to boys (2 755 kcalories). The 1985/86 HES shows that the incidence of stunting and wasting are greater for female children than for male children in both rural and urban areas.

While women are distinctly worse off than men as members of labor force and as consumers, there appears to have been some improvement in three areas. The first is life expectancy. In the 1960s, life expectancy of a man was 49.2 years as compared to 46.9 years for women. During 1982-84 life expectancy for men and women became roughly the same, although the situation was different in the rural as compared to the urban areas. That is, in the urban areas women lived nearly two years longer on average than men, whereas in the rural areas women lived 0.6 years less than men. In general, Bangladesh appears no longer to

Table 7.10 Selected indicators of sexual inequality

A. Wage rate		
Female wage rate in agriculture as per cent of male wage rate (1983/84)		48
Female wage rate in tea garden as per cent of male wage rate (1973/74–1983/84) average		
	Sylhet	98
	Chittagong	92

B. Consumption of calories as per cent of requirement (1975/76)

Age-group (year)	Male	Female
1– 3	42.3	50.4
4– 6	66.2	62.1
7– 9	69.5	67.9
10–12	76.5	75.7
13–15	81.5	86.3

C. Nutritional status (1985/86): per cent of children six months to six years

		Male	Female
Stunted (less than 90% of median height for age:	Urban	42.4	46.1
	Rural	56.3	59.1
Wasted (less than 80% of median weight-for-height	Urban	6.7	7.1
	Rural	6.8	9.8

D. Life expectancy in years: 1982-84 average

	Male	Female
Urban	59.6	61.5
Rural	54.0	53.4

Source: A: BBS, *Socio-Economic Indicators of Bangladesh,* July 1986, pages 94, 99. B: Nutrition Survey of 1975/76. Requirements for the two sexes are same until age 9 and higher for the male for the higher age groups, by 11 per cent for age 10–12 and by 24 per cent for age 13–15. C: the Nutrition Status Module of the 1985/86 HES. D: BBS, *Statistical yearbook,* 1986.

conform to the South Asian pattern of lower life expectancy for women than for men. This pattern persists in several neighboring countries, including India, Pakistan and Nepal. It should perhaps be added, by way of a qualification, that the data on life expectancy are not very reliable (see Chapter 6).

A comparison of the population censuses shows that between 1974 and 1981 the total literacy rate (per cent of population age 5 years or more who are literate) for men declined (from 32.9 per cent to 31.0 per cent) while that for women improved slighty (from 14.8 per cent to 16.0 per cent). Between those dates the adult literacy rate for women grew relatively faster (from 13.2 per cent to 18.0 per cent) than for men (from 37.2 per cent to 39.7 per cent)[14]. As discussed in Chapter 6, primary school enrollment for women also increased faster than for men.

Finally, an average woman today can expect under five live births during her entire reproductive life as compared to well over six in the 1960s. This is due largely to the increased mean age at marriage, from under 15 years in the 1960s to about 18 years in the mid-1980s[15].

Notes and References

1. For details of these differences see, BBS, *Report of the Child Nutrition Status Module, HES 1985/86,* Dhaka, January 1987.
2. Note however that household size and per capita income are not positively correlated. Per capita income distribution is not just a compressed version of the household income distribution. The ranking of individual households in the two distributions is very different. Of the two criteria used for ranking, per capita income would appear to be better. It does not however take into account economies of scale in consumption and to that extent fails to provide an ideal ranking of well-being. For example, a household with Tk 500 of income and two members almost certainly has a lower standard of living than a household with an income of Tk 2,450 and ten members although the former has a higher per capita income. Per capita income also fails to reflect differences in consumption requirements which can arise from differences in the age distribution among members of households and other factors.
3. One set of reasons for such a discrepancy arises from the methodology of indirect measurement which is based on the cost of a single, inter-temporally and cross-sectionally invariant bundle of food items (whereas in reality it would be possible to attain a given level of kcalories by varying the composition of consumption, often trading quality for quantity) and numerous interpolations involving approximations and errors. Another reason is that though income is the overwhelmingly important determinant of the level of nutrition, it is not the sole determinant. As discussed later, the HES shows that calorie "deficiency" is also characteristic of a proportion of high income households. The indirect method does not allow for this possibility. The bundle of goods used in estimating the poverty threshold and the total calories that it represents are arbitrary. It is impossible to resolve the question of what the appropriate level of energy requirement is and how it should be supplied. The present exercise, which is largely illustrative, did not appear to be the place for getting into these controversies.

4. Thus in 1981/82 90 per cent of the households in the poorest decile of the population (with a per capita income below Tk 100 per month) consumed less than 1 600 kcalories per capita per day while 2.3 per cent of the households belonging to the richest 5 per cent of the population (with a per capita income above Tk 500 per month) suffered from a similar calorie deficiency.
5. See A.R. Khan and Eddy Lee (eds), *Poverty in Rural Asia,* ILO/ARTEP, 1984, pp. 185-6.
6. The regression equation is
   Log $W = 2.44 - 0.017T$; R-squared $= 0.55$
   where W = real wage and T = time ($=1$ for 1949, 2 for 1950, ... 38.5 for 1986/87). The coefficient of T is significant at the one per cent level. Note that as an explanation of change in W over time, the above trend equation is under-specified. For more completely specified models, trying to explain the causes of wage movements, see, A.R. Khan and Eddy Lee (eds), *op. cit.,* pp. 185-204 and James Boyce and Martin Ravallion, *Inter-sectoral Terms of Trade and the Dynamics of Wage Determination in Rural Bangladesh,* University of Massachusetts, Amherst, October 1987 (Draft).
7. BBS publishes two sets of manufacturing industry wages. The one that provides a detailed classification of industries has been used. The other series, based on average industrial wages in four selected centers, has a time path that is substantially different from the one used here.
8. See, Government of Bangladesh, Ministry of Finance, *Bangladesh Economic Survey, 1986/87,* Dhaka, June 1987 (in Bengali), p. 528.
9. The increase in money wages was highest (61 per cent) in Mymensingh, the district in which the *increase* in jute acreage was the greatest as a per cent of net sown area (11 per cent). Three other districts – Rangpur, Jessore and Faridpur – produce more jute than does Mymensingh. In Jessore and Faridpur wage increases were respectively 24 per cent and 39 per cent, but in Rangpur only 9 per cent.
10. See Mahabub Hossain, *Credit for the Rural Poor: The Grameen Bank in Bangladesh,* The Bangladesh Institute of Development Studies Research Monograph No. 4, Dhaka, 1984.
11. There is a strong possibility that the data in Table 7.8 understate the degree of inequality. The reported "improvement" in the distribution between 1977 and 1983/84 must be judged in the light of the fact that the 1977 estimates are based on a very small sample of 30 households each in 137 sample villages (thereby having a large sampling error) whereas the 1983/84 estimates are based on a much more comprehensive agricultural census. The point to note is that inequality in the distribution of landownership is very high even in the latter year.
12. See A.R. Khan and Eddy Lee, *The Expansion of Productive Employment in Agriculture: The Relevance of the East Asian Experience for Developing Asian Countries,* ILO/ARTEP Occasional Paper, 1981, for some discussion of these factors.
13. See A.R. Khan, R. Islam and M. Huq, *Employment, Income and the Mobilization of Local Resources: A Study of Two Bangladesh Villages,* ILO/ARTEP, 1980, pp. 30-32.

14. These data are from BBS, *Socio-Economic Indicators of Bangladesh,* July 1986, p. 140. As discussed in Chapter 6, the two censuses used somewhat different standards of literacy, and it is believed that the use of a uniform standard would have shown a slightly less dismal picture.
15. Data on total fertility and mean age at marriage are from BBS, *Statistical Yearbook,* 1986, pp. 105 and 125.

8 Conclusions

In his latest book, the editor of this series of studies on economic development of and choices before the developing countries, Keith Griffin, identifies six strategies of economic development: Monetarist, Open Economy, Industrialization, Green Revolution, Redistributive, and Socialist[1]. A useful way to begin this concluding chapter is to ask how the Bangladesh experience fits into this classification of development strategies. Griffin notes that the strategies identified by him are "ideal types" which should be "viewed as points along a multi-dimensional spectrum". According to him no country "will in practice have followed a particular strategy consistently, without qualification, dilution or amendment." In most cases a country's strategy would in retrospect be seen to have constituted an identifiable approach to the problems of development, often incorporating elements from more than one of the ideal types.

A recurrent theme of the present study is that one of the major weaknesses of development policy in Bangladesh has arisen from the fact that successive governments have lacked the stability and authority needed to pursue economic development as the main goal of national policy. Though created as a consequence of massive popular opposition to an alien military rule, Bangladesh was deprived of political democracy soon after independence. Successive governments took power by force, not popular consent. To stay in power they created fragile alliances held together by distributing privileges and granting access to the process of financial accumulation as described in Chapter 4. The country has lacked an essential condition for a successful development strategy under any system, namely, a stable government which defines the rules of the game, enforces them with authority and then creates a coalition of entrepreneurial classes.

This does not mean that the governments had no economic strategy. Their actions did amount to a development strategy although policies sometimes lacked coherence because of the government's need to foster multitudes of alliances and to grant occasional concessions to those outside the main alliances in order to survive. Amid all the confusion and inconsistency, an identifiable approach to the problem of development can be discerned and the dominant elements of the approach can be related to some of the ideal types in Griffin's classification.

Government policy was dominated by a variant of what Griffin calls the Green Revolution strategy, a strategy of promoting agricultural growth with a primary focus on increasing the supply of foodgrains. Large-scale government subsidies for modern inputs within the framework of the existing distribution of land ownership and the prevailing social institutions were the main feature of the strategy for nearly a quarter of a century, starting almost a decade before independence. During the past decade, the development strategy in Bangladesh also came to be increasingly characterized by elements of what Griffin calls the Open Economy strategy. This strategy has stressed policies of allocative efficiency with special emphasis on improving incentives to export. Contrary to the rhetorical adherence to socialism by the Awami League regime immediately after independence, the actual strategy adopted during that period was not akin to the socialist strategy in Griffin's classification. The major objective of the nationalization program during the so-called socialist phase was to use state ownership and state power to promote private enrichment.

MACROECONOMIC PERFORMANCE

Since independence, the economy of Bangladesh has grown at an annual trend rate of more than 4 per cent. Per capita income has grown at an annual trend rate of one and two-thirds percent. These rates are substantially higher than the corresponding rates during the two decades before independence. However, the significantly higher rate of growth in the post-independence period is somewhat misleading. The point of departure for calculating the trend rate of growth in the post-independence period was an unusually depressed level of income reflecting the sharp initial decline in the level of GDP immediately after independence. The pre-independence peak in per capita GDP was regained only as recently as 1980/81. Had per capita GDP continued to grow at the pre-independence trend rate, income per head would have been slightly higher in 1986/87 than it actually was. Yet in retrospect the growth performance must have surprised many observers who, at the time of independence and during the serious political instability of 1975, predicted a much worse outcome.

The average rate of investment in the 1980s has been about 14 per cent of GDP. This is higher than the rate of investment in the pre-independence period. The rate of investment however began to decline at the beginning of the 1980s.

Most of the investment in the post-independence period was financed by external resources. In the 1980s only about 16 per cent of investment was financed by domestic savings. Nearly three-fifths of investment was accounted for by net foreign assistance while the remaining quarter was financed by remittances from Bangladeshis working abroad. This is in sharp contrast with the pre-independence period when domestic savings financed nearly three-quarters of investment. The domestic saving rate declined from over 8 per cent of GDP in the pre-independence period to about 2 per cent in the 1980s. This is one of the outstanding weaknesses of present development performance.

Per capita external assistance – averaging approximately $10 in recent years – is perhaps not unjustifiably high given the extreme poverty of the country. But rather than complementing domestic savings and contributing to raising the rate of investment, foreign assistance has been a substitute for domestic savings. In spite of the very favorable terms of external borrowing and a high proportion of grants in foreign assistance, the burden of debt service has increased rapidly. This could have been avoided if external resources had brought about a corresponding rise in investment, rather than a fall in domestic savings. The resulting rise in the rate of growth would have reduced the burden of debt servicing.

Instead of being used for such a positive purpose, the availability of foreign assistance gave policy makers an opportunity to reduce efforts to mobilize domestic savings. Moreover, the large inflow of foreign aid and the public sector imports permitted by such aid had a profound effect on industrial incentives and accumulation. Aid and public sector imports provided the basis for the rapid enrichment of a thin layer of society at the top of the urban pyramid. Few of the accumulated riches were channelled into productive investment.

In the early years after independence there was a significant reduction in the birth rate, perhaps partly induced by increased poverty. The progress in fertility reduction was not continued into the 1980s. Indeed, it is possible that the birth rate has increased somewhat during the last decade. Official claims of a rapid expansion in the rate of contraceptive acceptance is not consistent with either the available evidence on the estimates of the trend in fertility or the trend in public expenditure on the program.

THE GREEN REVOLUTION STRATEGY AND RURAL DEVELOPMENT

All governments in Bangladesh have considered self-sufficiency in food production as a foremost objective of development. To this end a policy of agricultural development, based on the green revolution technology, was adopted. There was heavy government involvement in the development of water resources, in providing subsidies for modern inputs and support to farmgate prices. No serious effort was made to redistribute land or to implement other institutional reforms in agriculture.

Per capita consumption of foodgrains fell immediately after independence. Since 1973 however growth in overall agricultural production was at least as high as the growth in population while the growth in foodgrains (cereal) production was higher than the growth in population. The rate of growth was however too low to prevent a further rise in the absolute level of foodgrains imports. In the early 1980s per capita consumption of foodgrains was significantly higher than in the 1970s but still significantly lower than in the immediate pre-independence years.

Agricultural growth has had an extremely narrow base. It was entirely accounted for by the growth in wheat and *boro* rice, based on the adoption of the high yielding technology. Other crops and livestock products increased at a slower rate than population. Import dependence on agricultural products other than foodgrains increased rapidly.

The pattern of agricultural growth has almost certainly aggravated inequality in the distribution of income. The benefits of fertilizer subsidies appear to have been rather widely distributed thanks to the high rate of HYV adoption by small farmers. The high rate of adoption, in turn, was facilitated by three things: the provision of irrigation water by the public sector, the instinct for survival on the part of small farmers faced with a declining land/man ratio and – in the case of tenants – by a push by the owners of land. Since the late 1970s the emphasis in irrigation has shifted to the promotion of private ownership of highly subsidized equipment. In more recent years subsidies on fertilizer have been drastically curtailed while the subsidies on irrigation were retained. Richer farmers have acquired irrigation equipment with the help of credit from public lending institutions. While massively defaulting on the repayment of credit, these farmers have sold water to the smaller farmers at very high prices. Growing land scarcity has raised the factor share of land in agricultural value added. In the absence of land reform and given the continuation of the high degree of inequality in the distribution of land, this growing share of output accruing as rents has continued to be very unequally distributed.

In recent years the area under wheat has begun to stagnate. The demand for irrigation equipment has slackened since the expansion of the credit program came to a halt, a halt that was induced by an attempt to tighten credit discipline and improve repayment rates. This in turn has led to concern that it may not be possible to maintain the moderate rate of progress achieved in agriculture since independence.

THE OPEN ECONOMY STRATEGY AND PRIVATIZATION

Development policy in Bangladesh has placed considerable emphasis on policies to improve allocative efficiency. The overvaluation of the exchange rate has been reduced sharply. Incentives for exports have been substantially enhanced. Interest rates have been raised to much higher levels than before and real rates of interest for loans and advances have become significantly positive. Subsidies on agricultural inputs and food rations have been reduced drastically.

The present study does not in any way suggest that the policies for greater allocative efficiency are either unnecessary or undesirable. They are necessary for any well-designed development strategy. It is, however, impossible to ignore the fact that these reforms have so far achieved little in Bangladesh. The main reason is that while they are necessary to make growth efficient, they can not promote growth. Their success depends on the fulfillment of the preconditions for growth, among them a stable environment conducive to investment in productive activities, the existence of institutions capable of designing and enforcing a non-arbitrary set of rules to guide economic activity, and an adequate infrastructure. In Bangladesh these preconditions have not been created.

Moreover, the adoption of policies to promote allocative efficiency has been selective. It has been easier to adopt reforms that remove benefits from the powerless and the poor than to reform policies that favor the rich. Policy distortions have in reality become fungible. Thus subsidies on fertilizer have been removed while those on irrigation equipment have been retained. Interest rates on loans to rich farmers and private capitalists have been raised, but massive defaults by borrowers have been tolerated.

Another reform in Bangladesh that is widely praised by the donor community and others is the large-scale privatization of industries, irrigation equipment, financial institutions and trade. One of the points arising from the present study is recognition that the nationalization program of the early 1970s did not in fact represent socialization. The operation of the nationalized industries was driven by the objective of appropriating their surplus for the enrichment of private individuals. Thus a comparison of the performance of the nationalized industries with that of the private sector proves nothing about the relative merits and demerits of the two alternative systems. Furthermore, available evidence suggests that the big private entrepreneurs in industry and agriculture who became the beneficiaries of the program of privatization have not performed significantly better so far. Once the massive defaults on the repayment of loans are taken into account, the cost to the society of financing the acquisition by the private sector of these formerly state-owned assets becomes apparent. The argument about the relative advantages and disadvantages of the private and public sectors is irrelevant unless there are appropriate rules of the game which are applied to enterprises in both sectors and enforced. The experience in Bangladesh makes it abundantly clear that the public sector is not alone in being prone to indiscipline when there is a "soft budget constraint"[2]. In recent years the private sector has outperformed the public sector in this respect.

While the policy of promoting private capitalists in modern industry and commerce and rich farmers in agriculture has led to the situation described above, small-scale producers in industry and agriculture, driven by ingenuity and the need to survive, have made a significant contribution to growth. Yet these small entrepreneurs have received little positive support from public policy.

INDUSTRY AND INFRASTRUCTURE

Industrial policy in post-independence Bangladesh has been characterized by the use of state power to create a mechanism for private enrichment. This is just as true of the early period of nationalization as of the later period of denationalization. Largely as a direct consequence of this strategy, the nationalized industries became a brake on development and operated at large losses and with widespread inefficiency.

The state failed to channel the accumulated riches in private hands into productive industrial investment. Among the reasons for this failure are the following: the absence of a political framework capable of enforcing sensible rules of the game and ensuring stability; the divorce between production and accumulation, with the process of accumulation itself reducing the incentive to invest; and the inadequacy of the physical and social infrastructure.

There is some controversy about the rate at which the industrial sector has grown. But however one may measure it, the rate of growth has not been particularly high by any standard. Moreover, much of the growth has originated in small-scale and cottage industries, which did not benefit significantly from the mechanism of accumulation fostered by government policy.

Inadequate physical infrastructure constitutes a serious obstacle to the development of the economy. Uncertain power supply is a major obstacle to the utilization of industrial capacity. The lack of access to power is an obstacle to the development of rural industries. The depletion of traditional energy sources and the high cost of transmission of commercial energy have created a serious shortage of energy in rural areas and have led to a considerable environmental imbalance caused by the indiscriminate felling of trees.

In transport, roads have expanded significantly, although the expansion has not been fast enough to keep up with the demand for road transport. The expansion of roads has also suffered from a serious imbalance. Feeder roads have received much less attention than arterial roads. As a result, agricultural marketing has faced serious bottlenecks. Railways have stagnated and the exploitation of the natural waterways has been limited by the inadequacy of investment.

The physical infrastructure is in urgent need of rehabilitation and expansion. To implement such a program the rate of investment must rise substantially above the present level. This, in turn, will require an increase in the rate of domestic saving.

INCOME DISTRIBUTION AND SOCIAL DEVELOPMENT

Compared to the pre-independence period the distribution of income is more unequal today and poverty is more widespread. There has been some recovery in real wages in agriculture since 1982/83 after a steady decline over a long period. Despite these improvements, real wages of agricultural workers in the 1980s are substantially lower than they were in the late 1960s. Real wages in industries and urban construction are also lower in the 1980s than in the pre-independence years.

The social sectors have made remarkably little progress. The evidence on trends in literacy is somewhat uncertain because of a change in the definition of literacy between different censuses. It is, however, clear that the literacy rate has not improved significantly. The rate of primary school enrollment has declined, disastrously for boys. The standard of higher general education has deteriorated greatly and the opportunity to enter all kinds of higher education has become more unequal. Higher technical education is the only part of the education system which has grown without a significant deterioration in quality. Available indications suggest that access to health services has also become more unequal.

The overall picture thus is not an encouraging one. The high hopes held by those who fought for independence have not materialized. Policy priority has been given to agricultural development within an unchanged institutional framework. During the last decade allocative efficiency and privatization have come to feature strongly in the development strategy without the simultaneous creation of a system of incentives conducive to productive investment and an adequate infrastructure. Per capita income has increased moderately, but this has been achieved by becoming dependent on external resources while allowing the domestic rate of saving to collapse. Inequality is greater today than at the time of independence and the number of people suffering from poverty is larger. Their plight on the whole has not been significantly alleviated by an expansion of public services and a redirection of public services to favor those most in need. Political democracy has been indefinitely postponed and the military has become firmly entrenched in the country's government.

Notes and References

1. Keith Griffin, *Alternative Strategies for Economic Development*, London, Macmillan, 1988, Chapter 2.
2. See J. Kornai, *Economics of Shortage*, Amsterdam, North-Holland, 1980, for an analysis of the behavior of the state enterprises when there is a soft budget constraint.

ANNEX TO CHAPTER 2

National Income Estimates

For the pre-independence period, GDP and GNP estimates are based on those in Alamgir and Berlage, *Bangladesh: National Income and Expenditure 1949/50-1969/70*, Bangladesh Institute of Development Studies, Dhaka, June 1974. These are at 1959/60 constant prices. For 1969/70, estimates of GDP at constant 1972/73 prices are published in the Ministry of Finance, *Bagladesh Economic Survey 1985/86*, Dhaka, June 1986. Comparison of the two estimates for 1969/70 gives the deflator for 1972/73 with 1959/60 as the base year. This is used to "convert" the pre-independence series into 1972/73 prices.

For the post-independence period, the primary source of the national income accounts is the Bangladesh Bureau of Statistics (BBS)[1]. Its constant 1972/73 price series (published in the annual *Statistical Yearbooks* and elsewhere) includes the following:

(a) Estimates of sectoral values added at *market prices* are made and added together to obtain GDP at market prices.
(b) Net indirect taxes (deflated by the GDP deflator) are subtracted from GDP at market prices to obtain GDP at factor cost. Estimates of sectoral values added at factor cost are, however, not shown.
(c) Net factor income from the rest of the world (deflated by the GDP deflator) is added to GDP at factor cost to arrive at GNP at factor cost.

A controversy has arisen about the performance of the industrial sector in Bangladesh. For example, recent work connected with a research project on trade and industry at the Bangladesh Planning Commission[2] shows that the official Quantum Index of Production for large and medium scale industries understates the actual growth in output, especially for recent years, due to the use of outdated weights which fail to reflect the importance of the more rapidly growing products. The study contains a revised index, based on more recent weights, which shows a much higher rate of growth for recent years than does the official index. In the national income accounts, value added in large- and medium-scale industries is estimated on the basis of the Censuses of Manufacturing Industries (CMI). There is a time lag before the census data become available and hence at any given date the estimates of industrial value added during the last few years are derived by applying the official Quantum Index of Industrial Production to the most recently available CMI value added. In the present series, this has resulted in an underestimation of value added in large- and medium-scale industries for the years since 1982/83. To make a correction for this, value added in large and medium industries has been re-estimated by applying to the 1981/82 estimate of the BBS the growth rate implied by the Revised Quantum Index of Industrial Production based on appropriate weights properly reflecting the growth of the rapidly expanding sectors[3]. In the GDP series used in this study, value added in large- and medium-scale industries grew much more rapidly than even the Revised Quantum Index referred to above until 1981/82, making any upward adjustment for that period unnecessary. For 1985/86 and 1986/87 no estimate of the Revised Quantum Index is available; hence the growth rates from the BBS estimates of sectoral value added have again been used for these years.

There are reasons to believe that the small-scale and cottage industries in Bangladesh have been more dynamic than is implied by the growth rate in their value added as estimated by the BBS. For this sector, the BBS uses the growth rate of employment between 1969/70 and 1976/77 as benchmarks to estimate employment in each year. Value added per employee, obtained from the 1976 sample survey, is deflated by the wage index to obtain the same at 1972/73 constant prices. Even if the principle of the BBS methodology is accepted, one might reject the growth rate of employment that it uses as being too low. Employment in manufacturing industries was 1 026 000 in 1973/74 (according to the 1974 census) and 2 483 000 in 1983/84 (according to the LFS Final Report for that year). Employment in large- and medium-scale industries was 309 500 in 1974/75 and 367 400 in 1982/83 (*Statistical Yearbook, 1984/85*). Using the average of the annual growth rates between these years to extrapolate, estimated employment in large and medium industries becomes 303 000 in 1973/74 and 375 000 in 1983/84. This means that the labor force in small and cottage industries must have been growing at an annual rate of 11.3 per cent. As discussed in Chapter 2, labor use in small and cottage industries probably increased a good deal less than the labor force, though it is impossible to know by how much. In the present case an arbitrary assumption has been made that the rate of growth of the former was about 80 per cent of the latter. On this basis, labor use in this sector increased at an annual rate of 9.1 per cent and this has been applied to the BBS estimate of value added in 1974/75 to obtain a revised series of value added in small-scale and cottage industries. Value added in 1973/74 was very low due to inadequate recovery from the dislocations of the independence war; it has been left unchanged.

The correction factors (the differences between the official estimates and the revised estimates made according to the methodology described above) for values added in large-scale and small-scale industries are at market prices since they have been derived from the BBS estimates of sectoral values added. These were converted to factor cost after making approximate allowance for indirect taxes.

Thus for each of GDP and GNP two estimates are available. These estimates are identical for the pre-independence period, but for the post-independence period they differ depending on whether their industrial values added have been adjusted upwards or not. The four estimates are:

(a) GDP;
(b) Revised GDP formed by adding the correction factor for value added in manufacturing to the BBS estimates;
(c) GNP; and
(d) Revised GNP formed by adding the correction factor for value added in manufacturing to the above.

The effect of the upward revision in the value added in manufacturing is to raise the trend rate of growth by about a quarter of a percentage point per year during the post-independence period.

Annex Table 2.1 contains the estimates of trend rates of growth of sectoral values added in the post-independence period. For trade and housing sectors, the BBS appears to have made major changes in estimation methods starting in 1977/78 but it failed to adjust the estimates of the previous years using the revised method. The result is a discontinuous change in sectoral values added for trade and housing between 1976/77 and 1977/78. In the case of trade there is a 29 per cent decline and in the case of housing a 92 per cent increase! In contrast, the *Statistical Yearbook 1980*, contains earlier estimates (based presumably on past methods), and reveals no such discontinuity: values added for the two sectors respectively are reported to have increased at 1.3 per cent and 6 per cent between the two years. Changes in methodology, leading to discontinuous changes in values added, were made later. For the trade sector, this discontinuity was preceded by another – an

Annex Table 2.1 Trend growth rates of sectoral values added, 1972/73-1985/86
(Per cent per year)

Agriculture	2.6
Manufacturing	5.3 (8.0)
Construction	7.8
Transport	4.1
Trade	1.5 (2.7)
Housing	8.6 (2.3)
Public administration and defense	11.3
Services	6.6

Note: Growth rate, b, is estimated by fitting the trend line: Log VA = a + bT where T is time. All the bs – except that for trade sector – are significant at the 1 per cent level. Far better estimates of trend growth rates for trade and housing – giving much higher explained variation – are shown in parentheses and calculated as follows: for trade it is c in the equation Log VA = a + bDummy + cT, where Dummy = 1 for 1975/76 and 1976/77 and 0 for other years. For housing the growth rate is c in the equation Log VA = a + bDummy + cT, where Dummy = 0 for years up to 1977/78 and 1 thereafter. The figure in parenthesis for manufacturing is the growth rate based on the series adjusted upwards for possible underestimation of value added. Sources of data are discussed in the text of the Annex.

upward one – in 1975/76, so that the time series of value added in this sector has a pronounced hump for two years, 1975/76 and 1976/77. The result is too low a trend growth rate (which, moreover, is not significantly different from zero) for the trade sector and an incredibly high trend growth rate for housing. As the note to the Annex Table indicates, by introducing appropriate dummy variables to take these arbitrary methodological changes into account, one can get a more reasonable estimate of sectoral growth rates for housing and trade (though for the latter it still appears to be an underestimate).

It is impossible to say whether on balance the discontinuity in the method of estimating the values added in housing and trade has created a downward or an upward bias in the estimate of the overall growth rate. In the absence of any basis for revision it is best to hope that the overestimation of the one cancels the underestimation of the other.

To conclude, it is clear that even with the existing statistical information in the country, it should be possible to improve the national income accounts by ensuring consistency of method over time and by using the available information more comprehensively. The revisions carried out above are no substitute for this task; their purpose is merely to avoid a possible, but by no means certain, underestimation of the post-independence growth rate.

The source of the population estimates, used in deriving per capita estimates from aggregate products, was discussed in Chapter 2 for the years after independence. For estimates for the pre-independence period, see A.R. Khan, *The Economy of Bangladesh,* Macmillan, London, 1972, Chapter 2.

Notes and References

1. The Planning Commission also produces a GDP series. This is not however based on primary sources. The trend rates of growth during the post-independence period according to this series are about the same as the ones based on the adjusted BBS series.
2. See W. I. Abraham's work and the World Bank report cited in note 6 to Chapter 2.
3. The Revised Quantum Index is contained in the World Bank report cited in note 6 to Chapter 2.

Bibliography of Works Cited

ABRAHAM, W.I.
Manufacturing Output and the Industrial Production Index, Industrial Statistics Improvement Unit, Dhaka, 1984 (mimeo).
Features of Bangladeshi Manufacturing Industries: Some New Perspectives, Industrial Statistics Improvement Unit, Dhaka, July 1984 (mimeo).

AHMED, J. U. et al
Paddy Rice Procurement System; Report to the Ministry of Agriculture, Dhaka, 1980.

AHMED, Raisudding
Agricultural Price Policies Under Complex Socio-Economic and Natural Constraints, Research Report No. 27, International Food Policy Research Institute (IFPRI), Washington, D.C., 1981.

ALAMGIR, Mohiuddin and L. BERLAGE
Bangladesh: National Income and Expenditure, 1949/50-1969/70, the Bangladesh Institute of Development Studies (BIDS), Dhaka, 1974.

BANGLADESH BANK, Dhaka
Monthly Bulletin, relevant issues.

BANGLADESH BUREAU OF STATISTICS (BBS), Dhaka
Monthly Statistical Bulletin, relevant issues.
Statistical Yearbook of Bangladesh, 1981, 1983/84, 1985 and 1986.
Statistical Pocketbook of Bangladesh, 1981 and 1986.
Report of Agricultural Census, 1977 and 1983/84.
Yearbook of Agricultural Statistics, 1985/86.
Report of the Child Nutrition Status Module, Household Expenditure Survey, January 1987.
Socio-Economic Indicators of Bangladesh, July 1986.
Agricultural Production Levels in Bangladesh, 1947-72, 1974.
Bangladesh Census of Manufacturing Industries, Detailed Report, 1981/82.
Final Report of the Labor Force Survey, 1983/84.
Household Expenditure Survey 1981/82.

THE BANGLADESH INSTITUTE OF DEVELOPMENT STUDIES AND THE INTERNATIONAL FOOD POLICY RESEARCH INSTITUTE (IFPRI)
Fertilizer Pricing Policy and Foodgrain Production Strategy in Bangladesh, Dhaka and Washington, D.C., 1985.

BANGLADESH SMALL AND COTTAGE INDUSTRIES CORPORATION (BSCIC), Dhaka
Survey Report on Small Industries of Bangladesh, 1982.
Cottage Industries of Bangladesh, A Survey, 1983.

BHALLA, G.S. and G.K. CHADHA
Green Revolution and the Small Peasant, Concept, New Delhi, 1983.

BHUYAN, A. R., A.T.M.Z. HAQ and M.A. RASHID
A Study on the Domestic Prices of Imports in Bangladesh and the Derivation of Shadow Prices of Foreign Exchange, Labor and Some Major Inputs and Commodities, The Planning Commission, February 1985.

BOYCE, James K.
"Water Control and Agricultural Performance in Bangladesh", *The Bangladesh Development Studies*, Vol. 14, No. 4, 1986.

BOYCE, James K. and Martin RAVALLION
Inter-sectoral Terms of Trade and the Dynamics of Wage Determination in Rural Bangladesh, University of Massachusetts, Amherst, October 1987, (Draft).

CUMMINGS, J.T.
"The Supply Responsiveness of Bangalee Rice and Cash Crop Cultivation", *The Bangladesh Development Studies*, Vol. 2, No. 4, 1974.

GHAI, D.P., A.R. KHAN, Eddy LEE and Samir RADWAN (eds)
Agrarian Systems and Rural Development, Macmillan, London, 1979.

THE GOVERNMENT OF BANGLADESH: PLANNING COMMISSION, Dhaka
The Annual Development Program, 1986/87.
Inter-modal Transport Study – Final Report, Transport Survey Wing, 1985.
The Second Five-Year Plan.
The Third Five-Year Plan.

THE GOVERNMENT OF BANGLADESH AND THE INTERNATIONAL DEVELOPMENT ASSOCIATION (IDA)
Joint Review of Agricultural Credit in Bangladesh, Dhaka 1983.

THE GOVERNMENT OF BANGLADESH: MINISTRY OF FINANCE, Dhaka
Bangladesh Economic Survey, 1985/86 and 1986/87 (in Bengali).

THE GOVERNMENT OF BANGLADESH: MINISTRY OF FOOD, PLANNING AND MONITORING UNIT
Food Situation Report, August 1987.

GRIFFIN, Keith
  The Political Economy of Agrarian Change, Macmillan, London, 1974.
  Alternative Strategies for Economic Development, Macmillan, London, 1989.
GRIFFIN, Keith and A.R. KHAN (eds)
  Growth and Inequality in Pakistan, Macmillan, London, 1972.
HAMID, M.A. et al.
  Low Lift Pumps under IDA Credit in South-East Bangladesh: A Socio-Economic Study, Rajshahi University, 1984.
HONG, Sawon
  Demographic Characteristics of Bangladesh, Dhaka, June 1980.
HOSSAIN, Mahabub
  "Agricultural Development in Bangladesh – A Historical Perspective", *The Bangladesh Development Studies*, Vol. 12, No. 4, 1984.
  "Irrigation and Agricultural Performance in Bangladesh: Some Further Results", *The Bangladesh Development Studies*, Vol. 14, No. 4, 1986.
  "Price Response of Fertilizer Demand in Bangladesh", *The Bangladesh Development Studies*, Vol. 13, Nos. 3&4, 1985.
  "Agricultural Growth Linkages – The Bangladesh Case", *The Bangladesh Development Studies*, Vol. 15, No. 1, 1987.
  Nature and Impact of Modern Rice Technology in Bangladesh, IFPRI Research Report, Washington, D.C., 1988.
  "Farm Size, Tenancy and Productivity: An Analysis of Farm Level Data in Bangladesh Agriculture", *The Bangladesh Development Studies*, Vol. 5, No. 3, 1977.
  Employment Generation through Cottage Industries – Potentials and Constraints: The Case of Bangladesh, ILO/ARTEP, Bangkok, June 1984.
  Credit for the Rural Poor: The Grameen Bank in Bangladesh, The Bangladesh Institute of Development Studies Research Monograph No. 4, Dhaka, 1984.
HUTCHESON, T.L.
  Effective Rates of Protection: An Input/Output Analysis, Trade and Industries Project, Planning Commission, Dhaka, June 1985.
THE INTERNATIONAL BANK FOR RECONSTRUCTION AND DEVELOPMENT (World Bank)
  Bangladesh: Recent Economic Developments and Medium Term Prospects, Vol. I, March 1986.
  The World Development Report, 1986 and 1987.

INTERNATIONAL FERTILIZER DEVELOPMENT CENTRE
Agricultural Production, Fertilizer Use and Equity Considerations: Results and Analysis of Farm Survey Data, 1979-80 and 1982-84, Alabama, 1982 and 1984.

ILO
Poverty and Landlessness in Rural Asia, Geneva, 1977.

ILO/ARTEP
Employment Expansion in Asian Agriculture: A Comparative Analysis of South Asian Countries, Bangkok, 1980.
Manpower Planning in Bangladesh, Bangkok, October, 1981.

JANNUZI, F.T. and J.T. PEACH
Agrarian Structure in Bangladesh: An Impediment to Development, Westview Press, 1980.

KAHNERT, F. et al.
Agriculture and Related Industries in Pakistan, OECD Development Center, Paris, 1970.

KHAN, A.R.
The Economy of Bangladesh, Macmillan, London, 1972.
"Real Wages of Agricultural Workers in Bangladesh" in A.R. Khan and Eddy Lee (eds), *Poverty in Rural Asia,* ILO/ARTEP, Bangkok, 1984.
"Population Growth and Access to Land: An Asian Perspective", in Ronald Lee *et al.* (eds), *Proceedings of the Seminar on Population and Rural Development,* see below for full citation.

KHAN, A.R. and Eddy LEE
The Expansion of Productive Employment in Agriculture: The Relevance of the East Asian Experience for Developing Asian Countries, ILO/ARTEP Occasional Paper, Bangkok, 1981.

KHAN, A.R. and Eddy LEE (eds)
Poverty in Rural Asia, ILO/ARTEP, Bangkok, 1984.

KHAN, A.R., R. ISLAM and M. HUQ
Employment, Income and the Mobilization of Local Resources: A Study of Two Bangladesh Villages, ILO/ARTEP, Bangkok, 1981.

KORNAI, Janos
Economics of Shortage, North-Holland, Amsterdam, 1980.

LEE, Ronald et al. (eds)
Proceedings of the Seminar on Population and Rural Development, held in New Delhi, December 1984 under the auspices of the International Union for the Scientific Study of Population, Oxford University Press (forthcoming).

LIPTON, Michael
  Poverty, Undernutrition and Hunger, World Bank Staff Working Papers, No. 597, 1983.
MAHMUD, Wahiduddin
  "Foodgrain Demand Elasticities for Rural Households in Bangladesh", *The Bangladesh Development Studies*, Vol. 7, No. 1, 1979.
MANDAL, M.A.S.
  "Farm Size, Tenancy and Productivity in an Area of Bangladesh", *The Bangladesh Journal of Agricultural Economics*, Vol. 3, December 1980.
THE MASTER PLAN ORGANIZATION
  National Water Plan Project – Final Report, Ministry of Irrigation and Flood Control, Dhaka, 1986.
McKAY, Lloyd
  Report of Readymade Garments Industry, Trade and Industry Reform Project, Government of Bangladesh, Dhaka, 1984 (mimeo).
OSMANI, S.R. and M.A. QUASEM
  Pricing and Subsidy Policies for Bangladesh Agriculture, BIDS, Dhaka, 1985 (mimeo).
PAKISTAN, AGRICULTURAL CENSUS ORGANIZATION
  Census of Agriculture 1960, Vol. II (East Pakistan), Karachi, 1962.
PAKISTAN, CENTRAL STATISTICAL OFFICE
  Twenty-Five Years of Statistics in Pakistan, Karachi, 1974.
  Quarterly Survey of Current Economic Conditions, various rounds.
PEARSE, Andrew
  Seeds of Plenty, Seeds of Want: Social and Economic Implications of the Green Revolutions, Clarendon Press, Oxford, 1980.
QUASEM, M.A.
  "Government Procurement of Paddy/Rice and Farmers' Participation in Bangladesh", *Asian Profile*, Vol. 8, No. 4, 1980.
QUASEM, M.A. et al.
  Impact of the New System of Distribution of Fertilizers and Irrigation Machines in Bangladesh, BIDS, Dhaka, 1984 (mimeo).
RAB, A.
  Export Performance and Prospects and Government Policy to Promote Exports in Bangladesh, Trade and Industry Reform Project, Government of Bangladesh, Dhaka, (mimeo).
RAHMAN, Atiq
  "Surplus Utilization and Capital Formation in Bangladesh Agriculture", *The Bangladesh Development Studies*, Vol. 8, No. 4, 1980.

RAHMAN, S.F.
"Road Development in Bangladesh under Roads and Highway Department", *The Bangladesh Times,* Dhaka, 14th April, 1987.

RAHMAN, S.H.
"Supply Response in Bangladesh Agriculture", *The Bangladesh Development Studies,* Vol. 14, No. 4, 1986.

ROY, P.
"Transition in Agriculture: Empirical Studies and Results", *Journal of Peasant Studies,* Vol. 8, No. 2, 1981.

SOBHAN, Rehman
"Distributive Regimes under Public Enterprise: A Case Study of the Bangladesh Experience", in Frances Stewart (ed), see below.

SOBHAN, Rehman and Muzaffer AHMED
Public Enterprise in an Intermediate Regime, BIDS, Dhaka, 1980.

SOBHAN, Rehman and S.A. MAHMOOD
The Economic Performance of Denationalized Industries in Bangladesh: The Case of the Jute and Cotton Textiles Industries, BIDS, Dhaka, June 1966 (mimeo).

SOBHAN, Rehman and Binayak SEN
The Crisis in the Repayment of Loans to the Development Finance Institutions: A Crisis in the Development of Capitalism in Bangladesh?, BIDS, Dhaka, June 1987 (mimeo in Bengali).

STERN, J.J., R.D. MALLON and T.L. HUTCHESON
Foreign Exchange Regimes and Industrial Growth in Bangladesh, Harvard Institute of International Development, March 1986 (mimeo).

STEWART, Frances (ed)
Work, Income and Inequality, Macmillan, London, 1983.

SUMMERS, Robert and Alan HESTON
"Improved International Comparisons of Real Product and Its Composition: 1950-1980", *The Review of Income and Wealth,* June 1984.

UN
Statistical Yearbook, 1960.

WENNERGREN, E.B.
An Assessment of the Agricultural Sector in Bangladesh, USAID, Dhaka, August 1983.

Index

Abraham, W.I., 29, 96, 97, 187
accumulation, process of, 88–92, 177
Africa, 8
agricultural census, 34, 36, 37, 54, 64
agricultural credit, 61–2, 120
agricultural marketing, 59–61
agricultural price support, 62
agricultural subsidies, *see* subsidies
agriculture, 31–65, 92
Ahmed, J.U., 66
Ahmed, Muzaffer, 97
Ahmed, R., 65
Alamgir, M., 28, 183
allocative efficiency, 95, 96, 121, 164, 176, 179, 182
amon rice, 40, 42, 43, 44, 47, 62, 138
Assam, 1
aus rice, 40, 43, 44, 47, 49
Awami League, 1, 2, 3, 79, 81, 85–6, 176

Bangladesh Agricultural Development Corporation (BADC), 57, 58, 59, 60
Bangladesh Bank, 117, 118, 119, 120
Bangladesh Institute of Development Studies (BIDS), 65, 84
Bangladesh Small and Cottage Industries Corporation (BSCIC), 69
Bangladesh Water Development Board (BWDB), 57, 58
bank credit, 117–21
Bengal, 1
Berlage, L., 28, 183
Bhalla, G.S., 66
Bhuyan, A.R., 98
birth rate, 8, 12, 14, 178
bonded warehouse, 93 107–08
boro rice, 40, 42, 43, 44, 62, 63, 138
borrowing, external, *also see* foreign aid, 24–5, 28–9
Boyce, J.K., 65, 172
Brahmaputra, 32
Burma, 8, 90

capital flight, 92
capital inflow, *see* foreign aid and borrowing, external
capital intensity of industries, 83
census, 14, 15, 17, 140

census of manufacturing industries (CMI), 69, 70, 76, 78, 79, 82, 83, 84, 96, 97, 184
Chadha, G.K., 66
China, 8
communications, 135–6
consumer price index, *see* price index
consumption, 26–8
contraception, 9, 13
coup d'état, 2
crop production, 40–8
Cummings, J.T., 65

death rate, 12
debt, external, 99–101
debt service, 25, 29, 110, 177
denationalization, 82, 84, 179–80
Disadvantaged Group Feeding (DGF), 165–6
distribution of income, 13, 31, 51–7, 147–68, 178, 181–2
drop out, primary school, 142
duty drawback, 107, 108

East Asia, 7
East Pakistan, 1, 2
East Pakistan Industrial Development Corporation (EPIDC), 79
education, 139–42
  primary, 139–42
  higher, 141–2
electricity, 125–9
employment, 4, 14, 15, 17, 75
energy, 124–9
entrepreneurs, 3, 91, 180
Ershad, General H.M., 2
Ethiopia, 1
exchange rate policy, 92–6
exchange rates, 94
  real effective, 93–5, 108
export, 100, 103–7
  of jute, 103–4, 105
  of garments, 104–6, 108–9
  policies and performance, 107–10
export performance benefit, 93, 107, 108
export performance licensing, 93, 107
Export Promotion Bureau, 103

famine, 11, 155

195

Index

FAO, 9
farm size, 33
   and land productivity, 54–5
fertility, *also see* birth rate, 13
   poverty-induced reduction in, 13
fertilizer, chemical, 45–8, 55–6
   subsidy on, 57–9, 63, 164
Finance Ministry of, 27, 97, 100, 102, 146, 172, 183
fishery, 37–9
flood, flood control, 33, 137–8
food consumption, 4, 5, 42, 178
Food-For-Work, 162, 165
foreign aid, 24–9, 81–91, 99, 177
foreign investment, direct, 8, 80
fragmentation of holdings, 33, 34
Ganga (Ganges), 32
gas, natural, 6, 8, 124–5
GDP, 4, 19–28, 183–7
Ghai, D.P., 168
Gini coefficients, 147, 149, 151–3
GNP, 19–23, 183–4
government expenditure, *see* public expenditure
government revenue, *see* public revenue
Grameen Bank, 165
green revolution, 45–8, 51, 175, 176, 178
Griffin, Keith, 9, 10, 66, 175, 176, 182
growth, trend rates of
   in GDP and per capita income, 22–3
   in agriculture, 36–8, 40–4
   in industry, 75–8
   in different sectors, 185–6
growth performance, 176–7

Hamid, M.A., 66
Haq, A.T.M.Z., 98
health, 142–4, 145
Heston, Alan, 10
high yielding variety (HYV), 33, 34, 45–8, 63
   and distribution of income, 51–7, 166
Hong, Sawon, 29
Hong Kong, 8
hospital beds, 143
Hossain, Mahabub, 53, 55, 57, 65, 66, 69 97, 172
Hutcheson, T., 94, 98, 121
Huq, M., 64, 97, 172

ILO, 159
ILO/ARTEP, 65, 146, 159
import, 100, 101–3
India, 1, 2, 7, 51, 54, 85

Indonesia, 7
industrialization, 67–98, 180–1
industries
   cottage, 6, 70, 72, 76–8
   handloom, 70, 76
   large and medium, 70, 71–2, 78–9
   small, 70, 72–7
   private sector, 79–84
   public sector, 79–84
inequality, rural–urban, 150, 165
infant mortality, 4, 143
inflation, 115–6
infrastructure, physical, 6, 8, 123–8, 144–5, 181
   social, 139–44, 145, 182
Inheritance, Islamic Law of, 33
interest rate, domestic, 118, 120–1
International Development Agency (IDA), 66
investment, rate of, 24–9, 177
Investment Corporation of Bangladesh, 81
irrigation, 32–3, 45–8, 57–9
   subsidy on, 57–9
Islam, 3
Islam, R., 64, 97, 172

Jannuzi, F.T., 64
Japan, 7
Java, 8
jute, *see* export of jute, 43–4

Kahnert, F., 66
Kenya, 8
Khan, A.R., 9, 10, 64, 65, 97, 143, 159, 168, 172, 187
Korea, South (Republic of), 7, 8, 90
Kornai, J., 182

labor force, 14–19, 168–9
Labor Force Survey (LFS), 14–17, 70, 71, 77, 168, 184
labor productivity, 16–9, 83
land, cultivated, 31–2, 33, 45
land productivity, 47
landholding, distribution of, 33–5, 166, 167, 176
land/labor ratio, 8, 166
landless laborers, 35, 167, 168
Lee, Eddy, 10, 65, 159, 168, 172
Lee, Ronald, 10
letters of credit, back-to-back, 108
life expectancy, 4, 5

Index

female and male, 169, 170
Lipton, Michael, 9
literacy, 139–40
  adult, 4, 5, 139–40
  female and male, 170, 171
livestock, 35–7

Mahmood, S.A., 97
Mahmud, W., 65
Mallon, Richard, 94, 98, 121
Mandal, M.A.S., 66
McKay, Lloyd, 121
medical graduates, 143
Meghna, 32
migration, from rural area, 167
modern variety (MV), *see* high yielding variety
monetary demand, 115
money supply, 115–20
  causative factors behind, 119–20
mortality, 13, 29

nationalization, 2, 79, 81, 84–8, 176
Nepal, 8
New Industrial Policy, 82
Nigeria, 1
nutrition, 148, 150, 156, 157
  of female and male children, 169, 170
nutrition survey, 39, 150, 170

Osmani, S.R., 58, 66
open economy strategy, 175, 176, 179–80

Pakistan, 1, 2, 7, 90, 103
Peach, J.T., 64
Pearse, Andrew, 66
Planning Commission, 9, 12, 13, 130, 136, 138, 146, 183, 187
political stability, 3–5, 90, 175
population, 4, 8, 11–14
  urban, 4
poverty, 5, 9, 13, 147–68, 178
  incidence of, 153–6
price index, 116
  consumer, 116
price level, 115–6
primary school enrollment, 4, 5, 139–41, 171
privatization, *see* denationalization
procurement price of rice, 62
protection, 91, 95
  effective, 94–5
public expenditure, 111–5

  on administration and defense, 113
  on social sectors, 113–4
  on economic services, 113–4
public investment, 114
public revenue, 110–11, 112, 114–15

quantum index of production, industry, 183–4, 187
Quasem, M.A., 58, 66

Rab, A., 121
Radwan, S., 168
Rahman, Atiq, 65
Rahman, S.F., 133
Rahman, S.H., 65
Rahman, Sheikh Mujibar, 2
Rahman, Ziaur, 2, 81
Rashid, M.A., 98
Ravallion, Martin, 172
real wages, 16–9, 148, 156–63
remittance, by workers employed abroad, 25–8, 99, 100, 106–7, 109, 177
road transport, 131–3
  feeder roads, 131–3
Roy, P., 66
"rules of the game", 90, 96, 175, 180
Rural Industries Study Project (RISP), 69

Sattar, President, A., 2
saving, domestic, 24–9, 110, 177
  foreign, 24–9
  private, 25–8, 110
  public, 25–9, 110, 111, 112
Second Five-Year Plan, 145
secularism, 3
Sen, Binayak, 97
sharecropping, 34
Singapore, 8
Six points program, 1
Sobhan, Rehman, 97, 98
socialist economy, 2, 175, 176
socialist transformation, 2, 84–5
soft budget constraint, 180
South Asia, 7
South-east Asia, 7
standard of living, 5, 6
  long-term change in, 6–7
Stern, Joseph, 94, 98, 121
Stewart, Frances, 98
subsidies
  on agricultural inputs, 57–8, 164
  distributional effects of, 59
Summers, Robert, 10
supply elasticity of rice, 48

surplus appropriation, 88–92
Survey of Cottage Industries, 70, 77
Survey of Small Industries, 70, 73, 97

tax holiday, 93, 108
tax revenue, 110–11, 112
  direct taxes, 110–11, 112
  indirect taxes, 110, 112
  land tax, 111, 112
tea, 44
tenancy, tenancy reform, 34–5
terms of trade
  of agriculture, 48–51, 163, 165
  of industries, 91–2
Tanzania, 90
Thailand, 7, 90
Third Five-Year Plan, 146
trade, foreign, 99–110
trade balance, 100

transport, 129–35
  railway, 134–5
  road, *see* road transport
  water, 133–4

underemployment, 168
unemployment, 168
United Nations, 7

wage earners' scheme (WES), 89, 106
wage rate, agriculture, 6, 55–7
  in industries, 74–5, 83
  female–male disparity, 169, 170
  also see real wages
Wennergren, E.B., 146
West Bengal, 6
women, discrimination against, 168–71
World Bank, 7, 66, 97, 121, 146, 187